OPPORTUNITIES FOR ICT IN THE PRIMARY SCHOOL

Helen Smith

Trentham Books

First published in 1999 by Trentham Books Limited

Trentham Books Limited
Westview House
734 London Road
Oakhill
Stoke on Trent
Staffordshire
England ST4 5NP

British Cataloguing in Publication Data
A catalogue record for this book is available from the British Library
ISBN: 1 85856 106 X (pb)
ISBN: 1 85856 151 5 (hb)

Designed and typeset by Trentham Print Design Ltd, Chester and
printed in Great Britain by The Cromwell Press Ltd., Wiltshire

Contents

Acknowledgements

I should like to thank all the teachers and children with whom I have worked over the years in carrying out the research which led to this book. I am particularly grateful to Sue Evans and her staff for their willingness to allow me into their classrooms. My work would not have been possible without the advice and encouragement of many friends and colleagues at King Alfred's College. Special thanks are due to David Argles for his unfailing support.

This book is dedicated to my parents, John and Beryl, and to Wendy, in gratitude and love.

CHAPTER 1
INTRODUCTION

New developments set against background issues

What are the opportunities for ICT within the core curriculum? What styles of teaching and learning are supported? How do pupils benefit? Are attitudes to learning, and ability to work independently, enhanced? This book explores contexts within Mathematics, English and Science at Key Stages 1 and 2. It considers the role of the computer as 'tutor', enabling teaching focused at developing core skills within these subjects. 'Legacy' software from the dawn of microcomputing in schools has a place, alongside new developments such as multimedia authoring and the World Wide Web. The balance of the book, however, is weighted towards the role of the computer as a tool for problem solving and inquiry, since this is where there appears to be the greatest need for curriculum development. For instance, inspection findings show that the majority of pupils gain some experience of ICT in handling data. However, opportunities to interpret results and draw conclusions are not always taken (Goldstein, 1997).

With rapid developments in multimedia and telecommunications, gaps between 'low-tech' and 'high-tech' learning environments in schools are set to increase. Practitioners may regard the pace of current change with considerable unease. As existing hardware becomes obsolete, will teachers' hard-won ICT capability be declared redundant? There is a real danger that the expertise of a generation of innovators will be discounted and swept aside. It is time to take stock of what we already know about the ways in which IT enhances and enriches teaching and learning. Teachers should look to the new technologies for better ways

1

of reaching established goals. We need to build upon, rather than discard, our existing professional knowledge.

Government initiatives to resource ICT across the curriculum and train teachers are long overdue. As the new Government took office, ministers faced a situation where the classroom computing 'revolution', fuelled by industrial developments in the early 1980s, had run out of steam. Prophecies that IT would change the face of education had not been fulfilled. Government statistics (DfE, 1995a) showed that only two-thirds of primary teachers use IT 'regularly', which could mean as little as twice a week. More than 50% of the computers in schools were at least five years old. Software development was restricted because applications had to run on older machines.

In contrast, technology has brought about irreversible change in the workplace. ICT increasingly impinges on our leisure and social activity. Today's personal computers are well over a hundred times faster and more capacious than the cumbersome machines installed in classrooms in the early 1980s, and are actually cheaper. Due to vastly improved interface design, they are considerably easier to use. The rate of development of new communications technologies has accelerated.

OFSTED inspections confirmed that teachers lack confidence and knowledge of applications (Goldstein, 1997). Opportunities for integrating ICT across the curriculum are undeveloped (SCAA, 1996a). Many teachers are unsure how to incorporate ICT in lesson planning, and have little experience of assessment and differentiation in IT. Inspection data shows that pupils' achievements in IT are lower than in any other subject. Only one in two schools are meeting IT curriculum requirements.

Nevertheless, OFSTED observed 'much valuable work' in primary classrooms. The challenge and motivational appeal of ICT has been demonstrated. 'Skilful and creative' work with graphics and multimedia has been in evidence. However, many pupils experience ICT in isolation. Opportunities for greater challenge are missed, due to a lack of teacher intervention. Many pupils have opportunities to use new technology to support research, but use is often 'superficial and un-structured'.

Today, a large portion of funding is devolved directly to schools, and the tradition of free help and advice has ended. There is a fragmented, commercialised pattern of local support. In any case, local centres were forced to reduce their staffing as 'spotlight' funding was directed onto other targets. Many school managers have been ill prepared for the transition and have not planned strategically for targeting funding at curriculum training. There has been reliance on internal support. Most IT co-ordinators have little or no non-teaching time in which to utilise external sources of support, train colleagues and monitor pupils' progress. A national strategy has been called for in co-ordinating services and improving quality, thus increasing the market through making services more attractive to schools (NCET, 1996a).

Early training courses focused on the workings of the machine. The dominant use of computers in classrooms both in this country and the U.S. in the early 1980s was for instruction in computer 'literacy' (Becker, 1985). Even then, it was recognised that the new literacy 'cannot be founded on the shifting sand of the technology itself' (Longworth, 1981). Pupils need to be taught information skills in the context of authentic tasks modelled on real life.

The rapid advance of the personal computer in the 1980s brought powerful generic tools such as word processors and spreadsheets into the workplace. This innovation had a profound effect on the development of IT in education (Heppell, 1993). The IT Curriculum reflects the predominance of business applications in the curricula of the late 1980s (Ball, 1990). Teachers may feel, with justification, that widely used terms such as 'computer literacy' and 'information skills' have not been adequately defined.

Teachers lack confidence in teaching IT and rate it highly as a training need (Hargreaves et al, 1996). Most teachers feel comfortable using a limited range of applications (Murray and Collison, 1995), and can demonstrate that some aspects of the statutory requirements are being met. There is a unique difficulty in that, as soon as most primary schools have reached a state of relative equilibrium, new technological change drives 'progress'.

Education for the 'information society' has become an urgent Government priority. Yet there is still no clear vision of the role of ICT in education. This can be traced to a lack of shared values and goals, and the failure of national bodies to agree common aspirations. The question of how we should use ICT in schools reaches to the very heart of issues which affect curriculum content, teaching methods and expectations of learners. What should children be taught? What is the nature of computer-mediated experience? How do children learn, and what can they achieve?

We use computers to perform tasks which would require many hours of intensive human activity. In freeing our time, we are given increased opportunities for thinking and reflection. It is the responsibility of educators to empower young people to use these tools purposefully, creatively and responsibly. Teaching, according to Davis and collaborators (1997), must be intentional, and must be informed by 'understanding of the power of the tool, its generative capacity and of the demands made on the user'.

There may be considerable diversity in the ICT-rich schools of the future. Older machines may be used for tasks which do not require state-of-the-art functionality, such as planning, note making, writing and redrafting, analysing data, producing graphs and preparing reports. Notebook computers, which can be used at pupils' desks or taken out of doors, may also be used for these tasks. Inexpensive networked computers may become the mainstay in schools of the future. They will derive their capacity not from ever more powerful processors, but from local servers connected via high-volume, two-way links.

Throughout this book, illustrative use has been made of evidence drawn from close observation of pupils' interaction with ICT. Analysis will assist readers in forming expectations. The author cannot offer universal generalisations from the small-scale studies which formed the basis of her research. It is not possible in a small volume to give complete descriptions of the circumstances in which data was obtained. However, teachers will recognise similarities in the broader context, and be able to judge whether it is likely that their own pupils will respond in similar ways.

This book is not solely concerned with innovative technology. In fact, most of the practical examples in this book were developed on 2Mb Acorn systems. It would be a colossal error to draw a line over all older machines, effectively consigning them to the skip. Where teachers have made a committed effort to introduce ICT, belittlement of ageing classroom computers must be profoundly discouraging. Our knowledge of the ways in which ICT supports learning, gained through practical experience of teaching with older systems, will be just as valuable and as relevant in years to come. We should look to new technological capability to improve what we are already trying to do, and build upon our existing achievements.

The role of the teacher should be carefully considered. When is explicit IT teaching called for, and what form should it take? An important issue is whether whole-class teaching through the medium of ICT is desirable, or even feasible. In many of the examples in this book, whole-class teaching was an important element of what took place. Metacognitive skills (organising knowledge, identifying goals, planning, checking results and evaluating outcomes) may be modelled by the teacher, then developed through computer group work combined with whole-class discussion and review.

A good example occurs in Chapter 4, where the whole class reviews the graphs of seedling growth produced by groups. Another instance arises in Chapter 6, where many salient teaching points are covered with the whole class rather than repeated nine or ten times.

The Curriculum for ICT in subject teaching (TTA, 1998) requires teachers to be able to employ a range of approaches, including whole-class teaching with ICT. However, it seems hardly worth attempting this when the typical classroom display is a fourteen-inch monitor. I have observed a Year 1 teacher, with her whole class in a circle on the floor, lead an interactive Maths session with the Roamer. She encouraged children to talk though the commands, and everyone could see the outcomes. Later, she reviewed *MyWorld* screens (Chapter 2) on the computer by the door, while the class were lined up for assembly. Even then, not all children could see the screen. No-one would dream of giving a commercial presentation to thirty colleagues using a desktop display, yet this is apparently what we are expected to do in the classroom.

Fortunately, portable data projectors are now available. They are virtually silent in operation and, in a normal classroom, do not require blackout. An alternative is the LCD panel which sits on top of an overhead projector. Used with a portable computer, it may quickly be set up virtually anywhere in school. The drawback is that these displays are costly, although prices are on a downward trend. Whichever option is chosen, schools will have to budget at least £2000 – for one unit! A cheaper alternative is the thirty-four inch Hantarex video monitor, but few primary classrooms have space for this type of equipment. Some LEAs have set aside a portion of NGfL money for a pool of central resources. Provision of data projectors to selected schools, for instance to pilot the use of ICT in Literacy and Numeracy Hours, would be a commendable move.

Applications of ICT in schools are expanding and diversifying. It is impossible in a book of this size to cover every aspect of ICT in primary education. ILS (Integrated Learning Systems) will be viewed by some as an important omission. Sadly, there is no space to review the enabling role of ICT in special education. However, the scope for differentiation through ICT is noted throughout the following chapters, and ways of supporting and extending pupils within the mainstream setting are suggested.

This book provides a unique insight into pupils' development of ICT capability and the wider potential for learning in the core subjects. The case studies themselves are intended to offer exemplars: other practical suggestions and recommendations are made in the light of outcomes. Space does not permit a detailed review of planning, assessment and recording, and ICT management issues. Many current publications offer detailed advice in these areas, and it is not my intention to duplicate these materials.

A number of LEA IT Centres have published high quality guides and frameworks for ICT in cross-curricular planning. Good examples are Oxfordshire's *Progression in IT* and *Opportunities Across the Curriculum* (Oxfordshire County Council, 1996) and *Making IT Manageable* (Hertfordshire Education Services, 1997). NCET's planning tool *Managing IT in Primary Schools* (NCET, 1996b) is strongly recommended. The Primary IT co-ordinator will find further support and a host of planning materials in the NAACE ring binder *Implementing IT* (NCET, 1997).

IT or ICT?

To put it simply, IT is the subject, ICT the tools. If pupils use CD-ROM to research a topic in Geography, they are using ICT. If the teacher sets up an overlay keyboard with initial consonant blends to match to pictures, she is using ICT to support literacy development. Other ICT applications include email, video conferencing and the use of the World Wide Web. In ICT, 'the focus is on the subject being taught or studied [...] rather than developing pupils' skills with, and knowledge of, the technologies themselves' (QCA, 1998). The QCA framework also refers to the important role of ICT in school management and administration.

On the other hand, IT 'comprises the knowledge, skills and understanding' to make appropriate, productive use of ICT. QCA cites the analogous relationship of literacy to books, journals and reading material. IT (the subject) includes knowledge of how information is structured in a database, and skills of using ICT to communicate ideas and information.

Teachers may feel the distinction is a very fine one. Whatever the ICT application, it is nearly always possible to identify some potential for the development of IT skills. Multimedia CD-ROMs which provide practice in early number skills such as counting, sequencing and simple addition are good examples. Young children learn to point and click with the mouse, and associate numbers with numerals on the keyboard. It is precisely because teachers need to select such opportunities for developing IT skills that the distinction between ICT and IT is important.

At the same time, it should be recognised that older pupils may use ICT to support learning in a subject, while hardly adding anything to their knowledge of IT. The computer controls the learning environment by presenting manageable tasks and prompting for responses. Steps are repeated if mistakes are made. Curriculum-related software may be a rich resource to support learning in the subject. However, it may do little to develop IT skills because there is too much cushioning against errors. IT capability means being able to cope with, and learn from, errors. Pupils need opportunities to review faulty strategies. They need to develop the confidence to regard mistakes, and their consequences, in a positive light.

Why is ICT problematic?

As the pace of technological development continues to exert pressure to innovate, there are many unresolved questions in teachers' minds. Why use these ICT tools? Are they manageable, in the typical classroom? What may pupils achieve with ICT, and what wider learning is involved? What IT skills need to be taught, and how? What are effective ways of organising opportunities and supporting pupils?

It is now widely accepted that schools cannot be offered the same solutions as industrial and commercial concerns, since there are critical differences in aims and expectations. A new office computer system may perform highly regulated operations which were previously carried out manually. While the transition may exact a heavy personal toll on employees, there are clear expectations, since routines are modelled on established practice.

The school's ICT objectives, on the other hand, may be unclear. Lack of knowledge of applications is compounded by a virtual absence of established models for new types of learner activity. Computers cannot be used to deliver the traditional curriculum, since an all-embracing range of instructional software does not exist.

Even in schools where ICT is in everyday use, it is difficult for busy teachers to probe beyond surface features. End products (a graph printed in colour; a page downloaded from CD-ROM) rarely lead to further investigation. Most teachers work in comparative isolation, and have not had the opportunity to observe colleagues and pupils in ICT-rich classrooms. Consequently, a body of pedagogic knowledge, grounded in classroom experience and professional practice, developed and communicated within the professional network, scarcely exists. No wonder many teachers find ICT threatening. The introduction of ICT necessitates changes in attitudes, changes in classroom practice and changes in the knowledge base of teachers. In other words, all three dimensions of educational change (Fullan, 1991) are involved.

Both the National Curriculum and NGfL targets make considerable demands on teachers' IT subject knowledge. SCAA have produced leaflets intended to assist teachers in recognising appropriate cross-curricular applications. While slimmed-down guidance, with clear practical exemplars, is welcome, there is a great risk of over-simpli-fication. Faced with the revised Programmes of Study (DfE, 1995b), there is still a great deal of unpacking for practitioners to do. Sophisti-cated ICT tools present complex teaching and learning environments. It was the desire to gain a better understanding of the nature of ICT, and the demands on teachers and pupils, that prompted the research which led to this book.

Styles of teaching and learning

Somekh (1997) defines three ways in which teachers may approach the use of the computer to support learning. At the first level, the machine is used chiefly in *tutorial* mode. The software is designed to teach specific subject content. The learner receives knowledge delivered by the system. However, the computer allows opportunities for interaction, and the learner may have a degree of control (for example, being able to request help). There may be automatic assessment and tracking of progress. Due to the structured nature of the learning environment, there are predictable demands on pupils and learning outcomes. These programs do not have the potential to transform teaching and learning, but 'do the same things that schools have traditionally done [...] perhaps more systematically and efficiently' (Means et al., 1993).

The second (intermediate) stage is in using the computer as a *neutral tool*. The pupil has the opportunity to use content-free software, allow-ing a far greater range of applications. However, the computer activity is modelled on familiar routines which remain fundamentally un-changed by the presence of technology. A good example is the use of a word processor to make a 'best copy' of work that has already been drafted and corrected on paper.

Finally, the computer is used as a *cognitive tool* to support inquiry-based research. Pupils are introduced to open-ended applications such as databases, spreadsheets and controlling and monitoring software. However, there may be a high degree of focus in their use. For example, the activity may be driven by questions such as, 'What are the best conditions for growing seedlings?' 'How effectively do various materials insulate a container of water?' In using ICT to store, process and present data, new approaches to teaching and learning are implicit.

Pupils need access to higher order skills: formulating questions, planning, organising, interpreting feedback, testing hypotheses and evaluating outcomes. At this level, pupils take increasing responsibility for their own learning as they become able to undertake inquiries independently.

Arguments in favour of inquiry-based approaches are based on the recognition that learners acquire process skills through interaction with the environment. Ideas and explanations are accepted, modified or rejected in the light of experience. Pupils actively raise and develop questions, gather information, formulate and test their explanations and ideas, and communicate their findings to others. Pupils are more likely to be motivated to engage in challenging inquiries if presented with authentic tasks, modelled on real-world problems (Sheingold, 1990).

Somekh acknowledges that the step from 'neutral tool' to 'cognitive tool' is massive. In practice, many teachers edge forward as they gain confidence in using a greater range of ICT applications. With increased familiarity, the teacher is better able to make links with learning in other subjects. Open-ended software may be used for particular tasks. Teaching is planned with the intention of developing pupils' IT skills and knowledge. For example, the teacher shows children how to cut and paste with a word processor, and encourages them to employ these techniques in re-drafting their writing on the screen.

It hardly needs to be said that the development of ICT in supporting pupil-directed inquiry places intensive demands on the teacher, as pupils gain familiarity with skills, concepts and strategies. Official sources do not always recognise that even the simplest 'tutorial' software imposes organisational challenge. The teacher must decide where to incorporate in medium-term planning; how to match to pupils' levels (e.g. by selecting options); how to organise groups; how to integrate into daily planning; how to monitor and record progress. The teacher will also wish to identify opportunities for questioning and review, and plan links with other tasks. At school level, there are immense resourcing demands, especially where there is a plan to use ICT for individualised learning.

Given the rapid emergence of multimedia and new communications technologies, there are new specialist demands, with even deeper implications for changing pedagogy. There are opportunities for teachers to produce their own interactive teaching materials, using multimedia presentation tools. Given the opportunity, the teacher is able to use communications networks, both as a professional resource and in providing planned access for pupils to curriculum materials on-line. Through electronic link-ups with other schools, the teacher engages in collaborative projects. Distance is immaterial as pupils collaborate with students overseas in tackling research projects of common interest. Classroom groups devise tasks for each other, and co-operate in electronically publishing their findings. The teacher finds that, as an expert in the use of classroom technology, s/he no longer works in isolation but is an active member of an international electronic community. S/he becomes a learner alongside the pupils (Riel, 1990; Means et al., 1993; Davis, 1997).

In the use of open-ended software, the role of the teacher is critical: the mere presence of technology may have little impact on learning. Through informed, sensitive intervention, and through providing appropriate tasks alongside (or away from) the computer, the teacher provides 'scaffolding' (Elliott, 1995). The computer environment provides further structuring and feedback. The teacher passes on models which guide pupils' notions of the type of inquiries they may pursue, and possible strategies. As pupils adapt these models to serve their own ends, they develop higher-order thinking skills. The success of any approach to investigative learning with ICT depends on the extent of the teacher's knowledge, both of the ICT tools themselves and the challenges and opportunities presented to pupils. A further critical factor lies in the quality of the teacher's insight into learners' interactions, and ability to intervene appropriately.

The National Grid for Learning

According to the Government's desired objectives, ICT will be commonplace, and routinely used across the curriculum. By the year 2002, the National Grid for Learning (NGfL) will link all schools with libraries, museums, higher education systems and the home. This will inevitably change the ways in which learning is delivered, but the prospect of a widening gap between ICT 'haves' and 'have nots' must be viewed with concern. OFSTED (Goldstein, 1997) have reported signs of a gulf between schools with good levels of resourcing and those which can only offer limited ICT access.

The importance of teacher training has been recognised, and will be supported through Millennium Commission funding. All Local Education Authorities have development plans for ICT, as a precondition for NGfL funding. Priority issues are the connection of schools with minimum access charges; the development of curriculum content to be published on the Grid; the overcoming of barriers which currently inhibit the development of ICT in schools.

What are the chances of success? Much depends on the quality of content and the willingness of teachers to explore ways of incorporating resource-based learning opportunities. Teachers who do not already draw on a wide range of resources in the classroom may scarcely be affected. An influential Government adviser anticipates gradual change through 'stepwise' development, with setbacks as well as progress (Stevenson, 1998). Schools will welcome a gradualist approach in a climate where continued funding will very much depend on demonstrable results. Schools should not be penalised for failing to attain targets which initially appeared achievable, provided that every reasonable effort has been made.

A major feature of NGfL is the *Virtual Teachers' Centre* website, which appeared online in January 1998. The development of the VTC is critical to the success of the Grid. Many believe that the VTC was launched too soon, in a prototype form which largely consisted of an archive of official documents and curriculum resources lifted from the former NCET site. The active participation of teachers' groups in developing VTC content is to be hoped for. Other organisations such as BBC Education and Channel 4 Schools are to provide materials. Pages will be 'badged' as a mark of the high standard expected of the VTC. The chief advantage will be in a single access point to a range of resources covering the full curriculum.

While the VTC will be an asset, materials on their own will not deliver all the teaching. The VTC must not be allowed to become a mere vehicle for dissemination of worksheets and lesson plans from central sources. We need to consider ways of using on-line sources in the classroom. What skills do pupils need to acquire? How may on-line resources be used to enrich and enhance teaching and learning? Above all, active participation by teachers in sharing experiences and contributing trialled materials will go a long way towards rectifying the prevailing lack of shared professional knowledge of 'what works'.

Summary of main sections

Opportunities for ICT in Mathematics

Materials and advice for teachers issued in the early 1980s still have some relevance today. Examples of 'legacy' software illustrate the ways in which ICT may provide an interactive class teaching aid and a tool for pupil-led investigation. Content-free applications with tools for manipulating graphics provide the teacher with opportunities to adapt tasks to meet specific objectives.

Roamers, Pixies and turtles provide early experience of controlling IT systems through sequences of commands. In this section, we look at the opportunities for supporting teaching and learning in numeracy and introducing angular turn. Once children progress to controlling the turtle on the screen, there are many possibilities for enriching knowledge of number, shape and spatial concepts through problem solving and exploration of pattern.

Graphing programs are a non-threatening and familiar use of ICT. Computer graphs are often regarded as attractive end products, rather than as tools to support further inquiry. Important issues concern interpretation, and the language children use in communicating what their graphs show. In this chapter, we see how spreadsheet tools overcome some of the limitations of simple graphing programs.

Pupils may find spreadsheets more accessible than databases. Ways of introducing the spreadsheet and developing its use as an investigative tool are explored. Where ICT helps to sheds light on a difficult concept, pupils may experience pleasure, excitement and deep satisfaction. Such experiences not only contribute to effective learning. They help to overcome some of the barriers surrounding the technology itself.

Year 5 pupils created and used a database in Mathematics as part of a study of 2D shapes. This case study shows how, in organising the data

initially and in carrying out database searches, pupils developed classificatory skills through identifying attributes. The opportunity appeared
to widen their understanding of the properties of plane shapes.

Opportunities for ICT in English

The first chapter in this section identifies ways in which ICT may
promote speaking and listening. In particular, we look at opportunities
provided by 'adventure' games at Key Stage 1. The role of talking
stories and talking word processors in the teaching of reading is discussed. We also see how overlay keyboards may provide a useful teaching aid in developing literacy.

The enabling skills which pupils need in order to make effective use of
the word processor at both Key Stages are identified. Does the medium
really serve as an 'ideas processor' for young writers, as has been
claimed? Research, including detailed evaluations by teachers, is
reviewed. Opportunities for ICT within the Literacy Framework (DfEE,
1998a) are identified.

At Key Stage 2, pupils may use overlay keyboards in storing and
accessing semi-structured texts. There is a strong link with the Literacy
Framework in supporting non-fiction text level work. Texts were manipulated on screen, using standard word processor facilities. Pupils
found that features of texts originating in other genres (such as pictorial
captions) needed adaptation. They began to gain greater awareness of
structural features and language patterns.

The contribution of CD-ROM in supporting topic work is investigated.
What information handling skills are demanded? How may pupils use
downloaded content in the classroom? We also look at the use of multimedia authoring tools by pupils. Integral approaches to presentation, in
the format of 'topic folders', have been established for many years.
What, uniquely, is contributed through the use of ICT?

Finding out through ICT

This section begins with a close look at the contribution of databases in
pupil-led inquiry. How may teachers identify curriculum contexts?
What are the critical issues for managing learning? What skills are

demanded, and what are the constraints? All stages of database creation and interrogation can be highly problematic. In making practical recommendations, the chapter draws on extensive observation of pupils engaged in computer group work.

Data logging systems enable pupils to view at first hand the direct plotting of readings obtained by continuous monitoring. Lower-ability pupils encountered some unexpected difficulties, and the experience helped them to come to terms with graphical models. Teaching strategies involving a high level of interaction with real-time displays are explored. We see how Year 6 pupils made extended use of data logging equipment in Science investigations.

Control technology is as daunting for teachers as it is exciting for children. We look at opportunities across the curriculum, and see how initial work with the Roamer may lead into sensing and control. Progression is defined and links with work in other subjects are made explicit. There are practical examples showing starting points at a range of levels.

Finally, we explore what is involved in seeking information on the Internet. Strategies that teachers may use in tracking down specific topics are discussed. Independent use by pupils is examined critically. Capable 11 year olds readily acquired on-line navigational skills, and were prepared to compare and evaluate information sources. Pupils' ability to plan an inquiry, and use retrieved information away from the computer, will prove critical. In contrast to CD-ROM, the Internet is open and unfenced, with no integral signposts. What are the implications for the role of the teacher?

CHAPTER 2

OPPORTUNITIES FOR ICT IN TEACHING MATHEMATICS

With up to half a day committed to meeting the new Literacy and Numeracy requirements, teachers may feel there is little time for computer group work. How can opportunities for ICT possibly be incorporated, given the current emphasis on whole-class teaching? Before addressing the practical problems, we need to understand the unique benefits of ICT. The final report of the Numeracy Task Force (DfEE, 1998b) is quite clear. A major contribution of ICT lies in teaching, whether to focus on specific aspects of number or to support general demonstration.

Starting with 'legacy' software: number grids and factors

To look at how the computer may uniquely support the teaching of numeracy, we begin with a simple program first distributed – on cassette tape! – in 1982. *Ergo* could hardly look less inviting. The introductory screen is primitive in the extreme. The Acorn version which I use can easily be crashed. Printing BBC screen dumps is a long-forgotten skill. Despite these drawbacks, *Ergo* proved its worth when I recently taught a Year 3 class.

The screen shows a 5 x 5 grid, with only one number revealed at the start. Vertical and horizontal patterns underlie the grid. A typical example of a completed grid is shown here:

9	12	15	18	21
7	10	13	16	19
5	8	11	14	17
3	6	9	12	15
1	4	7	10	13

The aim is for children to discover the patterns and use them to complete the grid. The first number which children enter is a guess: they are told if the number is too large or too small. Immediately, this presents a situation where children have to think strategically in order to find the first number.

In teacher-led lessons, there is much scope for interaction at different levels. Can children correctly predict an adjacent number or – for the most able – the numbers at the ends of rows or in the corners of the grid? Pressing D at the start gives a 'difficult' level with bigger numbers and more exacting patterns to discover. At any stage, the teacher may complete the grid by pressing Ctrl-W.

After several demonstrations, I asked children, in pairs, to make grids on squared paper. Each pair played their own game, with one child in the role of the computer while the other tried to work out the hidden pattern. Later, children investigated adding diagonally opposite corners.

The Association of Teachers of Mathematics published *Some Lessons In Mathematics With A Microcomputer* (the SLIMWAM booklets) in the early Eighties. The booklets contain lesson plans for using *Ergo* and similar software, with accounts by teachers of the ways in which activities away from the computer were developed. It is interesting to note that the emphasis is on *teaching* with the computer. Independent group use follows the initial lesson.

For example, a teacher works with a low ability Year 7 class. He pretends to know little more than the pupils about what *Ergo* does. He acts as operator and 'voice' for the machine. Initial discussion focuses on tactics for finding the first number quickly. Discovery of vertical and horizontal patterns leads to pupils looking for diagonal patterns, combining the 'across' and 'up' rules to form a diagonal rule.

Where pupils had difficulty in articulating the rule, it was helpful to ask, 'What happens when you move to the right?' The related question 'What happens when you move to the left?' introduces the idea of inverse operations in algebra. The teacher had prepared sheets with partially complete grids. Pupils had to identify and record the rules for up, down, right and left, then complete the grids.

The unique contribution of the computer was in enabling the modelling of grids in a whole-class lesson. The computer was more than a visual aid, in that it gave immediate, accurate feedback in response to pupils' suggestions. Children continued working on the program in pairs, gaining valuable practice at their own level. As well as practising mental subtraction and addition, they were engaged in identifying patterns and in applying their knowledge to a problem.

Today, spreadsheets may be used in Mathematics for the same purpose. There are advantages in that grids may be printed and patterns in columns may be displayed graphically. Chapter 5 introduces spreadsheets in the context of calculator work and number investigations. We shall see how valuable this experience is in developing algebraic ideas. Once pupils know how to enter a simple function such as 'subtract two from the value above' and copy it to other cells, they may construct their own grids.

Knowledge of the pattern enables us to construct and manipulate a mental *image* of the grid. Another program from the eighties, *Monty*, begins by revealing the complete grid, for pupils to discern its structure. The grid is then hidden. A 'python' slithers around the grid, then stops in a random position. Pupils have to find the numbers covered by the python.

It is extremely difficult to retain a visual 'snapshot' of the grid. It can only be reconstructed mentally by applying observed rules, for example, 'It goes up in tens from left to right. It goes down in ones from top to bottom.' In other words, a mathematical description is more efficient, and more easily remembered, than a visual image.

Circle generates patterns on a circle of equally spaced dots, by repeatedly counting a fixed step then joining the start and finish points. Initially, children may be asked to explore freely. Even at this 'play' level, structured teacher intervention is important. In the past, inappropriate 'discovery learning' may simply have masked the fact that teachers were too busy to sit down and explore the possibilities for themselves!

It is important to ask questions such as, 'What patterns can you make? What does the screen always tell you?' From the beginning, the teacher's questions focus pupils' attention on the information on screen. Numbers of points and step size are shown, and the number of rotations is also given. The ultimate aim will be to investigate connections between these values and the type of pattern that is produced.

Pupils may be given a structured series of investigations. For example, they may first be asked to enter a fixed number of points (say 12 or 24) and investigate the range of patterns that the computer will draw. From the beginning, it is important to record the results. On a circle of 12 points, a step of 3 draws a square. Why? What happens with a step of 9? Teachers' questions should focus on the interconnections between the numbers and the patterns produced.

The next step might be to focus on a particular outcome such as a hexagon. Which pairs of numbers give hexagons? Again, it is important to record the data. As soon as the child notices a pattern, prediction should be actively encouraged. (How do we account for the fourth result?)

Number of dots	Step size	Number of sides	Number of revolutions
6	1	6	1
12	2	6	1
18	3	6	1
6	5	6	5

A more advanced investigation focuses on 'stars'. Can the child discover, for example, five-pointed stars? (10,4), (20,8) are good examples. The pairs (number of dots, step size) are all in the ratio 5:2. Factors, multiples, ratios and equivalence can be extremely difficult to grasp, yet are related concepts. The problems presented by *Circle* broaden the child's experience, in providing opportunities to identify and use numeric relationships.

'Star' produced by a step size of 4 on a circle of 10 dots.

At an even higher level, the teacher may ask, 'What rules can we use to predict whether the pattern will be a polygon or a star?' The unique contribution of *Circle* is the speed with which it can generate a range of patterns. Capable children may quickly move to a more demanding problem. Unless pupils have some expertise with protractors, it is difficult to space dots evenly on paper. I do recall making similar 'clock faces' on a banda master, but I think I would rather use the computer! Unfortunately, software of this vintage does not run in Windows, ruling out the pasting of patterns into other applications and causing printing to be a nightmare.

ICT is not a substitute for practical activities of a concrete nature. The computer is simply one of a range of resources for teaching Mathematics. The ICT application may support or extend work begun away from the computer. It may, for example, be used to extend an ongoing investigation. The computer can do this by readily generating exemplars and providing feedback, as in the case of *Circle*.

Multimedia resources may provide 'scaffolding' through graphics, sound and animation. For example, there are animated sequences controlled by the child which show a ten exploding into ten ones. (*Mighty Maths Carnival Countdown* contains a good example.) CD-ROMs with colourful, appealing graphics may be of particular value in supporting children who do not find it easy to get to grips with mathematical ideas.

For example, some young children find it difficult to grasp concepts of pairing and counting in twos. Much practice is needed and the computer offers another experience. For example, *Caterpillar* in *Tizzy's Toybox* requires the child to match pairs of shoes.

MyWorld **Mathematics activities with infants**

We have looked ways in which ICT may be used in teaching the whole class, and in providing opportunities for investigation. A further advantage of ICT is that it may provide a framework to the teacher who is prepared to spend just a little time in adapting content to meet learners' needs. To illustrate, we look at ways in which *MyWorld* screens may be used in Mathematics at Key Stage 1.

MyWorld features a background on which children may place and arrange graphic images. The graphics are stored on the screen and are of two types, 'one-off' or 'copiable many times'. On some screens there is a text button, enabling pupils to add labels to the background. Unwanted objects may be disposed of in the 'bin'.

Since *MyWorld* is an open-ended *framework* program, it depends on a good supply of content to serve a range of teaching objectives. The quality and appropriateness of *MyWorld* screens varies widely. Screens developed to meet a particular need – for example, practice in coin recognition for pupils with learning difficulties – may not succeed in another situation. Many teachers have expressed disappointment that there is no feedback. If pupils make incorrect matches, say between objects and captions, there is no response from the system. Screens where there is a 'right answer', such as those featuring time and money, suffer from this drawback, although the teacher may print the correct results for comparison.

Learning outcomes depend on the precise activity. A screen may be used in different ways, as we shall see. Since it is possible to prepare and save screens in advance, the teacher may frame an activity to serve a particular objective. Learning is not confined to Mathematics. In enabling children to arrange pictures on a background, some screens also serve as vehicles for story telling (see Chapter 7).

It is important to appreciate the open-ended nature of *MyWorld* screens. The most effective screens are those where there is no 'right' answer. In the 'Teddies' screens on the *MyWorld Nursery* disc, children may move objects to find the concealed bear, then rearrange the room in any way they like so that the next group has no idea where Teddy is hiding.

Another simple example is *Bricks,* where children may arrange 3D 'bricks' to make their own pictures. A group of low ability Year 2 children agreed to build a 'castle'. Sam could not see which brick was needed to span the top of a door. Steven told him which one to use; he was able to visualise the brick in place, but Sam could not do this. The chance to experiment assisted Sam in discriminating between the bricks. Later, the picture was labelled.

Some activities enable self-checking. The objective may be to make, copy or finish a pattern, or set of objects. Children may check for themselves whether the pattern, or set, is complete. An example is the *Clowns* screen on the *MyWorld Maths* disc. There is an infinite supply of clowns: each may be given a red, blue or green hat, nose and tie. As with all *MyWorld* screens, the activity is essentially open ended: children may arrange the clowns as they please. However, if a rule is made that all clowns must be different, the screen offers a range of combinatorial problems.

A group of three Year 2 pupils set out to find all the clowns. It did not take them long to discover twelve different clowns. There are 27 possible combinations, but the task becomes much harder as fewer combinations remain unused. Away from the computer, the children made a list on paper of four further clowns. This was a difficult challenge, and it seemed unlikely that they would find any more clowns, due to the amount of checking that was now involved.

There was clearly a need to constrain the number of possible outcomes, by fixing one of the variables. One group chose to make clowns with blue hats. They quickly discovered five, and I asked if they could make any more. They succeeded in making all nine. The approach was one of trial and error, followed by careful checking against clowns already on the screen. There was much use of the bin during this activity.

I posed the problem, 'How many clowns can you make with red noses?' One group showed signs of a systematic approach. They began with three clowns, each with a different hat. But instead of sticking to the same colour tie, they mixed the colours up. Because they had not followed a pattern, finding the ninth clown proved hard. Jenna said, 'He can have a blue hat! You can have a green bow, and he'll be different.' Jenna was not reasoning that, because there were three red and three green hats, there should be three blue hats. She was simply telling the others something she had noticed. In the event, the other children ignored her, and the wrong colour was put on. Jenna seemed to lose track of her idea, but at the end she announced, 'There's three red hats and three green hats and three blue hats!'

We made 9 clowns with red noses.

3 clowns have got blue hats.
3 clowns have got red hats.
3 clowns have got green hats.

Figure 1: Year 2 children recorded the set of clowns with red noses.

Another challenge is to make a set of clowns, each with three colours. Again, the clowns must all be different. There are six possible combinations. Another Year 2 group could not discover the sixth clown. I prompted the children to tell me about the hats. They noticed that there were two green hats and two blue hats, but only one red. They were then able to solve the problem.

The group next used the *Flags* screen. Six flags were made, each flag containing the three coloured stripes in a different arrangement. Grace, who made the last of the six flags, noticed that there were two with red at the top and two with yellow at the top, but only one with blue at the top. She reasoned that the sixth flag had to have blue at the top

Older pupils may be asked to use *Clowns* or *Flags* with the objective of exploring different systematic approaches. For example, all nine clowns with red noses may be arranged in a 3x3 matrix. The pupils may opt to select an attribute (i.e. hat or tie) and vary its colour with each clown in the row.

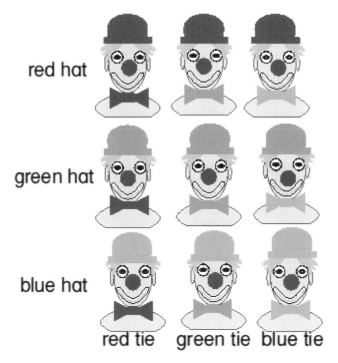

Figure 2: Clowns with red noses are arranged in a matrix.

Another useful yet simple screen is *Blocks*. Working on their own, Year 2 children began with random arrangements but then decided to follow a pattern. Rebecca made a tower with repeating red, yellow and blue blocks. Dean began with a random pattern, then 'binned' blocks as a repeating row began to emerge. Grace made a row of three, then extended her pattern into a two dimensional arrangement (Figure 3).

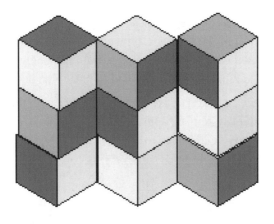

Figure 3: A Year 2 pupil's pattern of blocks

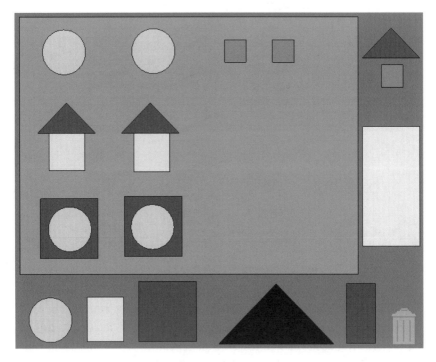

Figure 4: MyWorld Build (Nursery Disc)

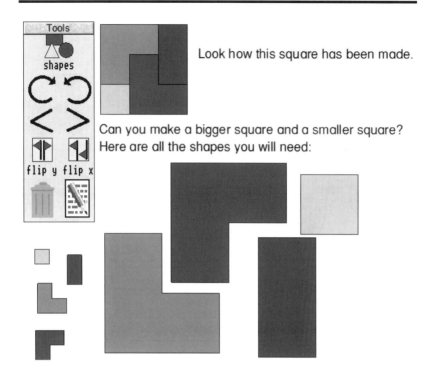

Figure 5: A screen prepared by a teacher using MyWorld2 Tiles

Some *MyWorld* screens provide sets of shapes for tessellation. One Year 2 group began with a pattern of equilateral triangles. When asked, they were unable to identify a hexagon within the tessellation they had made. One girl found a plastic hexagon and this was held up against the screen, to identify the shape. Other pupils needed no help, and made a number of separate hexagons. Children had to think hard about fitting the shapes together. These screens have an advantage over plastic shapes in that the rest of the arrangement is undisturbed while children try to fit a new shape into a gap.

The teacher may prepare and save a *MyWorld* screen to meet a particular objective, for example to give practice in organising objects in twos. Even the very simple *Build* screen on the *MyWorld Nursery* disc may be used in this way. The teacher may ask the child, 'Make me some pairs'. In the example (Figure 4), the teacher has prepared sequences for the child to finish. Children may use the unlimited supply of shapes in

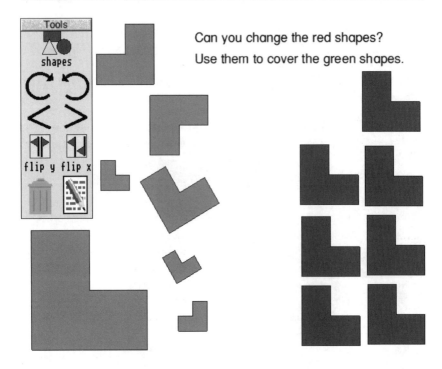

Figure 6: A screen prepared by the teacher. Can children transform the shapes on the right?

combination. The next step might be to make pairs of houses, or presents.

The teacher may set varied tasks for children who do not always progress readily from one step to the next. The *Tiles* screen and libraries are supplied with *MyWorld2*. Initially, children may choose freely from the four sets of shapes, which appear in a pop-up menu. There are tools which enable the shapes to be enlarged or reduced, flipped horizontally or vertically, and rotated in either direction. Children will discover for themselves what these tools do. However, the teacher may prepare a progression of screens which focus on a particular transformation. Activities may proceed step-by-step, supporting a pupil who has difficulty with the concept.

In Figure 5, the child is given the pieces needed to make a smaller and a larger copy of the pattern. Two pieces need to be rotated or flipped in order to fit. The teacher may plan a progression of tasks in which the level of challenge is increased, or support withdrawn, a step at a time. In the preceding task, the child may be asked to match the pattern exactly, with prepared jigsaw pieces. In the follow-up activity, shapes have to be selected from the pop-up menu and manipulated by the child to cover or copy the pattern.

In Figure 6, the red shapes on the right have to be manipulated to match the green shapes on the left. The full range of tools is used, and two shapes have to be transformed twice. The red shapes have been pre-selected from the pop-up menu, and the screen saved in advance by the teacher. This saves time, especially where the teacher plans to use this screen in the context of a whole-class interactive session. There is much scope for discussion: 'What do you think will happen?' 'Is there another way of making the green shape?' 'Can you describe other things we could do with the red shapes?'

Tasks specially prepared using 'content-free' IT applications often provide excellent assessment opportunities, because there is a visible end product. In preparing screens such as those above, the teacher may identify the skills, understanding and knowledge demonstrated by a child who completes the tasks successfully.

CHAPTER 3

ROAMERS, PIXIES AND SCREEN TURTLES

Floor robots in developing numeracy

Learning through ICT is not restricted to the computer. Technological developments in the early 1980s led to the invention of electronic toys which could be directly programmed by children. The Valiant Roamer was designed to build on the success of programmable toys and computer-controlled floor robots in introducing young children to IT concepts. At the simplest level, the Roamer is 'commanded' via a control panel to move in linear fashion or to turn right or left. When switched on, the unit of forward/backward movement is the Roamer's diameter. The default unit of turn is the degree. These units may all be re-set.

The Valiant Roamer

Initial 'play' is worthwhile, especially where children are meeting the Roamer for the first time. As initial curiosity and excitement subside, they become better able to concentrate on directed activities. Play also helps children acquire familiarity with the operation of the Roamer. They also gain a feel for predicting where the Roamer will stop. Levels of co-operation are high, and children are eager to help each other. Body language is often in evidence, as children use their hands to measure and estimate Roamer 'steps', and their whole bodies to enact the moves and turns it will make.

Cullen (1995) describes a simple 'beanstalk' number track activity, where children used large foam dice to generate forward 'steps' to be entered on the Roamer's control panel. She found that number track games were helpful for children with low level number skills. In a concrete way, children encountered different representations of number. For example, if 'four' has been thrown, children see the equivalence between:

- 'four' as the number of dots counted on the face of the die
- 4 as the number pressed on the Roamer's control panel
- 4 as the place on the number track where the Roamer stops.

Roamer games demand very few props. Masking tape is particularly useful to create tracks and grids. An area of the floor may be marked out and left for at least a few days. There are many possibilities for children to construct buildings, bridges etc., to add to the Roamer's environment.

With masking tape, a number track may easily be marked on the floor. Alternatively, a 'mat' can be made using thin cork tiles. The track needs to be marked out in Roamer 'steps'. The Roamer's unit of linear distance is 30cm, which is its diameter. The actual 'step' should be checked, because the nature of the floor covering makes a difference.

Straightforward addition may be modelled on the number track. Children may be asked to find ways of moving to 5 in two steps. They could, for example, move 'Forward 3' followed by 'Forward 2'. Subtraction may be modelled, as in 'Forward 6' followed by 'Backward 1'.

The Roamer stores commands. If you enter a new command without clearing memory, your command is added to the stored sequence. To begin afresh, you must press CM ('Clear memory') twice. At first, this seems tiresome. However, the feature can be used to advantage. Ask a child to enter 'Forward 2', then press Go repeatedly. What do children in the group think will happen?

At this stage, the children are discovering some important things about ICT. Microprocessor-controlled systems do whatever they are told! If a child enters 'Forward 90', the Roamer will try to do just that! Children are also beginning to appreciate that a device may store instructions and carry them out repeatedly. There are many parallels in the work and home environment. A good example to discuss with children is the photocopier outside the school office. We may make two copies by pressing '2' and 'Start'. If we press 'Start' again, we get another two copies.

Introducing turn

Early experience may be gained in the hall or playground, in games where children have to turn their bodies to face a new direction. Incorporating right and left quarter-turns on the Roamer may be the next step in the progression. A variation on the simple number track is to introduce a 'bend'. Children may now play simple games with the goal of staying on the track by turning the Roamer at the right place.

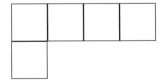

On a smooth surface, the commands 'Right 90' and 'Left 90' turn the Roamer through ninety degrees. Unfortunately, carpeted floors can present problems. In the room where I teach, 'Right 93' executes a perfect right angle! Also, young children may not yet be able to associate the idea of 'one turn' with the number 90.

The Roamer user guide explains how to re-set the unit of turn to a right angle[1]. Now, children simply enter 'Right 1' to turn through a right angle. The teacher may ask, 'What will Right 2 do?' 'What will Right 4 do?' Left as well as right turns are now re-defined, and the instruction will stay in the Roamer's memory until it is switched off.

At this level, children may use a simple method of recording their sequences. Already, they are programming. A 'program' is nothing more than a series of stored instructions which the device carries out in order, such as 'Forward 2, Right 1, Forward 3'.

Number tracks lend themselves to a great number of imaginative scenarios. For example, the Roamer may become a milk float, a bus or even the 'Jolly Postman' on his rounds. Children are learning to operate the Roamer while consolidating number track concepts. They are also gaining experience of counting and estimating Roamer units on the floor space.

Once the track is removed, pupils are faced with the challenge of estimating linear distance and turn. Here, the Roamer must be 'commanded' to land on the flower. Accurate estimation of the amount of turn is a considerable step, and pupils need some knowledge of what smaller angles such as 60, 45 or 30 degrees actually look like.

An extension of the simple number track is the two-dimensional grid. Again, it is vital that the grid unit is equal to the Roamer 'step'. There are many variations, setting the activity in a different context and enabling differentiation across a wide ability range. The basic grid may be labelled with co-ordinates. The child may be asked to move the Roamer from A1 to C3. The group may be asked to find different routes between these two points.

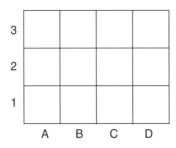

Again, a story scenario may be used. The grid may represent a farm or a zoo. Pictures of animals are placed in the cells. The child may be asked to take the Roamer to the monkeys then to the elephants. Different routes are possible. A constraint may be imposed, such as 'Don't go past the snakes on the way.'

Cork tiles may be laid out to represent supermarket aisles. Children may make a 'basket' to mount on the Roamer's back. 'Shopping lists' prepared by the teacher may be carefully differentiated. The simplest task is to collect one item and move straight to the checkout. At the hardest level, the child has to collect an item from each aisle. Keying in the commands to collect the items in order poses a considerable challenge. The child needs to construct an image of the journey from the Roamer's viewpoint. When the Roamer has turned round and is heading back towards you, it can be difficult to determine whether it should turn left or right!

The child may walk round the grid first. The total journey may now be built up in stages. This is possible since the Roamer accumulates instructions. First, the child commands the Roamer to land on the first target. The child does not clear the memory, but presses the commands to move to the second target. The Roamer is then placed right back at the start. When Go is pressed, the original sequence is carried out followed by the new commands. Now the commands to reach the third target are added. The Roamer is placed at the start, and the whole sequence trialled.

Similar grid activities may be designed for the Pixie, a small robot which may be used on a tabletop. Broad (1997) describes work in a Year 1 class studying the topic 'Materials'. Much use had been made of the story of the Three Little Pigs. On the floor was marked a track, representing a road leading to the houses of the Three Little Pigs.

The 'wolf' creeping along the road was a Pixie. The route had been planned to enable children to program the Pixie to stop at each house in turn. Turning left or right proved the greatest challenge initially. By default, the Pixie only moves in 90-degree turns. This proved helpful in limiting the demands on children. The pupils worked in pairs, in weekly 'bursts' of 15-20 minutes. While they were free to explore for themselves what the Pixie will do, they always returned to the map. Broad notes:

> It is interesting to watch as the children develop from giving simple instructions to building up ever longer and more complex chains of commands. The brighter children very quickly cotton on to the fact that you can program the Pixie to negotiate the complete track in one go. Then it becomes a challenge to see who can be the first to achieve this.

Extending children's understanding of angle

Grid activities, with the unit of turn set to 90 degrees, limit the child to a simple choice between left and right. An important step is taken when children realise that turns can be of different sizes. Planned use of the Roamer gives pupils opportunities to make and compare turns of different sizes.

Initially, targets may be placed to form a circle around the Roamer. A die may be thrown to give the number of the target the Roamer is to visit. Linear distance is fixed, but children have to estimate, then enter, turns in units of 60 degrees. In a similar way, compass directions may be marked out on the floor. This time, the unit turn is set to 45 degrees. With the Roamer in the 'home' position facing North, a child may be asked to move two steps North West, and so on. These games introduce a smaller unit of turn while avoiding difficult angular estimation.

The Roamer is supplied with a pen kit. It may be worth asking older pupils what they think will happen if the pen is attached to the Roamer's side, rather than fixed in the centre! There is a 'repeat' button on the panel. Some of the initial work with turtle graphics described in the next section may be carried out using the Roamer. For example, repeating 'Forward 1 Right 60' six times draws a hexagon.

Pupils who are able independently to construct squares and hexagons are ready to progress to turtle graphics on the screen. However, it is often worth returning to the Roamer, especially where problems arise. Constructing an equilateral triangle often presents difficulties. The angle through which the Roamer must turn is larger than many people expect! Again, the Roamer presents an effective problem-solving tool since pupils may be able to see the task from the floor robot's viewpoint.

It is important to discuss with Key Stage 2 pupils the advantages of using the screen version. On the computer, the whole sequence is not only stored, but can be saved to disc, listed on the screen, edited and printed. It is important, however, not to rush into this stage. The great advantage of the floor robot is that it moves in the child's own space. It is much harder to think of direction on the screen, since the turtle moves in a vertical plane. I have often seen children bending themselves double in an effort to look down the screen from the turtle's viewpoint!

Introducing the screen turtle

The 'floor turtle' originated in educational research based on the Logo programming language. Early developments are strongly associated with constructivist theories of learning (Papert, 1980). Computer-controlled turtles are used in schools today, notably the Valiant Turtle, which receives its commands remotely via a small unit attached to the computer. The software, which optionally may be used to control the floor robot, features its screen equivalent which moves around in response to exactly the same commands. The screen turtle has a 'pen', and will 'draw' as it moves, provided the pen is in the 'down' position.

When children first move from the Roamer or Pixie to the screen turtle, they encounter important differences. Perhaps the most significant is that the screen turtle moves in a vertical plane. This may challenge spatial thinking, as we see below. In nearly all versions of turtle graphics (the graphics subset of the full Logo language), linear units are quite small. The child used to instructing the Roamer to move 'Forward 3' now has to think in terms of 'Forward 30'. The unit of turn is, by default, the degree.

In most implementations, the basic commands may be entered using function key presses. A strip is supplied, to place along the top of the keyboard. There may be a panel on the screen, enabling commands to be clicked. Typing in commands is a last resort, since it greatly increases the likelihood of error.

At Key Stage 1, the floor robot is generally preferred for the very reason that it moves in the child's own space. As we have seen, it can be dressed up, assigned a role and incorporated in structured play. However, some six- and seven-year-olds in my experience have been able to progress to the full screen version. Vaughan (1997) has investigated turtle activities with even younger pupils, and challenges us to review our assumptions about five-year-olds' readiness to explore larger numbers.

Andrew, a Year 2 pupil, had drawn a square on the screen:

    Forward 30
    Right 90
    Forward 30
    Right 90
    Forward 30
    Right 90
    Forward 30
    Right 90

(There is a much quicker way of doing this, as we shall see.) Andrew wanted to draw a line diagonally across the square. He told his partner to enter Right 50. Andrew explained, 'It needs to be half of ninety. Ninety is nearly a hundred, and half of a hundred's fifty.' Andrew's teacher told me that he was working on number line addition and subtraction to twenty.

Initially, children command the screen turtle a step at a time. The next stage may be to introduce the *Repeat* command. *Repeat* is available on the Roamer, but teachers may prefer to wait until the screen turtle is introduced. The Roamer may take a long time to trace repeated steps. The screen turtle, which may be set to a range of speeds, can draw a complex pattern in a very short time.

Andrew's square would become:

    Repeat 4
    Forward 30
    Right 90
    Next

The *Next* command is important, signifying the end of the repeat *loop*. It tells the computer to keep going back, until the given number of repeats has been carried out. The precise terminology varies according to the software.

There is much scope at this level for constructing shapes, regular or otherwise. National guidance on assessing IT (SCAA, 1995) suggests that pupils investigate the Logo commands to draw regular polygons, starting with the equilateral triangle. If *number of sides* and *angle* are tabulated, a pattern emerges.

The teacher may ask able pupils to compare with the process of creating shapes on a locked grid with !Draw (see Chapter 6). It is of value to do this, since pupils have to think very differently about the properties of the shape in each case. There is a strong dynamic element in Logo, since angles are constructed by rotating the turtle. Another difference is that the nature of the !Draw grid constrains the shapes that may be drawn. Pupils may profitably be asked to reflect on this.

The next step in the progression is to define a *procedure*, or new Logo command. For example, we may want to draw repeated squares. It is frustrating in the extreme to have to keep entering the commands!

There are different approaches in the various turtle graphics packages. it may be necessary to click a 'Procedures' button, or type a special command. Whatever happens, the procedure must have a name. Let's call ours *Square*. (If you are invited to complete the box, 'Square with...', don't! Some implementations have provision for variables, but we have not quite reached that stage yet.)

In most programs, the commands to draw the square are typed into the *procedure window*. Since implementations vary, it is best to check the user guide very carefully at this point.

Once the procedure has been defined, it may be used just like any other Logo command. It may be included in *Repeat* instructions, even in other procedures. A simple 'whirly' pattern is made as follows:

Repeat 8
Square
Right 45
Next

Other 'shape' procedures may be used in similar repeat loops, with spectacular results. There are many opportunities for number work. To extend the pattern through a full 360 degrees, the angle of turn needs to be calculated according to the number of repeats.

Capable pupils who quickly develop Logo programming skills may be introduced to *variables*. If we take our procedure *Square*, we can see that it is a little restricted because it always draws a square with a fixed length of side. A new procedure with variable 'side' can be used to draw squares with any side whatever. (Note that, depending on your version of Logo, you may have to define a new procedure with a different name. Otherwise you may be told, 'Square already exists.')

Let's adopt the name *Newsquare*. The new procedure (depending on the implementation: check your user guide!) is named as:

Newsquare with side

The commands are:

Repeat 4
Forward side
Right 90
Next

When you run your procedure, you must give a value for *side*, for example:

Newsquare 10
Newsquare 50

New possibilities for mathematical pattern making, for example a series of squares growing from a point, are opened.

Thinking from the turtle's aspect may prove a challenge even to adults. A variety of situations may arise which extend children's spatial thinking by requiring them to *de-centre*, or adopt a different physical viewpoint. The simplest case of all arises where the turtle is pointing down the screen, and we wish to move it to *our* right. I have often observed Year 3 children standing by the screen, contorting themselves to look at the problem from the turtle's perspective!

It is worth taking a moment to consider how the turtle could be instructed to make this pattern:

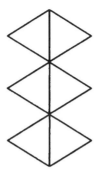

A group of student teachers had already programmed a 'right-handed' equilateral triangle called Tri:

Repeat 3
Forward 20
Right 120
Next

The students identified three right-handed triangles on the right of the pattern. They began at the base, with the turtle pointing up the screen. The column of triangles was drawn, as follows:

Repeat 3
Tri
Forward 20
Next

At this point, with the turtle at the top of the pattern, they decided to create a new procedure to draw a 'left-handed' triangle. The turtle would be moved back 20 to draw the new triangle, and this would be repeated three times. It took other students several moments to realise that this really would be rather a waste of effort! All that needs to be done is to turn the turtle 180 degrees, and repeat the above commands.

Faced with this type of problem, pupils should be taught first to model the turtle's movements, possibly by sketching on paper what has to be done. There may be several valid approaches, as in modelling this construction of four squares (Blyth, 1990):

41

The construction may be viewed as four adjacent squares, or as a pair of railway lines with sleepers. It may also be modelled in zig-zag fashion, with parallel edges added later:

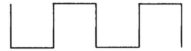

None of these models is intrinsically 'wrong'. Whatever pupils decide, it is important at least to talk through the process of construction step-by-step before attempting to translate into turtle commands. Children should be encouraged to make sure the computer does as much of the work as possible – that is what it is there for! In other words, they need to make sure they minimise their own effort by adopting a good plan which eliminates endless re-tracing of steps. If this modelling is undertaken as a whole-class activity, different approaches may later be compared. In each case, what do we have to tell the turtle to do?

Note

1. Press the right arrow, followed by the square bracket. Then enter 90 and press the square bracket again. Now press Go. Note that a value slightly higher than 90 may be given to compensate for the carpet!

CHAPTER 4

THE COMPUTER AS A GRAPHING TOOL

Graphing programs produce charts directly from data typed in by children. Axes are drawn automatically, and pupils are spared the effort of drawing and colouring graphs by hand. The emphasis is on interpretation rather than production. Once data has been gathered and prepared, graph production is straightforward. The same data may be seen in different representations. A bar graph may be transformed into a pie chart, for example. The use of ICT to 'represent data in graphs and charts' is recognised in the final report of the Numeracy Task Force (DfEE, 1998b) and strongly advocated in its recommendations.

When a Year 4 class investigated seedling growth they used *DataPlot*, a graphing program widely used in developing pupils' data handling skills. All were able to enter data independently. However, the interpretation of simple bar charts presented unexpected problems. On the other hand, the limitations of this simple program restricted its scope in supporting investigation. Children need opportunities to progress, both in ICT capability and inquiry skills. The next step may be to introduce the spreadsheet as a graphing tool.

Discrete and continuous variables

Pupils encounter different types of variables in a variety of situations. There are *discrete* categories: yes or no, months of the year, names of colours. A further type of discrete variable is numeric, and is obtained by counting: the number of leaves on a plant, scores in a test. From an early age, children learn the skills of measuring *continuous* variables such as length or mass. While their early work, with arbitrary units, gives rise to effectively discrete data, children progress to measure with increasing accuracy, using a continuous scale.

Height may be measured with cut-out paper 'feet'. Children progress to using standard units of measurement. The process still entails counting, until the concept is secure: only then are rules and measuring tapes introduced. Data is still effectively discrete, whether obtained by counting cubes or reading to the nearest centimetre on a tape or ruler. Children's first experience of truly continuous data may arise when they use highly accurate devices, such as electronic timers. The ordering, grouping and plotting of results rounded to two decimal places demands a considerable leap forward.

Many children have experienced frequency charts based on tallies. For example, they may have investigated jobs children do at home, or favourite playground games. At a more advanced level, pupils may group numeric data and plot the number of occurrences across the range, to produce a histogram. The frequency chart shows the *mode*, or likeliest value of any single entity within the data set. Histograms make greater demands, not least because data must be organised into appropriate groups.

Bar chart displays are most widely used. Pie charts are appropriate only where there are discrete categories within a defined set. The whole 'pie' must have meaning, as the complete set. *DataPlot* also has a line graph option, which is often used inappropriately. Line graphs are appropriate in charting continuously changing variables (McFarlane, 1997).

Interpreting and using computer graphs

It is vital that pupils learn to communicate and to read information displayed graphically. What does the tallest bar show? On the histogram, what are the bars at extremes of the range? The interpretation of graphs can be highly problematic. Few Year 4 pupils would have any difficulty in identifying the commonest mode of transport, or most popular colour, from a frequency chart. Histograms, however, present different demands. The x-axis is a continuum, and 'bars' represent grouped data.

Children are likely to equate the 'tallest' bar to the 'biggest' value, rather than the greatest number of occurrences.

In all frequency charts, there is a potential problem in articulating what the mode shows. It may not be true that *most* entities are in this category! Terms such as 'commonest', 'most popular' circumvent this problem but are not always appropriate. The confusion has spread to official guidance for teachers. *Expectations in IT* aims to exemplify attainment at the end of Years 2, 4 and 6 (SCAA, 1997). In one example, Year 2 pupils have produced a bar chart of children's favourite sports. The teacher asks, 'Which is most children's favourite?' The child replies, 'Football [...] because it's biggest on the graph.' In fact, *most* children prefer other sports. I have argued (Smith, 1997) that the language of sets is a convenient and accurate way of talking about what frequency bar charts actually show. In the SCAA example, the biggest set, or mode, is the set of children whose favourite sport is football.

Graphs are only one of the modes of representation that children may encounter. In the first instance, data may be recorded numerically, as a list or table. The presentation of the graph with written report is often the conclusion of the activity. There has been a call for active, rather than passive, use of graphing (Pratt, 1995). The computer graph is not merely an attractive end product: it should be used as evidence to inform an inquiry. Active graphing depends on children's ability to interpret with accuracy, and to articulate and communicate what the graph shows.

Using a graphing program with a Year 4 class

Pupils had planted bean seeds in different locations, to investigate the effects of extremes of light and temperature. They kept diaries of daily measurements and used *DataPlot* to chart the height of seedlings directly. Children were encouraged to look for trends, and to make predictions as the display took shape. The more able pupils collected heights of all seedlings on one day, and grouped data to produce a histogram.

Direct plots

Since growth is a continuous variable, *DataPlot's* line graph format was selected. This format shows continuous, rather than step-wise, change. Unfortunately, a serious difficulty arose because data was missing for certain days. No-one had wanted to come to school at weekends and on Bank Holiday Monday to measure bean plants! Where no data has been included, the value $y = 0$ is plotted by default. This is a problem in the design of the software. Children rejected the line graph option, because the line descended sharply to the x-axis. In using the spreadsheet as a graphing tool, the problem is overcome.

If the missing days were left out, there was a sudden rise in the graph, and nearly all children were aware that this could be misleading. I was told, 'People will think it's shot up in the night.'

Missing days must therefore be put in, to obtain the gradient which shows the rate of growth. This is a highly abstract concept. Even so, some children could identify *changes*. For example, they suggested that 'levelling off' meant the plant was 'slowing down'. Most, including the lowest ability pupils, were able to link the 'steepest' feature with the fastest growth. Of the nineteen who handed in finished reports, eighteen had labelled correctly where the plant had grown most slowly. All but five explained this in their writing. Imagery of 'steps', 'hills' and 'floors', suggested at the computer, featured strongly in their written work (McFarlane, 1997).

Two capable girls told me that the bean plant was slowing down and suggested reasons. They thought that, if they were to continue entering daily measurements, the steps would get smaller and smaller. They were able to extrapolate from the trend evident in their graph.

No-one showed intuitive understanding of *rate of growth*. Luke produced a ruler and laid it along the line of the 'steps' in Russell's graph. Russell observed, 'It's all in a line!' This was just a curiosity and nothing else was said.

As more bars are added to the display, autoscaling is carried out. The graph of 'Pets' shows clearly what happens when a large value is entered. Year 4 children understood that, although the display had been re-scaled, the *values* represented by each bar were unchanged. Some were keen to predict how the y-axis would look as larger values were

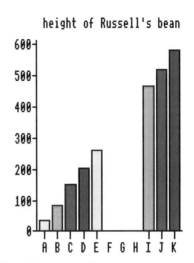

	Day:	Height(mm):
A	8	35
B	9	85
C	10	150
D	11	205
E	12	260
F	13	
G	14	
H	15	
I	16	470
J	17	520
K	18	585

DataPlot bar graph of plant growth

entered. On entering the first two measurements, two bars filled the display. A boy said, 'It looks like a very close view it.' This was a helpful insight into scale. I explained that it would look as though we were getting further and further away as the graph grew.

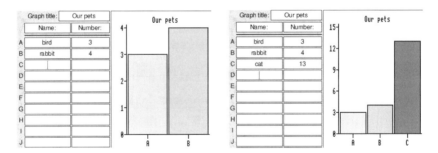

DataPlot bar charts which show the effects of autoscaling

Histograms

All the measurements taken on one day had been written on the board. The teacher asked the pupils to group the data. A child told me that, in a recent Mathematics lesson, 'we learned to group them in fifties.'

Christina said, 'The graph shows how many beans were at different heights.' Later, she explained, 'My graph is about the whole group of beans that have been grown in our class.' She added that her partner's graph was just about one plant.

I had to ask, 'What does the tallest bar show?' All agreed that the tallest column, 'E', had the highest bean plants. Pupils changed their minds after I asked them to locate the tallest bean on the display. I was then told that the tallest bar was 'the most'. Polly wrote on her graph: 'I found out that 200-249 is the most popular height for the beans.'

	Height(mm):	Number:
A	0-49	5
B	50-99	1
C	100-149	2
D	150-199	4
E	200-249	12
F	250-299	3
G	300-349	1
H	350-399	
I	400-449	1
J	450-499	
K	500-549	
L	550-649	1

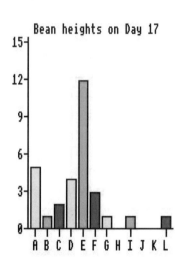

Bean heights on Day 17

Histogram derived from the heights of all plants.

There was heated discussion between Luke and Russell:

Russell   But E's tallest bar, it's got the most in one column.

Luke   There's 18 others and there's only 12 in there.

Russell   There's only six more in all the other groups put together!

Russell appeared to think that, because it was impossible for another group to outnumber 'E', it therefore is the most. Another boy was adamant that the tallest bar showed the 'most'. I asked whether there really are more in column E. 'No, because if you count up all the others there's more.' But he then reasserted that 'E' was 'most'. At this stage, children's understanding is not challenged because their understanding of 'most' encompasses 'the biggest', and is quite workable in this situation.

Georgina	Most beans grow up to 200-249. [I challenge:] Well, the beans that we've grown.
HS	What if I counted up all these other plants? Is it true that most of them are in that group?
Georgina	No! [laughter] A lot of them are.
HS	Apart from the ones that haven't grown at all, whereabouts are most of the beans?
Georgina	On this one. 'E'.
HS	Where are most of them gathered?
Georgina	Here. (She points to 'D', 'E', 'F'.)

Georgina added up the three columns to confirm. Three days later, Georgina urged another girl to write down that 'most' plants were in D, E and F. Computer graphs emphasise 'the tallest bar', rather than that *part* of the graph which features most occurrences in a normal distribution. Chopping up into bars is arbitrary. Yet the bars are perceived as entities and the children do not think of re-grouping the data.

Should we be concerned at this stage? At Key Stage 3, many pupils continue to find interpretation difficult, but the only guidance is limited to explanations in textbooks (Watson, 1993, p.80). It is important to develop a secure understanding at Key Stage 2. In any case, when pupils use database software, they will almost certainly encounter frequency histograms. A useful activity would be to produce a histogram of grouped data obtained from measuring children's heights. It could quickly be established, by asking the whole class, that most children were not represented by the mode.

When the graphing was complete, the whole class reviewed the work. A portable computer was set up with a display panel, mounted on an overhead projector. The large colour display could be seen by all. The image was projected onto a large sheet of white paper pinned to the wall. This allowed children to 'label' features of the graph with coloured chalk. The teacher was able to model the language we use in communicating what graphs show, and give children the opportunity to talk about their graphs with the whole class. This could not possibly have been done with the standard computer monitor.

Spreadsheet graphs

At the simplest level, the spreadsheet is a table, with rows and columns. Used simply as a graphing tool, the step in progression from *DataPlot* is a small one. Having used *DataPlot*, children are already familiar with entering data in columns. Depending on the spreadsheet software, the only new skill is that of dragging a selection over the data and clicking on a 'graph' button.

In the Year 4 'beans' investigation, the case for using a spreadsheet arose from a limitation of *DataPlot*. The same problem is reflected in *Expectations in IT* (SCAA, 1997) in an account of an investigation of cooling by Year 4 pupils. A *DataPlot* bar chart is selected for insulation data. Line graphs were dismissed because 'they joined up every point' – in other words, the line yo-yos up and down to the x-axis. The bar chart gives a 'clearer picture' of the falling temperature. This is a misleading exemplar. The line graph is the correct choice because the data, obtained by measuring temperature at timed intervals, is truly continuous. In fact the failing is in the software – the line plunges to the x-axis when there is a gap in the data. (Spot checks taken of a range of different containers would not be continuous.) It is important to discuss examples with pupils so that they understand when to join the points.

There are valid reasons why teachers may not want to rush into spreadsheet use. The overall concept of spreadsheets is more daunting, but there may be specific drawbacks. Adding a title and labelling axes may not be a task for the faint-hearted (especially in higher-level Acorn applications such as *Eureka*). Pupils may not see the graph being built. The graph appears instantaneously on command, and it may be harder for children to relate the graph to the data. With *Excel*, it is possible to view the graph in a window. As the sheet is updated, changes are automatically made to the chart. Children can see how entering or amending data affects the display.

Eureka's comparative line graphs enabled children to compare the progress made by plants growing in different conditions. Though highly abstract, the representation was directly related to the actual plants which children had observed daily. Even the lower ability pupils were able to point out features:

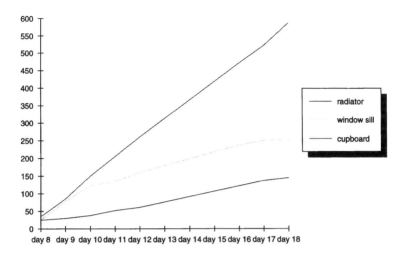

Comparative chart which shows the growth of seedlings in different environments.

Becky	That's probably when it was a seedling there. That's
the	steepest –
Sonia	That's where it's grown most.

For older children, spreadsheets offer a further advantage in that one variable may be plotted against another. There are pitfalls: it is easy to select the wrong block of cells to be graphed, for example. As with so many new ICT skills, it is helpful to model the process to the whole class and train peer tutors beforehand. An instruction card by the computer may show exactly what has to be done.

In plotting one variable against another, children are able to investigate connections within the data. In work with Year 5 / 6 pupils, personal data was used, since it is readily obtained. One teacher, for example, made use of sports timings. Great care should be taken, and the private nature of personal data should be respected. No teacher can justify high-lighting the slowest, weakest, shortest or heaviest member of the class. Groups working on their own investigations should ask permission for any individual's data to be used. There is often no need to use data from the whole class, and the teacher may intervene to suggest a sample.

Year 5 children entered timings from sports events onto a spreadsheet. A bar chart was displayed, of 800m run times. I asked whether the tallest bar showed the fastest time. Pupils were not misled! I was told, 'No, it's the slowest [...] which is 320 seconds.'

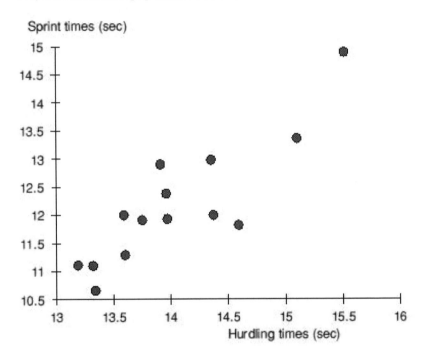

Scattergraph of sprint times plotted against hurdles times.

I asked pupils to select sprint and hurdles times. Luke and Alex were able to identify points plotted on the scattergraph. They identified the fastest sprinter, Tim, 'at the bottom'. They checked the data to find that Tim was runner-up in the hurdles. The fastest hurdles time was then found on the scattergraph. I asked, 'Are the points just anywhere, or are they in a pattern?' I was told that the points were 'together', 'nearly in line'. Luke suggested that they were in a diagonal line. I commented that I would be able to paint a broad stripe through the points.

I asked whether, if somebody has a high time in one race, they are likely to have a high time in the other? The two children were unsure. I asked, 'Looking at the points there, is there anyone who's got a high time in one race and a low time in the other?' They could not answer.

I asked them to imagine a point in the upper left quadrant. Alex promptly replied, 'They'd be fast on one and slow on the other. That person would be fast at the hurdles and slow at the sprint.' They agreed that there were no children in the sample who were slow at one event and fast at the other. They confirmed the parts of the 'scatter' which showed slow/fast times in both events.

Alex noticed that one person did not fit the pattern: 'If you got quite a broad brush and it went over all of those, that would be odd because he's further across.' They agreed that this person was a slower hurdler.

The pair suggested that high jump and long jump performance could be connected. On the scattergraph, they were quick to identify a good high jumper whose long jump was poor. The children were aware that the best performances were now indicated by the *higher* values.

An excellent introductory spreadsheet activity is 'Apes and Kangaroos' (Cobden and Longley, 1996). If your arm span, measured from the tips of one outstretched hand to the other, is greater than your height, you are an 'ape'. If the reverse is true, you are a 'kangaroo'. It may of course be possible that these measurements are identical, in which case you are a 'square'!

The data is entered onto the spreadsheet in columns, in the usual way. Pupils may be shown how to enter a formula to compute the difference between arm span and height. For 'kangaroos', the difference between height and arm span is negative.

Height was plotted against arm span. I discussed the slope, and how it shows that, as we go up in order of children's heights, arm spans generally get bigger as well. Year 5 pupils of above average ability had no difficulty in interpreting points in different areas of the graph, in terms of 'short with small arm span', 'tall with small arm span', etc.

Summary

Nearly all the pupils could use *DataPlot* unaided. While the software has limitations, it is a useful resource in that both discrete and pre-grouped data may be conveniently plotted with no need to scale axes beforehand. Most children are keenly interested in the visual display. The interactive element appears to contribute to understanding of important mathematical ideas. In seeing the construction of the graph, children notice the effects of scale.

Unless someone comes into school to take measurements at weekends, there will always be gaps in this type of data. If missing days are excluded, a misleading picture is presented. Most children were aware of this.

Year 4 pupils could identify where the plant had grown quickest, and where it had slowed down. Most children (with the exception of the lower ability group) showed that they could interpolate and extrapolate to make predictions. It was evident to most that the plants had slowed down markedly. Suggestions were made, such as re-potting and training up a support.

The dominant feature of a computer histogram is the tallest *bar*. This is fully equated with 'most'. It is difficult for children mentally to re-group the data and consider which part of the graph includes most occurrences.

Simple graphing programs are limited tools for purposeful investigation. While they provide a good starting point, there must be the opportunity for progression as children acquire skills.

Where data is entered on a spreadsheet, comparative line graphs may be produced, showing *on one display* the different rates of growth for selected plants. This enabled Year 4 pupils to compare the effect of different growing conditions.

More advanced spreadsheet applications enable scattergraphs. Children may investigate whether two variables are related. After some intro-ductory teaching, Year 5 pupils of above average ability had no difficulty in interpreting 'scatters' and in relating parts of the display to high/low values.

The value of a large display system was demonstrated. Where the image was projected onto the wall, pupils were able to label features of the graph. The teacher may discuss graph features with the whole class, model the language of interpretation, and provide opportunities for inter-action. The availability of a large display will be critical in enabling the use of graphing software within the National Numeracy Framework.

CHAPTER 5

SPREADSHEETS AND INVESTIGATIONS IN MATHEMATICS AND SCIENCE

Introduction

An anecdote best shows the accessibility and relevance of spreadsheets in the primary classroom. When I visited a Year 6 class to help the teacher introduce spreadsheets, two girls were chosen to work with me. They stood close together, chins tucked in, their apprehension tangible. We sat round the computer and I asked them to tell me about their experience of calculators. Discussion quickly turned to their dislike of mathematics. They thought that I had come to test them!

I asked the girls to enter a number on the screen. We then talked about the things we could do to that number. In a very short time, a pattern of multiples had been produced. One girl suggested adding two to a number, then multiplying it by two. The result was not as expected, and I prompted them to use brackets. Both girls became excited and animated. They told me that they had come across brackets in a maths test, but had not understood. Below the first row, they generated a row of results:

1	2	3	4	5	6
6	8	10	12	14	16

The girls were keen to predict how the pattern would continue. They quickly learned how to copy and paste their formula, and wanted to generate more ambitious patterns. Later, the teacher asked them to show others what they had done. Later that day, one of the girls showed her parents, on the PC at home, what she had done on the Acorn at school[1].

A simple starting point, closely linked to familiar work with calculators, led to a positive learning experience. An elusive feature of mathematical notation now made sense. The opportunity to teach peers contributed to the girls' self-esteem. The experience may have helped to counter their negative attitude towards mathematics.

A counter-productive feature of the development of IT in British schools has been the lack of compatibility between the major platforms. However, with spreadsheets, there is such uniformity that it makes little difference which platform, or package for that matter, is used. The availability of laptop computers has increased access. There are excellent publications at an introductory level for teachers who plan to use spreadsheets in Mathematics and Science (Ainley, 1996; Green and Graham, 1994, Frost, 1993).

Despite this, spreadsheet applications are little used in primary schools. Reasons include lack of inclusion in Inset courses and association with Key Stage 3. There is no specific mention in the Key Stage 2 Programmes of Study. Where database use is specified in the curriculum, the option of using a spreadsheet is implied. In many respects, spreadsheets are easier to use than tabular databases. Worthwhile results may be achieved in much less time.

There are important advantages in introducing spreadsheets in the context of Mathematics. Firstly, pupils may work with familiar data, such as the numbers 0,1,2,3! This simplicity makes it much easier to focus on mastering new skills. It is easier for pupils to keep track of processes, and see what the computer has done in calculating a result.

Secondly, there are important teaching and learning benefits, entirely compatible with the National Numeracy Framework. The spreadsheet offers a highly interactive environment which gives instant feedback. Pupils may experiment, using and extending their knowledge of number facts and laws of arithmetic. Mental calculation is encouraged, as pupils are motivated to predict and check results. The modelling of patterns and grids is particularly beneficial in establishing the idea of a linear function, a focal concept in algebra.

In Science, there are many contexts where pupils measure variables as part of an investigation. Where data consists of numeric values, a spreadsheet may be a better choice than a tabular database (Chapter 11). We saw in the last chapter how the spreadsheet may be introduced as a graphing tool, especially where data is continuous. In this chapter, we shall see how spreadsheet calculation enables pupils to find other results such as the mean of a set of values. Pupils may also investigate relationships between variables through, for example, calculating ratio.

Keeling and Whiteman (1990) have identified the following uses of spreadsheets in supporting teaching and learning in Mathematics and Science:

- Investigations into number patterns and sequences

- Construction of mathematical models

- Investigations involving the collection of data, analysis, interpretation and presentation in order to test a hypothesis

- Modelling: exploring what happens if variables are changed.

We look first at ways of generating mathematical patterns, in order to gain a feel for the ways in which spreadsheets manipulate data. Then we consider introductory strategies in the classroom. This section addresses important questions: what are appropriate starting points? What needs to be taught initially? How should work be structured to develop pupils' skills? We then look in turn at the other uses of spreadsheets, as defined by Keeling and Whiteman.

An introduction to modelling in Mathematics

We begin with the following simple pattern:

1   2

2   4

3   6

The pattern is entered onto a spreadsheet, in columns A and B:

	A	B
1	1	2
2	2	4
3	3	6

There are two ways of describing this simple grid. The first is to describe it in terms of repeated addition. As we look down Column A, we see that 1 has been added repeatedly. In Column B, 2 has been added repeatedly. It's easy to see how the grid will extend:

	A	B	C	D
1	1	2	3	4
2	2	4	6	8
3	3	6	9	12
4	4	8	12	16

The second approach to the original grid is to employ a multiplication model. Each number in Column A has been multiplied by 2, to give the results in Column B. If the rule is repeated, the grid will look very different from our earlier example:

	A	B	C	D
1	1	2	4	8
2	2	4	8	16
3	3	6	12	24
4	4	8	16	32

In order to generate these grids on a spreadsheet, we need to identify the rule that has been repeatedly applied. In the first grid, each cell is calculated by taking the number above and adding. 1 is added in the first column, 2 in the second, and so on. In the second grid, the number to the left is multiplied by 2. This is consistent across the whole grid.

Now we see the hidden formulae in the first grid:

	A	B	C
1	1	2	3
2	=A1+1	=B1+2	=C1+3
3	=A2+1	=B2+2	=C2+3

If you are unfamiliar with spreadsheets, it is worth spending a moment here to ensure that you really do understand how the values in the first grid have been calculated.

Here are the formulae which underlie the second grid:

	A	B	C
1	1	=A1*2	=B1*2
2	2	=A2*2	=B2*2
3	3	=A3*2	=B3*2

Each formula is signified by the = symbol. We are effectively telling the computer, 'This is a formula. Work it out.' There is no need to type A2, B3 etc. Clicking on any cell will enter its address into the formula. I encourage pupils to do this from the very start since it reinforces the idea of relative position. In the above example, we take 'the value in the cell to the left', wherever we are on the sheet.

As Noss (1986) pointed out, spreadsheet formulae are cell references rather than true variables. The values they generate do not stay fixed (try altering the values in Column A and see what happens!) but their *functions* remain unchanged. In the second grid, all formulae mean, 'Take whatever is in the cell to the left and multiply it by 2.'

Since the second grid features essentially only one formula, it need only be entered once. Provided that it has been manually entered (into B1, for example), it can be copied then pasted to other selected cells.[2]

When the formula is copied, its precise expression is changed *relatively* to the new position on the sheet. Hence =A1*2 becomes =B1*2, and so on. The function is always, 'Take the value stored in the cell to the left and multiply it by 2.' You will of course see the calculated results, not the copied formulae. If you click on any cell you will see the formula that it contains.

Note that, in the first of our grids, each column contains a *different* formula. This is because 1 is added in the first column, 2 in the second, and so on. Once each formula has been entered in A2, B2, C2 etc., it can be copied down the column.

Children are gaining an intuitive feel for linear functions such as $f(x)=2x$ through modelling number patterns. While formal abstraction lies some years ahead, pupils are beginning to see the effects of algebraic transformations on familiar numbers. In Chapter 2, we saw how *Ergo* could be used to lay foundations. The question asked in the *Ergo* lesson was, 'How do we get from one number to the next?' This idea is the whole basis of the spreadsheet formula. An instruction may be entered, then copied to generate the entire row or column. In telling the computer what to do, children begin to think algebraically.

Note that the *origin* must be given, for each spreadsheet pattern. In my multiplication example, the initial values in Column A must be typed in directly. The Fibonacci sequence is a worthwhile spreadsheet challenge for upper primary pupils. It originates with two numbers, 0 and 1. Adjacent pairs of numbers are added to generate the sequence:

0   1   1   2   3   5   8   13   21   34   ...

Older pupils may also calculate the constant ratio which emerges as the sequence grows. This ratio, 'the golden mean', was used in classical art and architecture and is also found in natural forms.

Introducing spreadsheets in Mathematics

Introduction of spreadsheets calls for careful planning. Preparatory work may involve pupils making *Ergo*-style grids on squared paper, and playing games in pairs (Chapter 2). A whole class introduction may involve pupil interaction as the teacher models each number grid, asking, 'What pattern is this?' 'What will we get in this cell?'

The unfamiliar use of = to label a formula presents a difficulty at the outset. Pupils will be greatly assisted if they have experience of calculators. On the calculator the 'equals sign' also has a dynamic function. It effectively instructs the machine, 'Now work out everything I have put in and display the result.' This is quite different to the meaning of *balancing* in an equation such as $2 + 2 = 10 - 6$. It is hardly surprising that children become confused. After all, they often see:

$1 + 3 =$

Here, the 'equals sign' effectively means, 'Write the answer here!'

I found that, once pupils had grasped the idea of the formula as a function, the commonest error was in forgetting the equals sign. Printed examples on display, and by the computer, are helpful in providing constant reminders.

There seems no reason why children should not interact with prepared spreadsheets at a younger age. The teacher may enter the formula, while children enter the data themselves. This can be as simple as adding a small value to an input number. The aim can be for children to discover what the computer is doing. However simple, it seems important right from the start to allow children to enter their own data, so they can explore at first hand what the spreadsheet does and make links with calculator work.

In introducing the spreadsheet in mathematics, there are three initial stages:

1. Children experiment with the sheet, entering numbers and text before printing. The aim is simply to gain a feel for clicking on cells and entering data.

2. Formulae are introduced. Children use the spreadsheet as a simple calculator.

3. Formulae are used repeatedly to generate simple patterns, such as tables by repeated addition.

Year 4 pupils began by entering simple formulae such as =A1+B1+C1 to add three numbers. Columns of numbers were entered, then each row added. Each formula was entered manually. There is no need to introduce 'copy' at this early stage. Pupils need practice, and will learn from their errors in this interactive environment. The chief problem lay in forgetting to select the cell to contain the result. Cell contents were lost as children overtyped earlier results.

Two Year 4 girls made columns of numbers which added to 14. I intervened, asking whether they could now make their numbers add to 24. Siobhan thought that she would have to do the work all over again, but Kara said, 'That's easy, all you've got to do is add 10 to all the first numbers.' They were delighted to see the instant change. While this activity was very simple, and could have just as well been carried out using pencil and paper, children had been introduced to an important feature of the spreadsheet.

It is important not to rush through these stages. Pupils need to develop a secure understanding of why we use addresses in formulae. I asked Year 5 pupils to enter two numbers side by side, anywhere on the sheet. They entered two small values in F1 and F2. I asked them to click in F3, to place the result there. I asked them to enter: =F1*F2

They repeated the operation using a calculator. They typed different numbers into the cells F1 and F2. They discovered that they had made a simple multiplication machine. The numbers 3 and 6 were entered into F1 and F2. I asked the pupils to change the formula in F3 to: =3*6

Children were surprised to see no change to the result in F3. When they entered new values F1 and F2, the result 18 remained unchanged in F3. Pupils commented, 'That's what we've told it to do!' Then one observed, '[It will be different if] we put F1*F2 again!' Clearly, they were beginning to understand why cell addresses, rather than fixed values, are used in formulae.

The numbers 6 and 7 were entered on a fresh sheet:

	A	B
1	6	7
2	=A1*4+3	

We talked through the formula and children worked out mentally, 'Six times four, add three.' As expected, the value 27 appeared in A2. I showed children how to copy A2 to B2. I asked, 'Why is it 31 now? Why hasn't it just copied 27?'

Children clicked on B2 to see that it contained =B1*4+3. Danny, a 10 year old of average ability, told me, 'It's got a greater number than the last one. It's 7, not 6.' Later, the formula was changed to =B1*(4+3). Children were keen to investigate the effect of inserting brackets into other formulae.

From the beginning, it is helpful to teach pupils to enter references by clicking on cells. Again, it is important to talk through a range of exemplars. 'How did the computer work out the number in C3?' 'What did it then do to get the number in C4?'

Year 6 pupils were asked to calculate the mean of a set of results. There is a special 'Average' function for a range of cells. However, the children were not told this, since the teacher wished to see whether they could successfully compute the mean. The pupils entered:

=B3+B4+B5+B6/4

They were quick to realise that the computer had only divided B6 by 4. They saw the need for brackets and corrected the formula. It is always possible to go back and view formulae. Pupils should be encouraged to take a positive approach to spreadsheet errors – we all make them! It is important to review what the computer has done.

There is no need to rush into copying and pasting formulae. Year 6 pupils, well in command of the mathematics, needed much practice in entering formulae individually. I intervened frequently, asking them to tell me what each formula did. It is preferable to confine initial exploration to familiar number patterns. There is, after all, enough to challenge the novice in generating the two times table on a spreadsheet!

Depending on the application, keyboard shortcuts may be the quickest way to copy and paste. Pupils quickly grasped the idea of Ctrl-C (copy) and Ctrl-V (paste), although they had not come across these before. When generating a pattern, they chanted together: 'Go to the one next door – press Control C.' This appeared beneficial, reinforcing the idea of the formula as a *function* applied (in this case) to the number to the left.

Peer tutoring may present a good opportunity for pupils who have understood the process to explain to others, thus consolidating their own learning. Careful monitoring and sensitive handling by the teacher is needed, since it is very easy for peer tutors in this highly regulated environment to resort to a didactic approach. One pair became quite irritated with their tutees: 'You have to put equals and click on the one above!' There was no attempt to explain *why*.

In one action, a formula copied from a single cell may be pasted into an entire column, row or block, with impressive results. However, at this early stage there is no urgency to introduce this feature. It is better for children to consolidate copying to individual cells before rushing ahead. Also, they were fully prepared to work out the result for themselves before clicking 'Paste'. They set their own mental arithmetic challenges by choosing appropriate 'start numbers'.

Investigations into number patterns and relationships

When I told a Year 6 class we were going to make number patterns, 'tables' were promptly suggested. We have already seen that these patterns may be readily generated by repeated addition, demonstrating the power of the spreadsheet tool.

Preliminary work with calculators is beneficial. Starting with 0 on a clear display, children may generate a pattern of multiples by adding then repeatedly pressing the equals sign. The teacher may set challenges such as, 'Find which tables have the number 63.' Which patterns can immediately be discounted? Can other children see why?

Another useful calculator challenge is, 'Display the 13 times table up to 91. Have a race with your partner.' This requires some thought, since children have to anticipate when to stop! These calculator activities help to consolidate the vitally important idea that we are adding on to the *previous* number each time.

The teacher should continue to ask questions about the formulae which underlie the pattern. Can children predict what exactly will be shown when they click on a cell? Take advantage of any opportunity to ask questions such as, 'What has the computer done?' 'What did we *tell* it to do?' 'How has that number been made?'

Patterns which run down columns may be investigated, and used as a basis for predicting the next results. Year 6 pupils were very excited by this. Emma said, 'We've done the nine times table and the units column goes 9,8,7 [...] and the tens column goes up 1,2,3,4,5, and we think it's going to be 63 next.' Pupils were keen to predict other sets of multiples which would yield similar patterns.

Many well-known number investigations may be carried out using squared paper or apparatus such as centimetre cubes or Multilink. So why use a spreadsheet? Many of these activities involve children in intensive use of formulae and copying. Consolidation of new skills is an important IT objective. But what does the spreadsheet contribute uniquely to learning in Mathematics?

In a well-known example, pupils investigate the area of rectangles of constant perimeter. This table shows the dimensions and areas of a set of rectangles of perimeter 20 cm:

Width (cm)	9	8	7	6	5	4	3	2	1
Length (cm)	1	2	3	4	5	6	7	8	9
Area (cm^2)	9	16	21	24	25	24	21	16	9

There are many practical approaches. Pupils may be asked to make 'fields' using paper strips of constant length for 'fencing'. Rectangles may be drawn on squared paper, and dimensions tabulated. So what are the advantages of using a spreadsheet? The data generates an impressive graph from which pupils may deduce other rectangles through interpolation. Another benefit lies in the speed of calculation, enabling pupils to investigate many other rectangles in the time available.

For example, pupils may proceed to investigate rectangles of perimeter 18 cm. They will need to interpolate to find the dimensions of the rectangle with the largest area. The values in question are not whole numbers. Why is this? (To give the greatest area, length and width are the same. In the former case, 20 divides neatly by 4 to give us a 5x5 square!)

Another well-known investigation involves the generation of consecutive number patterns. Initially, children were asked to write down all numbers to 30 as the sum of consecutive numbers (for example, 2+3=5; 1+2+3=6).

	Adding 2 numbers	Adding 3 numbers	Adding 4 numbers	Adding 5 numbers
1				
2	3			
3	5	6		
4	7	9	10	
5	9	12	14	15
6	11	15	18	20
7	13	18	22	25
8	15	21	26	30
9	17	24	30	35
10	19	27	34	40
11	21	30	38	45
12	23	33	42	50

Year 6 children of above average ability had a firm grasp of the mathematics, and were quick to spot patterns and analyse the growth of the overall grid. Children noted the diagonal row of triangular numbers, and keen to predict what would happen in each new column.

Again, we have to ask, 'Why use a spreadsheet?' Certainly, from the IT standpoint, this activity gave valuable practice in entering and copying formulae. Mathematically, children needed a firm grasp of the rules underlying the grid in order to build formulae correctly. However, this was one case where speed could not be claimed to be an advantage.

I felt that these capable pupils would have been able to generate the pattern more quickly using pencil and paper. They saw that they could obtain the start value for each column by continuing the triangular sequence. They discovered that they could use emerging patterns, rather than add lengthening strings of numbers, to continue the grid. Teachers may like to consider this point with older pupils. Humans are more intelligent than computers, in that we can detect and use patterns. The computer has to perform routine addition to fill each cell (although it does it very quickly!).

Incidentally, many interesting outcomes of this investigation can be pursued away from the computer. For example, which numbers *cannot* be found in this way? Why are all the sums of two consecutive numbers odd? Why can any multiple of three be written as the sum of three consecutive numbers?

Investigations using data obtained by pupils

1. Are small bananas better value?
In the local supermarket, small bananas cost more by weight than large bananas. Could shoppers possibly believe that, because they are getting more fruits, small bananas are better value? Children thought that parents prefer to buy small bananas because they fit into lunchboxes. Also, large bananas have so much skin on them that there is more waste. Are small bananas in fact better value?

To investigate this hypothesis, two kilos of large and small bananas were purchased. Each fruit was weighed, then peeled. The pulp was eagerly consumed, then the skin weighed. The data for large and small bananas was entered onto a spreadsheet under the headings:

Mass of whole banana (g)   Mass of skin (g)

What can now be done with the data? This is the most difficult part, and the teacher must consider in advance how to analyse the data. The mass of edible pulp may readily be calculated, but does this actually get us anywhere? Further analysis is needed.

Pupils may suggest calculating the average (mean) mass. This can be done, for both large and small bananas. It still doesn't show which is the better value. It may be helpful to go back to the original observation that led to the hypothesis. A pupil had said, 'There's more waste with bigger bananas. There's so much skin on them.'

At this stage, we need to decide what to compare in order to get an indication of 'value'. As the child said, there is more skin on a large banana, but there is also more to eat. We need to find what *proportion* of each banana is inedible. Difficult mathematical concepts underlie this investigation, and it is important that the pupils understand what is going on. There are links with Mathematics: the activity presents an excellent opportunity to re-cap earlier work with fractions, percentages and ratio.

In tackling this type of problem, it is always worth considering some grossly simplified examples. If the skin of a freak 200g banana weighs 100g, dividing skin mass by total mass gives 0.5, or $1/2$. Half the banana is inedible. What if the skin weighs 50g? The same calculation shows that a quarter of the fruit consists of skin. If we multiply these results by 100, we obtain the *percentage* waste. In the first case, it is 50%. In the second, it is 25%.

From these special cases, we see that we first need to calculate the ratio of skin mass to the whole, obtained by dividing skin mass by total mass. If multiplication by 100 is included in the formula, the part we can't eat is expressed as a percentage:

Mass of whole banana (g)   Mass of skin (g)   Waste (%)

It is important to work through sufficient 'special cases' for the pupils to be able to understand the calculation: (skin mass / whole mass) x 100.

Pupils also need to be able to attach meaning to the results. In our survey, we found higher waste values for small bananas. This unexpected result showed that they are poorer value for money, and that the supermarket may be pulling a fast one!

The economics behind the supermarket's pricing policy are another matter, but there is a link here to the decreasing ratio of surface area to volume, as size increases. This complex idea has a familiar manifestation. Small mammals are furry, but larger ones such as hippos and elephants do not need fur, despite cold winter nights in the bush! For small mammals, the ratio of surface area to volume is greater, and they will lose their body heat without insulation.

2. *Investigating the ratio of surface area to volume for cubes of increasing size.*

The next stage may be to model the same idea mathematically. Again, the spreadsheet is used to support the investigation through its facility to display stored data, calculate and tabulate results.

Pupils are asked to find the volume and surface area of cubes. Approaches will depend on previous work in Mathematics. Some pupils may build cubes while the more able investigate on paper, sketching a square 'layer' and working out the number of units in the entire cube.

The spreadsheet is introduced. Depending on the ability and previous experience of pupils, they may be asked to enter formulae in all rows, so that only the linear dimension of each cube has to be entered:

Length of edge (cm)	1	2	3	4
Area of each face (cm^2)	1	4	9	16
Total surface area (cm^2)	6	24	54	96
Volume (cm^3)	1	8	27	64
Ratio:				
Surface area/volume	6	3	2	1.5

The final row shows clearly how the ratio decreases with size. Although a spreadsheet is not strictly necessary for this investigation, it is a helpful means of tabulating and displaying all calculated results. Able pupils may continue to extend the sequence through inserting and copying formulae.

Modelling using a spreadsheet

One of the most widespread 'real world' uses of the spreadsheet is in financial modelling. Provided that the model is straightforward, Key Stage 2 pupils will enjoy exploring real examples. Keeping data (such as amounts of money) as simple and as manageable as possible will assist, in that children will be better able to follow how the spreadsheet manipulates the data, and check results mentally.

There are many contexts where children have the opportunity to plan spending within a budget, or make a profit through selling goods they have made. In this hypothetical example, pupils are given £2, and challenged to make a profit of £5. The spreadsheet is used to calculate profit in advance. Since data may readily be changed, pupils may explore different selling prices to see the effects on proceeds.

The children decide to make balloon 'stress toys'. A plastic bottle is cut in half and used as a funnel. The mouth of the balloon is stretched over the bottle top and filled with flour, taking care to squeeze out all air. The balloon is tied off and the mouth may be decorated with 'eyes' and other adornments. When complete, the toy may be squeezed into a variety of shapes.

At the craft shop, Jumbo balloons are 20 pence each. 'Goggly eyes' are 25p per pair. We assume that the flour has been donated, and is not therefore a cost to the pupils. Other decorations (coloured wool, pipe cleaners, buttons, stickers) are available free of charge.

Children first use the spreadsheet to find the cost of making toys. Then, they enter trial selling prices, to see how much profit each will yield.

One pair of eyes costs:	£0.25			
One Jumbo balloon costs:	£0.20			
Number of toys made:	4	5	6	7
Cost of eyes	£1.00	£1.25	£1.50	£1.75
Cost of balloons	£0.80	£1.00	£1.20	£1.40
Total cost:	£1.80	£2.25	£2.70	£3.15
Selling price:	**£1.25**	**£1.25**	**£1.25**	**£1.25**
Total income:	£5.00	£6.25	£7.50	£8.75
PROFIT	£3.20	£4.00	£4.80	£5.60

The pupils start with £2. The sheet shows that they can only make four toys. If the toys are sold at £2 each, an instant profit of £6.20 is made. However, other children feel that this is far too high a price. If £1 is charged, the profit is cut to £2.20.

The sheet may be put to further use. Pupils may enter different selling prices in the shaded cells shown above, and keep a separate note of the profit yielded:

Selling price	Profit
£1.00	£2.20
£1.25	£3.20
£1.50	£4.20

The teacher suggests that they make a first batch, sell the four toys and plough the proceeds straight back into making a second batch. The children decide to charge £1.25. The sheet shows that they can make seven more toys for £3.20, the profit they will make by selling the first batch. Selling a further seven toys will realise a profit of £5.60.

Summary

Calculator work provides a good introduction, enabling pupils to appreciate similarities and differences. Unlike a calculator display, results remain on the sheet, enabling patterns to be more easily recognised.

The role of the equals sign in labelling a formula may confuse pupils. It is important to talk about what formulae actually do. We are instructing the computer, 'Now work this out and display the result here.' Discussion of the role of the 'equals' button on the calculator may be helpful.

Children readily absorb automated routines, for example in repeatedly copying a formula. They do not have to think mathematically. Routines may quickly be forgotten without practice. A card should always be available for reference, and the teacher may quickly re-cap procedures when talking to the whole class.

There is no need to rush into copying and pasting formulae with relative addressing. If pupils enter the formula each time, they have to click on the actual values used in each calculation. This helps to build a sound understanding of what is happening.

Children accepted that cell references, rather than absolute values, are used in formulae. Sound understanding develops with practice. The idea of a function, consistently applied across the sequence, is paramount. Pupils should be encouraged to think in terms of, for example, 'taking the number to the left and multiplying by 2.'

In mathematical sequences, the originating value may be altered to change the whole row or column. Children are fascinated by the speed of recalculation. I was told, 'It's a good way of learning your tables.' I also overheard the comment, 'This is fun! It's better than doing maths!'

Spreadsheet use does not counteract the development of numeracy. In fact, mental calculation is encouraged, as children enjoy checking results. One child called out, 'Let's predict what it's going to be!'

There is a risk of rushing into excessive abstraction. Pupils need to make links with things they understand: familiar number patterns, physical objects, the data they have collected, the questions driving the investigation. If children have been involved in collecting and organising the data, they are better able to relate to what is going on, and form a clearer understanding of why we use the computer.

Notes

1   We had used *Eureka*: the processes of selecting cells, entering values and formulae, copying and pasting cell contents are identical in *Excel* and other Windows applications.

2   If you are using *Excel*, the copy and paste buttons are on the toolbar. Alternatively, select B1 (the cell containing the formula) and type Ctrl-C (Control-C). Select other cells and type Ctrl-V. If an irritating flashing highlight remains after copying and pasting a cell or block of cells, press Esc (Escape). These 'control' keys work with many Acorn applications, but not the very simplest. Users of primary spreadsheets such as *DataCalc*, *DataSheet* and *Sheetwise* should consult the documentation.

3   Spreadsheets are a useful resource for whole-class teaching, provided that children can all see the display! It is vital to 'zoom' the grid, possibly to 200%. *Eureka* offers this feature, as of course does *Excel*.

CHAPTER 6

CREATING AND INTERROGATING A DATABASE IN MATHEMATICS

This chapter describes the creation and use of a database by 9-10 year olds in the context of a Mathematics topic. Databases are discussed in more detail in Chapter 11, which contains a fuller explanation of the processes of file creation and data retrieval. Readers with general awareness of how data is structured in a file, and the type of searches that may be undertaken, will have no difficulty with this chapter. Others may prefer to read Chapter 11 first, and return to this section.

In the Year 5 class, the creation of a database to investigate the properties of 2D shapes is planned into the Mathematics curriculum. The project took place over a period of two weeks. In supporting the teacher while conducting my own research, I worked with individuals, groups and the whole class. I particularly wished to explore organisational issues. What support is needed? How many children may be involved in the activity, or the framing task, at one time? Where may whole-class teaching be appropriate? Can this work be supported by the class teacher alone, or is help necessary?

In the *Puzzling Shapes Database* (Keeling and Whiteman, 1993), 2D shapes have been given imaginary names. The only way of locating a shape is by searching for its properties. For example, the first step in finding the 'kite' may be to search for all shapes with four sides. A further search (e.g. for one line of mirror symmetry) narrows down the retrieved selection. The process is repeated until the selection contains only one record.

Rather than use the published database, Year 5 pupils created their own shapes. Preliminary work was designed to enable children to abstract attributes of shapes in order to suggest 'headings' or fields for the database, and use the field structure in subsequent searching.

The school is situated in an urban environment, and draws its pupils from a socially diverse area. While there are a few pupils of high ability, there are a significant number who achieve below the national expectation. Joint planning, supported by the IT co-ordinator, has enabled integration of IT into the programme of cross-curricular topics taught throughout the school. Little data handling work had been attempted, but staff were keen to develop this area.

The data handling application used by the school is *Junior Pinpoint*. The Year 5 classroom, with 34 pupils, has two Acorn computers. The children had no previous experience of databases. Pupils had just begun related work with the Roamer, constructing shapes such as squares, rectangles and equilateral triangles.

Outline of activities

Pupils originated shapes on geoboards by stretching rubber bands over pegs. Next, the shapes were drawn on paper, directly onto a centimetre grid. I asked children to investigate shapes with mirrors for bilateral symmetry, and to make notes on their properties. Pupils then used *!Draw*, a graphics utility, to create the shapes on screen. It was essential to display and lock the grid.

There was a strong correspondence between stretching out a line on the screen with the mouse, and pulling a rubber band over pegs on the geoboard. Children rapidly learned how to select and delete shapes, and colour-fill and copy. With the grid turned off but still locked, pupils were able to select and drag shapes to investigate tessellation.

!Draw would be inappropriate for younger children exploring tessellation for the first time. It would not be evident to them when shapes overlap on the screen. But, for older pupils, it is a valued alternative to drawing on squared paper. Each shape is identical and quickly replicated. There is scope for trial and error, and considerably greater productivity.

The class had previous experience of tessellation. However, there were important ideas that appeared quite new to them. Robert was the only child to point out rotational symmetry. He showed me that he could turn his board round 'four times [...] and the square looks the same'. Two children had produced a trapezium but were unable to say what was special about this shape. I introduced the new shape to the whole class, in the context of a discussion of parallel lines. Jenny held up a truncated cone from a box of 3D shapes. She observed correctly, 'If you cut it down through the middle you will get a trapezium.'

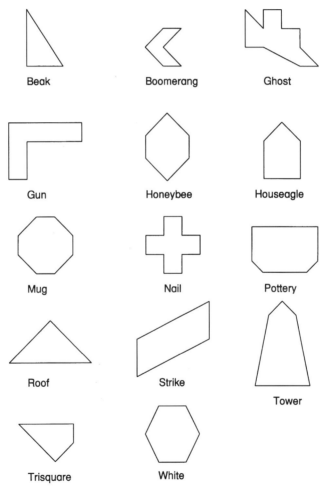

Examples of the shapes produced by the class, with 'mystery names'.

The next step was to discuss *Junior PinPoint* form design. I asked children to suggest questions we could ask about the shapes. Individually, they prepared 'questionnaires' on paper. I asked groups to review them, before we discussed the design of a standard form. As data was added, the need for changes arose. This again was discussed with the whole class, and amendments were made.

What is the name of your shape?	Houseagle
Can you fold it so that the sides meet exactly?	☒ Yes ☐ No
Does it look the same if you rotate it?	☐ Yes ☒ No
How many sets of parallel sides has it got?	1
How many right angles has it got?	3
How many corners has it got?	5
How many lines of mirror symmetry has your shape got?	1
Does it tessellate?	☒ Yes ☐ No
What shapes is it made up of?	A triangle and a square

Junior PinPoint questionnaire.

Shapes were printed and cut out. The shapes on paper could be folded, or tested with mirrors, to identify lines of symmetry. The paper from which each shape had been cut was conserved, and mounted on card. This enabled investigation of rotational symmetry: could the shape be partially rotated to fit the hole? Paper shapes and cards were carefully stored in plastic inserts in a ring binder.

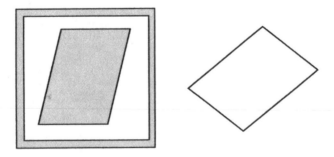

Printed shape, with the cut-away remnant stuck on card.

Each pair chose a paper shape, and interrogated the file to find its name. With the class, I discussed strategies for identifying shapes. Finally, children had the opportunity to hypothesise connections. With the whole class, I discussed how the computer could be used to test ideas such as 'Do all shapes with four corners tessellate?' Later, groups put their hypotheses to the test.

Creating the database

The next stage was to create the database structure. In *Junior PinPoint*, a 'form', analogous to a questionnaire, is designed. Once data has been entered on copies of the form, the tabular structure is created automatically. Children needed to think of attributes as questions they could ask about all 2D shapes.

In whole-class discussion, children suggested questions such as:

> Does it tessellate?
> How many corners has it got?
> What shapes is it made up of?

James ventured the question: 'Can you turn it round and round with it looking the same?' I rephrased this: 'Does it look the same if you rotate it?' I decided against quantifying rotational symmetry, as the idea was so new to them. Some pupils found it difficult to abstract general properties of shapes. Simon had produced a square. He asked, 'Shall I put what colour is it?' I replied that squares can be all sorts of colours: he had to think what squares always have.

Precise wording needed careful consideration. Matthew asked: 'How many times can you fold it over and it will be the same?' James suggested: 'Can you fold it with it looking the same?' Children had all performed folding, so knew what was meant, but found it very difficult to articulate this question. I suggested we look together at what happens when a rectangle is folded. One child observed, 'The edges all come together when you fold it.' This led to the question being accepted: 'Can you fold it so that the edges meet exactly?'

There is no statutory requirement at Key Stage 2 for pupils to construct a new database. However, one group quickly grasped the process. They completed the form themselves after I had assisted them in entering the first two questions. Data entry soon caused the need for review. Certain questions could not be applied to all shapes. For example, the form asked, 'How many pairs of sides are the same?' This had seemed an obvious question: we had compared *pairs* of sides in talking about the square, rectangle and trapezium. However, the question must be answerable for all 2D shapes. Ghost (page 75) has seven sides the same! The question 'How many equal sides?' is inappropriate. For many shapes, such as a rectangle, there is no single value.

Pupils had asked, 'How many pairs of parallel sides has your shape got?' I drew a rectangle and the shape Gun (page 75) on the board. I asked children to show me the rectangle's parallel edges. This was repeated for Gun. Children identified three horizontal edges. I coloured them red, then asked a child to colour parallel vertical edges in blue. I asked why we couldn't say *pair* any more. I wrote: 'How many ___ of parallel sides does the shape have?'

Rachel   Lines.
Catherine   Twos and threes.
Luke   Threes.

I pointed out that we could not ask the question 'How many threes of parallel sides?' about the rectangle. I asked them to think again. I turned to Stephen, who looked particularly eager: 'Sets!' he called out, confidently. Other children quickly warmed to his idea. This was a rewarding moment, for Stephen, a low achiever with poor manipulative skills, had experienced extreme difficulty in creating shapes.

Interrogation

Part of the completed database, in tabular format, is shown below. In *Junior PinPoint*, searches must be broken into steps, and carried out in succession. For example, to retrieve the trapezium, pupils might enter:

    Right angles / equal to / 0
    Parallel / equal to / 1

Only two types of search condition were needed: 'equal to' followed by a value, or the selection of 'Yes' or 'No'. Children quickly mastered the process. Following the search, they were keen to go through the collection of printed shapes, to see what else the computer might have found. Manual searches through the collection served to model the process.

Showing:	26 sheets of:	26			
Sorted by:	(No order).				

name	fold	rotate	parallel	right angles
Houseagle	Yes	No	1	3
Bun	No	No	2	5
Contrast	Yes	No	2	0
Ghost	No	No	2	4
Platform	Yes	Yes	2	4
Sausage	Yes	Yes	2	4
boat	Yes	No	1	0
Paper	Yes	No	0	0
Strike	No	Yes	2	0
Mug	Yes	Yes	4	0

Part of the database shown on screen in tabular format.

Children enjoyed searching: it was a game to them. Scott, who had not found using the computer easy, commented, 'The computer finds the things it's got. It's like a competition really.' He added, ' Say there's only 5 that can't fold, so the computer's found all the ones that can't fold and he's put them all into one place.'

Difficulties in interrogation were mainly due to mathematical uncertainty, not to lack of facility with IT. The chief problems lay in identifying the number of right angles and number of sets of parallel sides. Children needed a means of checking that they had found the right shape. The field *Which shapes is it made up of?* provided a useful check. Unfortunately, it was not possible to store a unique graphic on each record.

Investigations

This stage was introduced through a whole-class lesson. Children readily recalled the questions we had asked about *individual* shapes. I explained that we were now going to ask questions about all the shapes. For example, I might think that all four sided shapes have at least one right angle. Did anyone think this idea might be true? Alexis disagreed, pointing out that the trapezium has no right angles. Again, I might think that shapes with rotational symmetry tessellate. No one was sure about this. I explained that we could use the computer to investigate.

I asked them to suggest questions to investigate. A number of children were aware of the connection between 'folding' and bilateral symmetry. Matthew explained that the mirror can be placed on the fold.

Children were asked to write three questions. I wrote all the attributes on the board. Thirty-one children carried out the task. Nineteen clearly understood, devising questions such as:

Does every shape with mirror symmetry fold equally?
Does every shape with at least two sets of parallel lines have mirror symmatry [sic]?
Does most shapes with mirrer symmetry have rotational symmentry.

Children of all abilities were in this group. Stephen wrote, 'bis eveery chap with 4 canrers tessalate?' Jane, who clearly had the same idea, wrote, 'Do a shapes with foru shide tesulat?' Six children included questions about individual shapes. Lucy wrote:

All shapes with 4 corners do thay rotational simytrey?
Has every [shape] with parallel lines have mirror simytery?
Can you fold it so sides meet?

Three children asked questions about the profile of the data as a whole:

How many shapes with [right angles] tessellate?
Does most shapes tessellate.

Perhaps we should have started with this type of question. I noted at the time: 'There's not much time, and I'm leap-frogging.' To the pupils' credit, they had grasped that we were asking about *all* the shapes in the database.

Three children asked questions about individual shapes. Matthew, despite having explained to me why 'folding' shapes have mirror symmetry, repeated his earlier questions:

Dos it hav ritanols
how mene shav it got
wolsaps is yor sap mad artov

Thomas wrote:

Can you fold the edges.
Do shape's tessellate.
is it symmetry.

Thomas may not have understood the class lesson at all. Whole-class teaching cannot be guaranteed to result in effective learning for all children. However, talking to the whole class saved me from repeating myself many times to small groups. The lesson needs to be followed by a task enabling the teacher to monitor and assess what has been learned. Subsequent support may be given to groups or individuals. After watching others at the computer, Thomas suggested: 'Do shapes with four corners tessellate?' He showed me tessellations on the wall display.

To check Thomas' idea, the records were retrieved as follows:

Corners / equal to / 4

Selected records were shown in tabular format. The *tessellation* field was inspected to check whether all entries were 'Yes'. Other lower ability pupils successfully undertook this search, with minimal help from me. Great excitement was aroused: 'We've found that all the ones with four corners have got 'Yes' all the way down.' These pupils, however, needed help in expressing their finding formally. As a group, pupils need to agree what they are going to record. The process of recording will encourage them to check what they have found. Otherwise they are inclined to carry on, with no reflection on outcomes, unless there is a constant adult presence.

It was important to stress that our finding was only true of the shapes in the file. Further testing would be necessary before we could claim that, on the basis of our evidence, it is *likely* that all quadrilaterals tessellate. Pupils learned that, in hypothesis testing, one exception is sufficient to invalidate the idea:

Caroline   There's one "No", so it's no.
Sarah   That one hasn't got it, so [...] the answer is no.

Generally, hypothesis testing made greater demands. For instance, children wanted to search for shapes with right angles. These shapes have a non-zero value in the *right angles field*. Less able pupils found it difficult to conceptualise the search *right angles / greater than / 0*.

On rare occasions, the viability of a hypothesis was challenged before using the computer:

Lucy   Do all shapes with four corners rotate?
Leanne   No it doesn't, because of the trapezium.

The 'discoveries' will rapidly be forgotten unless the child can make some meaning of them. Jodie and Nicole investigated whether folding shapes have mirror symmetry. About ten minutes later, I asked whether they had found 'Yes'. Jodie replied with uncertainty, 'Think so.' While it was her suggestion in the first place, she had no ideas about *why* the outcome was 'Yes', and had already begun to forget.

All the groups I observed were able to conduct searches on their own. However, few were prepared to adopt a strategy. Children were simply searching the fields in order. They made good use of paper shapes in identifying and confirming properties. I felt that they might be amenable to a more considered approach because they were clearly disappointed when their first search retrieved a large sample.

Building on the 'game' element may encourage a more planful approach: can they isolate the shape in as few searches as possible? It will be helpful first to consider whether the shape has any unusual properties. Russell quickly adopted this idea. Given a hexagon, he told his partner not to search the corners field, because he had noticed before that there were a number of these shapes. There were better ways of narrowing down the sample.

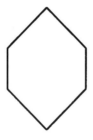

Russell   What's peculiar about it? [...] Yes, it folds. Does it tessellate? [He takes the paper shape out of the folder, and manipulates it.] Yeh, it does!

Lee   Tessellate – yes.

Russell thinks that this will not be a good narrowing-down search, 'because we need to find something unusual about it'.

Lee   Does it rotate?

Russell   Yes, you can do it some of the way, you can do it from there to there. [He rotates the paper shape 180 degrees.]

Lee   OK. Rotate. Yes.

A large selection is retrieved. Russell and Lee inspect the tabular format on the screen. They look for ways in which the shapes differ, in order to plan their next search.

Russell   No, it's not Strike. That's one thing it's not. Does it fold?

Lee   Mirror symmetry! Look –

Russell   Yes, [our shape's] got mirror symmetry, two lines of mirror symmetry. So *mirror* 2, that's right.

Lee wants to check for further lines of symmetry. Russell tries to persuade him that there's no need, but agrees to testing with a mirror. Lee confirms that there are only two lines of bilateral symmetry. The search is entered, and two shapes are retrieved.

Russell   Yes, done it! Yes, we're down to two. They both fold – they both rotate – they both got mirror symmetry – ah – one's got more right angles than the other. [He counts the *corners* of the paper shape.] Six.

Lee   [It's got] no right angles!

Russell   Oh yes. Corners – six. This is Honeybee.

Since the other shape has four corners, Russell is correct. Lee didn't notice that Honeybee has two right angles!

Needless to say, some searches were unsuccessful. Luke and Joshua entered five successive queries, leading to '0 records selected'. They lacked strategies for reviewing a failed search. I pointed out that each search was retained on the screen. Using the paper shape, they checked its properties against the searches they had made. They quickly spotted the error, and proceeded to find the shape in two steps.

The game-like, competitive element appeared to encourage a considered approach. The goal was to isolate a shape in as few searches as possible. Paul saw that Trisquare (page 75) could be singled out in this way:

Right angles / equal to / 2
Parallel / equal to / 0

James became very interested in the paper shapes in the collection. He was able to identify the two right angles in Trisquare.

A child asked, 'Have all the shapes with mirror symmetry got more than three corners?' Group members were unaware that it would follow, if this were true, that no triangles have mirror symmetry. This question could usefully be the basis of a class or group discussion. Children might use geoboards to find triangles with mirror symmetry. If questions are generated away from the computer as a group activity, there is greater likelihood that children will explain to others, justify and refine. This may well give rise to better questions. As Carter and Monaco (1987) found, pupils readily acquire the skills of data retrieval, but not the art of critical reflection.

Group work

There was a high level of discussion, particulary when two rather than three worked together. Space around the computers was limited, making it difficult for three to collaborate. I switched to working with pairs for interrogation. Even though the group had to study the shape they had been given carefully, the work involved more 'hands on' action than reflection. As Eraut (1993) found, such activities work best for small groups: larger groups are more appropriate where there is a need to explore problems or debate alternatives.

A group of five boys were restless at first. They only began to warm to the task when they began investigating with mirrors. The computer did not act as a catalyst for collaboration. At one of the computers, a boy used !Draw while his partners drifted off. Later, all five co-operated on the tessellation of crosses. This tessellation was highly problematic, and all were fully involved in making suggestions. Once they had discovered a system of placing the crosses, however, the task became routine. One pupil drifted back to the geoboards. The remaining boys showed keen interest in investigating other tessellations at the computer.

Not all data handling tasks stimulate high levels of discussion and collaboration. Certain girls seemed more concerned over matters such as whose turn it was. In many pairs, one partner tended to dominate.

Teacher intervention

The teacher may need to be quite persistent in questioning, in order to direct children's thinking. Focused questioning plays an important part in promoting the development of pupils' critical reflection. In asking children to think more deeply about their own observations, the teacher models the type of questions which individuals should ask of themselves, in interpreting outcomes or in checking out assertions.

Inevitably, the pattern of intervention changes where the teacher is in sole charge of the whole class. There is less opportunity to talk through problems in depth, and much pressure to make a rapid appraisal. The skilled teacher makes a well-targeted observation, with the aim of prompting children to see for themselves what may be amiss.

The most appropriate intervention in some circumstances is simply to offer a hint. Leanne was having great difficulty in tessellating kites in *!Draw*. She started by making a row of kites, but did not make a second row.

HS   Move the blue kite so it's on top of the orange one.

Leanne   On the point?

HS   Yes!

Leanne   I've got room for another one!

Having made three rows of kites, Leanne called for me. 'I've got to turn my kite upside down and I don't know how to do it.' At this stage, Leanne knew exactly what she had to do to complete her tessellation. She needed to be offered a new tool. I showed her how to select and rotate objects. She needed no further help.

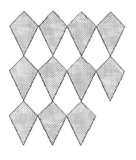

My first intervention enabled Leanne to make a good deal of progress. Such assistance needs to be kept to a minimum, or you are doing the thinking for the child. If help is not offered, the child may quickly become frustrated. It is important for the teacher to monitor at frequent intervals, in order to intervene where necessary.

Children's mathematical difficulties: right angles

The study of any IT-supported activity in the classroom is heavily contextualised. Here, we look at how a specific mathematical difficulty impinged on the IT activity. While the IT activity did not teach the concept *per se*, it provided a rich opportunity for children to apply new ideas after whole-class teaching had taken place.

In my original planning, I wrote: 'To find the square, children may first search for shapes with four right angles.' To an adult, this property of a square is virtually self-evident. But no child could initially tell me what was special about a square. I was merely told, 'It has four sides.' The teacher was surprised that her new class had such difficulty in identifying right angles, as, to her, right angles are so obviously what they are.

Pupils found the identification of right angles harder than anything else. I was told a right angle is 'a quarter'. Pupils had no idea how to measure or compare angles. The angles of the kite were all called right angles. Several children told me that lines meeting to form a right angle had to be horizontal and vertical. Geoboard use contributed in generating many shapes with right angles. The children did not expect nor recognise them, especially where they were not formed by vertical and horizontal lines.

Robert was convinced that Tower (page 75) had no right angles. He maintained that the apex could not be a right angle because it was not formed by 'straight' (in other words, vertical and horizontal) lines. Later, Robert rotated the shape through 45 degrees so that the apex 'became' a right angle.

I asked the whole class, 'What is a right angle?' Catherine made a connection with her recent experience with the Roamer. To other children, it was conceived in terms of 'straight' lines:

Alexis   A right angle is when there's – er – straight corners.

John   It's a bit like a square but it's made longer.

Catherine It's a 90 degrees turn.

David   It's a square like if there was a line going down and a line going across.

Lee   It's very straight.

We then looked at large paper shapes with right-angled corners at various inclinations. I also demonstrated angles made by turning hands on a clock. Problems persisted, especially where children continued to believe that right angles could only be made by horizontal and vertical lines.

Children need to understand angle not only as a static property of a shape. They should be introduced to the dynamic concept of an angle as a measure of turn. These pupils, given their apparent difficulties with the concept, need to connect with their past experience of enacting whole, half and quarter turns. Some children who had begun to use the Roamer were able to conceptualise a right angle as an *amount* of turn. (It is of benefit to use a pen in the Roamer so that pupils can see the resulting right angle on paper.)

Evaluation

The relationship between computer work and non-computer based 'framing' activities (Somekh and Davies, 1991) is demonstrated in this case. The starting point was in the geoboard activity. This framing task could have been extended, especially where children found it difficult to identify the properties of their shapes. There were points when additional framing activities could have supported computer work. An obvious example is the further investigation of right angles, embracing the construction of shapes with the Roamer. Framing activities may also extend children's thinking: for example, Alexis made geoboard shapes that he thought would be difficult to find if added to the database. He minimised the number of aspects in which they differed from each other.

The project sparked a high level of decision-making in small groups. However, the use of IT did not always inspire collaboration. Some pupils needed active encouragement to discuss the task as a group: there were occasions where single children remained at the computer while partners drifted away. Computer work began with the individual task of drawing one shape each. It might have been better to have set up the activity as a group project in the first instance, in order to stimulate collaboration.

Data file design is a task for the experienced user. Each question must be answerable for every entity in the file. Primary children lack the experience on which to base decisions on what to include, what to leave out and how to phrase questions. It is of benefit to discuss possibilities with the whole class. My approach was to accept ideas, and suggest a version that everyone could understand. Mercer (1993) calls such interventions 'reconstructive recaps'.

The constrained nature of initial inquiries, involving straightforward numerical searching or simple selection of *yes* or *no*, provided a good starting point. Children could progress to investigation using a wider repertoire.

No child ventured a hypothesis prior to the class lesson introducing investigations. However, on that occasion, some children were aware of a particular relationship that could have become evident through practical work as well as through database interrogation. If the shape can be folded so that the edges meet exactly, then it will have mirror symmetry. In encouraging children to formulate and test hypotheses, there are options available to the teacher: to 'plant' the idea, to wait until it is suggested, or to suggest the idea directly.

The collection of printed shapes in a ring binder served to model the database, and could be used away from the computer. Children could study a shape, to see how they might distinguish it from others. It would be useful to have a durable collection of shapes mounted on thick card. This could be manually sorted prior to a database search.

When other tools were to hand, some children were prepared to use them to check an idea. For example, Lee was keen to use the mirror to check symmetry. James, a pupil of below average ability, also used the collection of paper shapes to check. This did not always happen. Teachers need to consider how metacognitive skills (reflecting on outcomes, strategic thinking) could be developed. It is worth insisting that children write down their findings. The precise articulation of outcomes may be negotiated within the group. In discussion, children have the opportunity to rehearse what they may write on paper.

There is a tension between IT group work and a commitment to whole-class teaching. Reviewing IT with the whole class can be problematic, since a week may have elapsed since some pupils touched the computer.

Framing the database work within related tasks enabled large groups of up to twelve or more to be engaged at any one time. All children had access at least once each day. This enabled me to talk to the whole class, rather than having to repeat myself to each group.

Whole-class teaching provided the most efficient means to review progress, explain new work, refine questions and demonstrate new ideas. However, it was essential to provide support for group work at the computer. For example, when investigation began, I commenced by discussing children's questions, looking with the pupils through the folder of shapes for supporting evidence. I could not have done this with the whole class.

Class teaching needs to be followed by tasks which are planned to allow careful monitoring. The teacher needs to organise opportunities to work with individuals and groups. This may necessitate support from other staff, freeing the teacher for this purpose.

In many comparable situations, an IT specialist initiates database work with the whole class. Even where a number of pupils can cope with the computer activity on their own, the class teacher may be too worried about the prospect of something going wrong. The teacher may nevertheless play a vital part through developing framing activities away from the computer. For example, pupils could be asked to sort printed shapes into various categories, such as those with two right angles, or one set of parallel sides. At the very least, work produced with specialist support can be displayed, and discussed in class.

Clearly, the number of pupils who may engage in computer work at one time depends on accessibility. Portable or laptop computers offer many advantages for this type of project. Groups would be able to continue investigations using graphics software. Graphics could be incorporated, together with retrieved data in tabular format, in word-processed reports.

CHAPTER 7

OPPORTUNITIES FOR ICT IN TEACHING ENGLISH

Speaking and listening

The leaflet *Information Technology and the use of language* (SCAA, 1996b) draws attention to links that can be made between the IT and English Programmes of Study. For example, opportunities for speaking and listening arise when pupils 'use IT-based models or simulations to explore aspects of real and imaginary situations'. Computer-based explorations and interactive stories are an excellent stimulus for the development of speaking and listening skills.

A well-known example is 4Mation's *Flossy the Frog*. As Flossy undertakes some improbable journeys, children explore each 'scene', clicking objects to trigger events. There are different routes through the story, and there are points where groups have to discover a short sequence of actions in order to get to the next screen. There are numerous opportunities for decision-making and prediction.

Simple text, describing the scene and Flossy's thoughts and actions, is displayed below the main picture. The reading level is appropriately pitched for many Year 2 pupils. I have seen children desperate to return after the initial excitement has died down, to explore a scene more fully and read all the messages. Non-readers are not barred from exploring the scenes, and younger children enjoy triggering the animations and sounds.

Once children have explored the screen, the challenge is to get to the next scene. Careful reading may give a clue. 'Flossy wants to jump up to that star. I wonder if she can jump that far.' Clicking on Flossy takes the group to the 'planet' scene. Moving on from this scene is less straightforward. It may take children a few minutes to discover that, once they have set off the alarm clock to wake the inhabitants, they have to click *in* the big crater to call a robot to rescue Flossy. Even so, it is unlikely that they will be stuck for long. Young children are far less inhibited than adults in clicking around the screen. Later, the teacher may ask the group to relate for others' benefit how they moved on from this scene.

A scene from 4Mation's Flossy the Frog

Group exploration is important, since it may take just one suggestion to free the whole group in a difficult situation. Real-world problems typically demand the gathering of information and sequencing of actions. Adventure programs for young children are rich in such opportunities, as Whitebread (1997) demonstrates.

The teacher must know the likely pitfalls, in order to make a constructive hint if children encounter difficulties. The user booklet contains an 'Adults' Route Guide'. The aim is to enable a hard-pressed teacher to complete the game in five or ten minutes. It is always worth exploring at least some of the scenes on one's own, to gain a better feel for the experience.

Another well-known interactive story is *A Mouse in Holland*. Martin the Mouse lives in a windmill, and children may go on a trip to Amsterdam after exploring Martin's home. Again, improbable and highly entertaining events are built in to each scene. There are hidden objects and a scoring system. Additional text may be displayed by clicking objects with the right button. While very young children are able to interact with the scenes, a full exploration demands tenacity.

In the kitchen: a scene from A Mouse in Holland

Careful questioning encourages children to focus thoughts, articulate ideas and explain details. There are many possible questions, open and closed, that an adult may ask about a particular scene. Closed questions assist the child in focusing on details. Open questions encourage the pupil to reflect on experience and verbalise personal thoughts. For example, we could ask about the 'kitchen' scene:

> Where was the chicken?
> What was strange about the egg?
> What was your favourite food on the table?
> Why should you keep the door shut?

In the tunnel, we may ask:

How did the spider get its own back on the worm?
What was in the tunnel?
Where does the tunnel go?
What else do you think might be in the tunnel?
Have you ever been in a tunnel?

Once children have explored a scene, they may use a word processor with the aid of a specially prepared word list. The teacher may profitably use these programs as part of the Literacy Hour, especially if a large display is available. In text level work in Year 2, children should be taught 'to discuss story settings: to compare differences [...] to prepare and re-tell stories individually' (DfEE, 1998). Each encounter with a computer-based adventure is slightly different, because, although scenes are linked, there is no fixed order of events. It is highly unlikely that groups will discover all the animations on their first attempt. Each child's version of the story may therefore be unique.

Acorn users have an advantage in getting the best value from these programs. A built-in utility, *Paint*, has a 'snapshot' facility. When *Paint* is loaded, clicking the menu button on the icon gives the *Snapshot* option. The pointer is dragged over part of the screen and released. The resulting 'snapshot' may be named and saved to disc. In this way, a collection of images from various scenes may be built up.

With a multimedia word processor such as *Textease*, the graphic icons are dragged from the directory window onto the writing page. Children may arrange them and re-size them as they please. The images provide scaffolding for writing, since they may easily be arranged in sequence. The pupil then clicks below each picture to write the narrative. Other writing may arise from collections of graphics produced by scanning children's work, or from pupils' own use of graphics software. At the simplest level, children may add captions to images they have chosen. It is far less daunting to add a caption to a screen full of pictures than to compose text on a blank word processor screen!

Flossy and *Martin* are among the first examples of multimedia for education. They run from floppy disk on some of the oldest machines. On a technical note, setting the Acorn to a 256-colour mode makes a considerable difference, and I recommend finding out how to do this!

Reading

Talking stories

Multimedia talking stories, with animations and spoken text, aim to model the process of the adult reading with the child. Many are based on previously published books. Text, illustrations and other features, such as page numbers, are presented on the screen just as in the printed version. In the *Oxford Reading Tree* talking stories, even the cover and credits are faithfully replicated on screen. Words or phrases are highlighted when spoken, reinforcing the child's grasp of left-to-right progression through the text. Individual words are also sounded when clicked.

In all talking stories, clicking certain parts of the picture may trigger animations, music and sound effects. There are limits on how much can be packed onto a floppy disc, but the field is wide open with CD-ROM. The Brøderbund *Living Books* CD-ROMs feature extensive multimedia animation which is highly attractive to children. Characters 'speak' when clicked, providing insights into their actions and additional background to the events on the page. While active exploration is encouraged, some animation may not be central to the narrative.

The medium aims to present information in different ways, deepening the engagement of the reader and assisting subsequent recall. The opportunity to reinforce high frequency and newly familiar words may help in building sight vocabulary. Through repeated listening, children link the sound of the word to its printed form. The richness of the interactive screen, and the additional information obtained by clicking on characters, may help children to understand the stories.

The involvement of the adult in reading aloud with the child is known to be of critical importance in early literacy development. The adult models the process of reading, revealing why we read and demonstrating what reading involves. As the child gains familiarity with common words, reading becomes a joint activity. Adult and child read together: the adult intervenes to discuss the meaning of the story and to ask questions such as, 'What do you think will happen next?' As the child makes further progress, the adult relinquishes the lead, intervening to support where necessary.

Talking stories aim to 'scaffold' the reader in a similar way. In the early stages, the child may listen to the whole story being read. Then, the child may click on individual words where needed. The support provided by the computer builds confidence as the child begins to read independently.

Medwell (1996) has considered talking stories in the context of recent developments in publication for children. Generally, content has greatly improved, and the importance of structural features and genre has been recognised. For some years, publishers have included support materials with reading schemes. It is now the norm for CD-ROM titles, featuring talking versions of the books and associated interactive tasks, to accompany new schemes.

Can talking stories replace the teacher? Are they used more effectively by teacher and child together, or as a preparation for reading the printed version to the teacher? When pupils explored the talking version prior to reading to the teacher, Medwell found a significant increase in word accuracy. However, there was no difference when it came to recognising the same words in another context.

When the teacher used the talking story *with* the child, there were gains in another context. Evidence suggested that children probably made much use of semantic and contextual clues when using the talking stories. The computer versions help children understand the stories. Medwell concludes that talking books are used most effectively to support reading with the teacher, not as a replacement.

In a study of 8 year olds using one of the *Living Books* (Underwood and Underwood, 1996), girl/girl pairs proved better at recalling story events than boys or mixed pairs. There was much interest in interactive features, but these were often not essential to the story. However, in their own stories, key events rather than descriptions of animations featured. Pairs of girls appeared more relaxed in working together. Girls regarded their partners as a source of information and advice. This may have contributed significantly to girls' superior recall of the story.

Carr (1996) used talking stories within the genre of myth and folktale to explore structure and focus on character development. A further aspect was the use of description in creating atmosphere and imagery.

Carr describes the use she made of *Kiyeko and the Lost Night*, a South American folk tale.

Groups of pupils explored the talking story. The teacher then discussed features of the genre, asking questions such as:

- How are the mood and atmosphere created?
- What moves the story on?
- What do the 'hot spots' (interactive parts of the screen) add to the story?

From children's answers, 'story maps' were built up to show the basic structure. Comparisons were made with other stories in the same genre. Each group selected one screen. They had to write a speech for Kiyeko, to convey information and/or move the story on. Each group had to take account of what others were doing, so that the new version of the story had continuity and coherence. Away from the computer, pupils combined the speech with their own descriptions to produce their own texts for each screen. The development is fully described in Carr's on-line article.

Overlay keyboards and text retrieval

Overlay keyboards, used in conjunction with a word processor, have an important role in areas of literacy development such as modelling texts, making links between reading and writing, and developing awareness of structural features in various genres. The overlay editor is a program which enables the entry of texts, each associated with a particular location on the overlay surface. Several styles of overlay keyboard and editor programs exist, and there is no space to review them here. Local advisory services will be able to make recommendations.

The texts are saved as an *overlay file*. Subsequently, this is used side-by-side with a main application such as a word processor. When the overlay keyboard is pressed, the text linked to that location is entered at the cursor position, just as though it had been typed by an invisible friend at the keyboard. Fuller details are given in Chapter 8, which looks at the use of the overlay editor by older pupils to store their own texts.

Concept keyboard overlay allowing children to build a sentence by choosing a beginning and end.

In the simple example above, children match the character and action to compose up to four sentences: 'The troll is standing. The billy goat is eating.' However, the stored texts may be much longer then this. The overlay may contain a whole story, in paragraphs associated with pictures. The pupil may press the pictures in the chosen order to retell the story. The pictures drawn or stuck on the overlay support the child's recall of events and assist in sequencing the texts. The main story line is presented through the stored texts. Additional ideas may be added at any stage by typing on the standard keyboard.

Overlay keyboards provide a valuable source of support in the context of developing oracy. Texts may originate from children's spoken suggestions. Children in a Nursery class contributed their own ideas to an overlay based on the story of *Mrs Mopple's Washing Line* (Minns, 1991). A nursery assistant worked with a small group throughout a week. Children drew pictures for the overlay. The assistant acted as scribe while children re-told each part of the story. Linked text was then developed, giving three levels which could be accessed by pressing the overlay. In the second level, the texts reveal what the characters may have been thinking. The third level is captioned, 'What happens next?'

Initially, the story was read and discussed, with emphasis on the order of events. This helped children to decide the order of pictures on the overlay, to re-tell the story in the same sequence as in the book. Children were delighted when their own words appeared on the screen. They became familiar with certain words and phrases repeated throughout the story and even began to memorise some of these.

In the second level, the assistant worked with one or two children at a time. The aim was to encourage the children to develop empathy for the characters, and get a little deeper into the meaning of the story. The third level, 'What happens next?' was more difficult. Children were able to say what happened next in the story, but could not yet suggest their own versions. When the group showed their work to another adult, several children were able to read words from the screen. Children had learned some of the special words associated with the computer, and already were showing a positive, fearless attitude to using ICT.

Even at this very simple level, pupils learn that ICT allows them to exercise control over what happens. The order of displayed texts depends on the choices made by the child. The text can be altered or extended using the normal word processor facilities.

The above account shows just one of the ways in which an adult working closely with children may use the overlay keyboard to model the writing process, by capturing, storing and extending the children's thoughts. The content-free overlay software provides a tool for older pupils' to store and display their own information. The word processor may again be employed, allowing rapid generation of 'reports' from texts stored by pupils. This use is investigated in Chapter 8.

The overlay keyboard may be used with a talking word processor. Selected texts are 'read' to the child as they are displayed on screen. Children enjoy hearing their stories being read, and do not seem to be put off by the robotic voice. The association of pictures on the overlay, words on the screen together with speech constitutes a valuable literacy aid. With practice, many teachers have found that they can produce simple overlays quickly. I have seen large collections in ring binders, many of which have been designed to meet individual learning needs.

Talking word processors

Word processing software such as *Textease, Full Phases* or *Talking PenDown* enables words, whole sentences or the entire passage to be 'spoken'. The incorporation of synthesised speech provides the young writer with immediate feedback. Words are highlighted in a different colour as they are sounded, reinforcing directionality and enabling the child to follow the text.

In her study based on a rigorous evaluation of *Talking PenDown*, Joy (1994) identifies a number of benefits for pupils across the age range with below average reading scores. These include:

- Increased confidence, concentration and self-esteem
- Improved use of full stops, capitals and spaces between words
- More successful attempts at phonologically regular spelling

Pupils improved their reading age by an average of 7.63 months over the four-week programme, during which they worked on the computer for twenty minutes each day. Use was made of a 'Look, cover, write, check' approach using specially prepared sentence cards. Rehearsal was built into the programme, in that children would be given opportunities to re-type the words that they remembered, or type sets of words with similar letter strings. In *Talking PenDown*, the word is spoken as soon as the space bar is pressed.

A special needs co-ordinator in a project school observed that pupils were 'talking to themselves, analysing their spellings and self-correcting far more' at the end of the programme (Sharp, 1995). The key element appeared to be that instant feedback encouraged a more reflective approach through making the links between letters and corresponding sounds less abstract. Children who had difficulty with vowels in their reading benefited from hearing the words which they had typed. A pupil commented, 'It's making me think of sounds more.'

Joy points out that the costs of purchasing site-licensed software are low in comparison to other remediation schemes. She says, 'All these findings confirm *Talking PenDown* to be an effective tool for improving standards of literacy.'

Writing

Word processors were widely hailed in the 1980s as tools with the power to transform the ways in which young learners approach writing tasks. The ease of editing and the potential for moving text offers opportunities for experimentation with creative ideas. The Kingman Report (DES, 1988) noted the potential for motivating pupils to talk about structure, spelling and punctuation as well as the nature of their writing. Is the word processor fulfilling its promise? What skills should be taught? Given that computers are a shared resource, what are appropriate writing tasks?

In the initial stages, pupils must learn to:

- Identify letters on the keyboard
- Put a space after each word – but not before a comma, full stop etc.
- Use the shift key correctly to produce capitals and certain punctuation marks
- Use the backspace key correctly to make changes as text is entered
- Break a line with the Enter key.

For young writers, the above actions are unique. You do not physically have to make a space between the words when writing by hand! Pupils need to understand that, while a new line can be forced with the Enter key, continuous text flows onto the next line automatically.

Early writing activities should be simple but purposeful. In a Reception class, for example, each child may ask for a word. The teacher writes the chosen word on a card. The child thinks of a sentence including the word. The child types the sentence then clicks on the 'Print' button. The text is illustrated and stuck in a book. The finished book, with everyone's contributions, is displayed in the classroom.

As children make progress, simple writing tasks enable small groups to take turns at the computer over the course of two or three days. Lists are quickly compiled, and children gain experience of the skills identified above. The teacher may model the writing task initially, brainstorming ideas with the class. For example, a Year 1 class undertook various writing activities on the theme of 'Pirates'. The teacher began, 'The pirates landed at Southampton. They went to the supermarket. What was on their shopping list?' Children watched as the teacher typed their suggestions. She explained how each new line was made, and what she should do when she made a mistake. Later, the children wrote and printed their own lists.

At a slightly more advanced stage, children may compile acrostics, riddles or shape poetry (eg. the *Apple* poems described in Chapter 14). After hearing a favourite story, pupils may choose a character and describe his or her weekly routine. There are many potential contexts within the Literacy Framework. For example, in text level work in Year 2, children should be taught 'to use structures from poems as a basis for writing, by extending or substituting elements, inventing own lines, verses; to make class collections, illustrate with captions.'

If a large display is available, the writing activity may be modelled by the teacher in the context of the Literacy Hour. This riddle was written by two student teachers, to model a particular form to children:

On Monday I was a knight. I used my shield to fight off the dragon.

On Tuesday I was in a band. I played the drums, with one of mum's wooden spoons.

On Wednesday it rained. I got out my boats and they sailed on the lake.

On Thursday the men from outer space landed. I flew with them in my flying saucer.

On Friday I made my secret camp. The only way out was through the round trap door.

On Saturday I was the driver of a big red bus. I drove my passengers to the shops.

On Sunday my mummy said I should put the lid back on the dustbin.

Another approach is to prepare a framework to which children may add their own ideas. An outline plot can be built up, after discussing the start of the story with the whole class. Once the key events have been agreed, the teacher can type the starting sentence of each section. Each group may then work on their own version. The word processor assists writing with frameworks since it enables any amount of text to be inserted at the correct place. The work does not have to be finished in one session.

By Year 2, children may begin to acquire the skills of editing text anywhere on the screen, as the following example shows. This story was written jointly by three seven year olds during a forty minute session:

> One day a tiger was hidding from the
> sun, because it was to hot, he hid in
> the long grass, he saw a dinarsoir he
> asked him what he was doing down
> there, the dinasoir said I'm searching
> for worms to eat he found one worm.
>
> the dinasoir picked up a tree
> and he covered the tiger with it . the
> tiger was very small and the tree was
> very wide so the sun could'nt get in
> and the tiger was cooled down.

On finishing the story, the group reviewed the whole. Corrections were suggested and a title added. The children then took turns to edit the text. The story remained unchanged, and the corrections, though important, were at surface level. Finally, a different font was selected and the title emboldened:

> **The Tiger**
>
> One day a tiger was hiding from
> the sun, because it was too hot, he hid in
> the long grass. He saw a dinosaur, he
> asked him what he was doing down
> there. The Dinosaur said I'm
> searching for worms to eat. He
> found one worm.
>
> The Dinosaur picked up a tree
> and he covered the tiger with it. The
> tiger was very small and the tree was
> very wide so the sun could'nt get in
> and the tiger was cooled down.

Robson (1987) carried out a study of word processing by six and seven year olds. Were children prepared to redraft their work? How far would their editing go? Could they be encouraged to develop the ideas in their stories?

Children worked in pairs. There were initial difficulties in finding keys, but speed improved fairly quickly. At first, the emphasis was on acquiring technical skills. Robson goes on to note 'the marked effect [the word processor] has had on how children construct their stories and their use of punctuation'. Because the stories were to be mounted in books, children had to split the text into sections, each block to go on a separate page. After discussion with the teacher, they were able to eliminate repeated use of 'and'. An example is Sam's story:

Superman was flying in the air
and he saw a baby and he
flew down to pick him up and
he flew up with the baby in the
sky and the baddy said put
him down and a laser came
from the supermans eyes and
killed the baddy.

In making pages for the book, Sam changed this to:

Superman was flying in the air
and he saw a baby.

He flew down to pick him up.

He flew up with the baby in
the sky.

Put him down said the baddy.

A laser came from superman's
eyes and killed the baddy.

Each block was cut and mounted on a new page, with a picture. When other pupils adopted this approach, the teacher noted a marked decline in the use of 'and' in their stories. Robson goes on to discuss the improvement in Sam's handwriting which took place after he started to use the computer. This may have been due in part to his success with the word processor. On the computer, his stories became longer and more imaginative. Sam was better prepared to revise because he found it far easier to re-read his computer work. Robson suggests that this is one of 'the most valuable aspects'.

Only the most able pupils managed to develop their stories by inserting material. The majority spent the following session in adding to the end of the story, correcting errors and formatting the text. Robson suggests that pupils have been conditioned to focus on spelling, punctuation and appearance in improving their work. I suggest that, in addition, the technical demands of developing ideas through insertion and revision place a burden on young writers. The majority of children in Years 2 and 3 are at an intermediate stage where corrections tend to involve deletion and insertion of one or two characters, as in the 'Tiger' example.

At the computer, Robson noted sustained concentration and improved willingness to finish work. Resourcing problems and lack of time were barriers to fuller use. Each pair typically needed three or four half-hour sessions to compose and re-draft a story. Not all children were prepared to co-operate initially and collaborative working had to be encouraged. Provided the teacher is able to maintain an overview of group work, the computer is a catalyst for discussion (Blake, 1989). There were opportunities for critical appraisal during the development of children's stories, not just at the end.

Robson notes that, while most children wanted to transcribe stories written by hand, they found it difficult to focus on the copy as well as the keyboard and screen, and fresh errors were introduced. In a well-resourced Year 6 class, I found that nearly all pupils preferred to re-work their notes in rough books, rather than reformulate and draft the full text directly onto the screen. This is despite the fact that five computers were available most of the time. One girl told me that she would rather 'practise' in her rough book. When I negotiated with pupils to persuade them to write straight onto the computer, this led to discussion of alternatives, and joint acceptance. Pairs who had drafted their texts in advance took turns, one sitting passively while the other typed. I asked for their views:

Vicky	It's better writing it in rough first, because if you did it on the computer you don't know what to write and you get it all mixed up.
Theresa	It's harder writing it on the computer, because it takes ages.

Vicky   If you write something wrong [in your rough book] you can just go over the top of it.

I pointed out that you can correct mistakes on the computer. Vicky insisted, 'It still takes longer.'

The girls are quite right: it can be very difficult indeed to formulate and organise ideas while faced with the demands of composing on screen. Nearly all professional writers engage in some form of pre-writing, whether this consists of lists, diagrams with loops, or fully developed sketches. Many OFSTED reports have been rightly critical of word processing that is confined to typing up final drafts. This does not mean, however, that preparatory writing on paper should be banned. Pupils often want to see what their ideas look like before developing them further on the computer screen.

However, the most significant advantage of the word processor to many mature writers is the freedom that it allows in experimenting with written ideas. Are children inspired to redraft and extend their stories? Jessel (1997) observed that eight and nine year olds, despite their positive approach to using the computer, tended not to discuss each others' ideas as their joint writing took shape. They were also reluctant to engage in redrafting. As Jessel points out, the process may impose considerable intellectual demands. Vicky, the Year 6 pupil quoted above, appears to be saying that she finds manipulation of screen text quite difficult, and would prefer to make changes in her rough book beforehand.

I observed three boys working on a page for their World War II newspaper (Chapter 10). Two of the boys dictated to Tim, the typist. Tim's spelling errors were promptly picked up by the other two, who continually checked the source. The real difficulty was that Tim constantly forgot to reposition the cursor after correcting an error. On several occasions, he carried on entering text with the cursor in the wrong place, necessitating further correction. In marked contrast, Tim showed considerable skill in manipulating the authoring software and the Acorn desktop environment. With no help whatever from me, he carried out these steps:

Create a new page.

Draw frames for text and picture.

Draw frames for 'back' and 'home' buttons, and adjust size of frames.

Re-size the window, to show the page below.

Drag the link icon from the link on the previous page, to the new page.

Link the 'back' frame to the previous page.

Drag the window back to its original size.

Test both links.

Save both pages.

The above process took 37 seconds. Later, entry of the three words 'available in Stalingrad' took 55 seconds. This was mainly due to the group's insistence on correcting mistakes on the spot. The three boys sought a flawless product from the outset, and could not bear to leave mistakes for later correction. Robson (op.cit.) also noticed this in her study of Year 2 pupils.

As pupils' writing skills develop, they will be able to make far more efficient use of a word processor if they can make changes anywhere on the screen. If a mistake is spotted on a line above, it is simply not worth deleting then re-typing everything. Editing on the screen is more difficult than many teachers perhaps realise, in view of the skills and knowledge demanded. Pupils need to know and understand:

- The function of the cursor (caret), and why its placement is so important

- The use of the arrow keys, *Home, End, Page Up / Down*

- That spaces and line breaks can be deleted in the same way as letters

- The correct use of the Delete key

- How to use the mouse to position the cursor

- How to drag-select to delete and re-type.

In many cases, deletion as well as insertion is demanded. The position of the cursor, as the entry point of new text, is critical. For some pupils, identifying *what* needs to be deleted is a challenge. Mistakes often pass unnoticed because attention is on the keyboard. Only when the pupils look up are the errors spotted. In Tim's case, his partners urged him to correct mistakes as he typed. Constant stopping to make changes may, however, disrupt the flow of ideas. Once young writers become able to make amendments anywhere within the document, they should be encouraged to let superficial errors pass. At the end of each paragraph or section, the pupils should stop to review what they have just written. Leaving errors for later correction relies on confidence and a positive attitude. Where the screen is in full public view, children may be highly reluctant to leave mistakes for all to see.

Would the teaching of touch typing eliminate the problems experienced by pupils? Jarvis (1997) reviews touch typing tutorial software, but warns that the chief problem for teachers is lack of time. Even so, the acquisition of typing skills by pupils with impaired motor control is so important that tuition, with targets, has been built into Individual Education Plans.

Jarvis' article is available on-line and contains helpful advice. The importance of good posture is stressed. The monitor should be positioned at eye level. The use of coloured dots (blue for t, g, b and red for y, h, n) may help pupils position their hands correctly. The thumbs should be used for the space bar. Given regular opportunities for 10 to 15 minute sessions, repeated typing of short words has enabled children to learn keyboard layout and the correct fingering.

Bad habits, once learned, are difficult to correct. In one Year 5 class, pupils showed a range of inefficient techniques. Some still preferred to use Caps Lock rather than the shift key, a habit which the teacher believed had been acquired in the Infants school. Invariably the arrow keys were used to move the caret. The mouse was pushed right out of the way. One boy needed to insert 'fr' in front of 'om'. Instead of entering the two characters together, he typed r, then pressed the left arrow before inserting f.

Claire moved her finger across the blank screen as she made a suggestion, as though the words were already there! Later, on re-reading the story, she used her finger to trace where an insertion would go. It is possible that this highly visual writing medium was actively helping her to envisage her ideas taking shape. Claire and her partner, of average ability, frequently paused to review the text. This was not to look for errors, but to prompt the next idea. Other pupils tended only to read back the last sentence. Very few were prepared to review critically, check for inconsistencies or incorporate detail once they thought they had 'finished'. I had to spend time with each pair to persuade them to develop what they had written.

Between sessions, I asked the pupils to make corrections and suggestions for improvement on their printout in order to save time at the computer. Many did this thoroughly, marking spelling corrections and paying particular attention to punctuation. While this was welcome, in retrospect my approach may have counteracted any preparedness on their part to use the screen as an exploratory writing medium. Since they were correcting on paper, there was no change to the established procedure of drafting in rough books. Where insertions were suggested, they were to clarify or explain what was already present. These insertions rarely extended beyond three or four words.

Presentation is an important element. At an early stage, children may be taught to insert, centre and underline a title. Many pupils enjoy experimenting with fonts and character format. The public nature of the medium encourages strong awareness of audience. For example, nine to eleven year olds (Chapter 10) thought that ornate fonts and bold, riotous styles conveyed the wrong message. Teachers may welcome this awareness of the impact on the reader. However, the use of ICT may give such emphasis to the communicative function of writing that pupils fail to see the opportunity for experimentation and development of tentative ideas. Jessel (op.cit.) suggests that the priority given to conventions such as spelling and punctuation leads pupils to approach their initial draft as though it were a final version. In their perception, subsequent drafts simply give them the chance to correct mistakes. It is therefore highly likely that ICT will be incorporated into the established pattern of writing in the classroom.

Teachers are unlikely to find that pupils are receptive to the notion of the word processor as a tool for thinking. There are several reasons for this. We have seen that pupils are anxious to draft error-free text that will be included in the final form. Until pupils have control over a range of editing skills and techniques, redrafting remains a daunting task. While collaborative work provides opportunities for discussion, the cognitive demands of composing jointly while thinking up ideas are considerable, as Jessel (op.cit.) has shown.

Nevertheless, the word processor offers significant advantages as a drafting and presentation tool. The very fact that pupils are motivated from the start to attend to surface detail may be turned to advantage. Another benefit lies in the clarity of printed text, especially for pupils with poor handwriting. This visual medium is an excellent aid to the teacher in modelling the writing process. While there are scant references to ICT in the Literacy Framework, many contexts for the use of the word processor may be identified, especially in writing composition across both Key Stages.

CHAPTER 8

OVERLAY KEYBOARDS AND NON-FICTION WRITING COMPOSITION

This chapter is based on two case studies in contrasted settings. In the context of History topic work, pupils used overlay keyboards to store and retrieve non-fiction texts which they had researched and written themselves.

The overlay keyboard (or Concept keyboard, from the longest-established design) is a flat tablet with a sensitive surface. The keyboard is connected to the computer, and software is run to enable communication. In the last chapter, we saw examples of overlays prepared by teachers. Using special editor software, the teacher specifies the grid location of each 'message' or block of text. The texts are entered and the overlay file saved.

As we saw in the last chapter, the overlay file may be then used with a word processing package to enter stored words and phrases at the cursor position. The full range of word processor facilities are available, allowing pupils to correct errors, add to, delete or move blocks of text. The word processor gives control over presentational features, such as choice of font and size.

Overlay keyboards are most frequently associated with the early years and special education. However, the accessibility of editing software enables Key Stage 2 pupils to design and create their own overlays. Gomersall (1994) used this approach to develop skills of 'picture reading' in History. Contemporary images such as portraits and paintings of events were mounted on overlays. Pupils pressed the overlay to access information and questions. A talking word processor was used to display retrieved text. Subsequently, children chose pictures and made their own overlays. The process of formulating critical questions about the pictures contributed to children's awareness of the nature of historical evidence. Skills of interpretation were developed.

How can pupils make use of overlay keyboards in storing, organising and presenting the results of their research? What skills need to be taught? What are the learning benefits? In particular, how does this type of activity support literacy teaching objectives?

Using the overlay keyboard to store researched information

Year 4 pupils in Charlton, South East London, investigated changes over the last ninety years in the local high street. The A3 overlay consisted of a picture map, with children's drawings of all the buildings. Five text files were created for the years 1899, 1921, 1945, 1973 and 1989. Each contained details of businesses and residents. The editor software allowed the files to be linked, enabling layered information to be built up. To access the file for each date, children simply had to press the date on the overlay. Texts were then displayed by pressing on each building.

For 1899, the texts include:

> Robert Martin was the owner of a toolmaking and mechanical horse clipping business. He had thirteen men and five boys working for him.

> Number 21: John Osborn, Domestic Supply Stores. He would have sold brushes, soap, fly paper, mops, lamps and candles.

Children's research, drawn from visits and from street directories from the local library, enabled insights into the changing environment. In days gone by, there were no fast food outlets or estate agents. However, the pubs have altered not at all! Children began to speculate how everyday life may have changed.

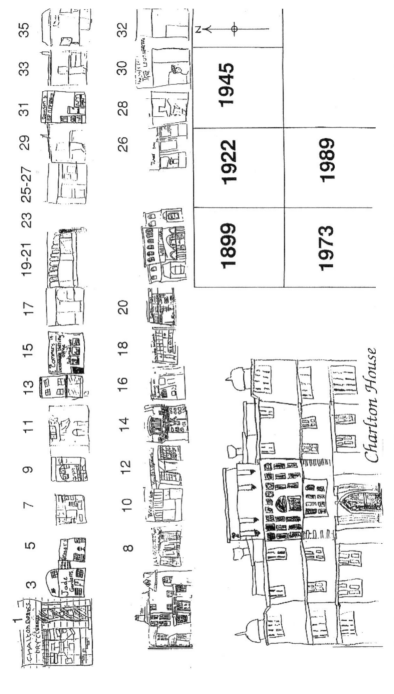

Overlay based on a picture map of Charlton Village. A date and a building are pressed to display information.

To see how each location has changed over time, users may press a building, then any of the five dates displayed on the overlay. We find that only one business has remained in the same family since 1899. By 1973, other family businesses had been taken over by chains with names such as Pricerite Ltd.

Parents showed great interest in the children's work. After school, Judith showed her father the completed overlay. He was particularly interested in No. 35, the premises of a staff recruitment agency. He was sure that he had once had his hair cut there. The date 1973 was pressed, to reveal that No. 35 had indeed been a barber's shop. Children had noticed that some premises were up for sale: this led them to speculate how the high street would continue to change.

Following the Charlton project, I worked with eleven Year 5 pupils in a mixed-age class. The pupils were engaged in a study of an Iron Age hill fort near Andover, Hampshire. While they had no previous experience of making their own overlays, they had at least had the opportunity to explore the Charlton overlay. This gave them a feel for the task and, most importantly, the type of information they would need to research.

The pupils were organised into three groups. Following visits to Danebury Ring and to the Museum of the Iron Age in Andover, they were given photocopied maps of the hill fort, on A3 paper. Two computers were available, with additional access to a third elsewhere in the school. One group thus had to work in relative isolation; in fact, the arrangement encouraged a high degree of independence and autonomy.

Pupils experienced little difficulty in using the maps to create their overlays. They added many details to the maps, and began composing texts to associate with each location on the map. Much use was made of notes taken at the museum, and from books. The desire to attach messages to all areas of the map motivated pupils to think hard about what other aspects of Iron Age life they could include. One message reads:

> This is where the burials are. Iron Age people believed in life after death. They were buried with swords, drinking vessels and food needed in the next world.

At the same location, another group wrote:

When people died the celts belived that their bones were dedicated to the gods. Enemies skulls were kept nailed up over the gate of the fort.

Pupils were well motivated and fully prepared to co-operate with minimum supervision. Faced with a problem which they could not solve, they explored it sufficiently to ensure that I was met with a precise request. For example, one group asked me how to copy a text to another place. A fence surrounded the hill fort, and they wanted the same text to appear wherever the fence on the map was touched.

At first, children took turns to sort through pooled notes, instructing another group member what to type. As familiarity with the process grew, there was a greater degree of collaboration. Discussion focused more on content rather than the mechanics of entry. Here, pupils decide to add a message about weaving. Great care is taken over wording: there is concern not to copy from the museum guide. All three members contribute equally, and there is less apparent division into roles than in earlier instances:

Lisa   Put 'probably' because we don't really know –

Alexa   They probably did weaving in their homes –

Penny   – at their houses.

Lisa   They're not going to do it in the middle of the street!

Penny   So what are we going to put then? (All read museum guide.)

Penny   'The tools they used included needles, weights' –

Alexa   The needles they used were all shapes and sizes.

Penny   We could put the tools they used for weaving were – (All read the guide closely.)

Lisa   The tools they used for weaving were made from bone and antler.

Penny suggests 'weaving and spinning'. There is further reference to the booklet. The final text reads:

The women probably did weaving in their homes. The tools they used for weaving and spinning were made from bone and antler. They had tools like needles, combs and weights etc.

Pupils were eager to press on the map to look at the texts. Some had been reluctant to review their writing during the creation stage. However, the process of exploring the map appeared to motivate them to correct and refine text. Errors and ambiguities were pointed out and noted for later correction. Spelling and punctuation were frequently discussed. These features were carefully checked when pupils reviewed other groups' work.

The class teacher noted the high levels of motivation and productivity shown throughout the week. She believed that children's success in coping with computer demands was largely due to their having been freed from all other tasks. Following the visits, they had been able to work without interruption. However, long-term planning is essential if blocked time is to be made available for this type of project.

In their own evaluation, Year 5 children commented on the benefits of group work. Alexa said, 'If I didn't know what something meant, or I couldn't find something, then one of these two might know something about it.' Lisa maintained, 'If you're writing your arm begins to ache [...] but when you're on the computer you can let somebody else have a go!'

After Year 6 classmates had seen the overlays, I asked them if they thought that this was a good way of presenting information.

Fiona   Yes, because you can see where it is as well as read a good description of it.

Allan   Usually when you look at books you hardly ever find anything –

Scott   It's so boring!

Allan   But on this, most people want to use it –

Scott   Everybody wants to use the computer!

Allan   – and when someone says, can you find out about Danebury, you can say, use the computer, it's all there.

Year 6 pupils compared the overlay keyboard with their experience of multimedia presentation. They agreed the latter was more suitable for younger children: older users would prefer the overlay keyboard. Grant commented, 'The way it was set out was much more technical.' Scott explained, 'Instead of just moving the mouse around [...] you just press the Concept Keyboard and it comes straight up.' Grant added that it was more 'efficient'. Other children thought that it was better to press a map to find information, than to click haphazardly around the screen.

The Year 6 pupils thought that the overlay keyboard allows a very high level of interactivity and access to information, and therefore is more 'technical' than the mouse. In other words, it embodies a higher level of technical sophistication. Surprisingly, Grant believed that the overlay keyboard had an advantage in that it only displays text, not pictures. He said, 'You have to build it in your mind.'

Researching the overlay content had enabled the Year 5 pupils to build up personal knowledge through pooling information. This may well have happened anyway, but the response of the Year 6 'audience' shows that the overlay had succeeded in making the pupils' texts readily accessible to others. The following study was undertaken to investigate whether the process of authoring and retrieving overlay texts may assist in the development of writing skills and awareness of genre.

Creating overlays to support writing in non-fiction genres

There are many references within the National Literacy Strategy (DfEE, 1998) to the teaching of writing composition in different genres. For instance, in Year 6 Term 3, pupils should be taught 'to select the appropriate style and form to suit a specific purpose and audience, drawing on knowledge of different non-fiction text types'.

In any genre, such as factual report writing, there is a characteristic schematic structure (Derewianka, 1990). Each section has a particular function. For example, the introduction may serve to locate the theme within a wider context. Key ideas may need to be explained, facts presented and implications considered along with other related information.

When children use the overlay editor to store their findings from research, they are not faced with the structuring task required in executing a longer piece of written work. Short texts may be produced in any order. Each text is stored in connection with a picture, or map location, on the paper overlay. This serves the function of the heading in notemaking. In the Danebury study, the process of overlay design helped focus the research, in the same way as preparing a list of headings. Children had to think in advance about topics and questions.

Used with a standard word processing application, a document is rapidly generated as the overlay keyboard is pressed. To facilitate experimentation, 'cutting and pasting' techniques must be taught. Children must be prepared, and able, to select text, make block deletions and move text about the page. Pupils are enabled to experiment with existing texts, which they have written themselves. In working with their own texts, they may become better able to make informed choices in future writing in non-fiction genres.

Researching life in Hampshire in World War II

Year 6 pupils were engaged in a study of the effects of the war on the people of Hampshire. To support the project, the class teacher had obtained resource packs from the Hampshire County Records Office. The packs contained photographs and facsimiles of documents. Texts explaining the materials (written for teachers, not children) were included in the pack, with background notes to assist teachers' planning. Beforehand, the class teacher and I grouped materials according to themes, comprising people at work, evacuation, air raids, rationing, salvage and effects on home life.

The setting was in marked contrast to that of the previous study. In statutory assessment of English at the end of the year, only six of the thirty Year 6 pupils reached Level 4. Most were achieving well below national expectations. A great effort had been made by the whole school community in improving behaviour and social skills. Despite the positive ethos of the school, many pupils continued to manifest low self-esteem, taking little pride in much of their work.

The six most capable pupils were girls. They were better able to plan and organise a task. They possessed the language skills which this activity demanded, and took greater pride in their work. Some boys showed refreshing enthusiasm, but were hampered by poor literacy skills, and needed much support. Mixed-ability pairings were selected by the class teacher, giving each group a better chance of being able to accomplish something independently. Not all pairings worked. In particular, girls did not like working with boys of lower ability.

Not all pupils were enthusiastic at the prospect of computer work. Emily rejected the activity but agreed to make a few notes on paper. At the computer, she preferred to slump in her chair and switch off. Staff assured me that resistance is not aroused solely by ICT. Any demanding tasks are resisted, especially where writing is involved.

Throughout the week, there was access to one computer in the classroom, and four machines in the adjoining shared area. Two computers had the benefit of hard disks, on which pupils had their own work directories. Despite the relatively high level of resourcing, I was unable to support work on more than three computers at any time. I needed to observe and monitor activity closely. Some pupils needed constant help. They became fractious and frustrated if left for a few moments. They were poorly prepared to cope with unexpected hitches.

Initially, I distributed photographs and posters on a particular theme: air raids, evacuation, workers, food and rationing. Children were aware that the aim was to find out about how the war affected ordinary people.

A poster entitled *County Salvage Drive* attracted attention. The text was highly informative. Children could read to find which materials were needed, and why. Peter showed infectious enthusiasm, but his level of literacy was poor. He was not assisted by his partner's manifest apathy. I helped the pair to use the salvage poster to answer questions: What was salvaged? What was it needed for? A reduced photocopy of the poster was stuck onto an A3 sheet to make the overlay. With support, the following text was composed:

> that old tin will help to make a tank.
> your metal will help win the war.
> save your waste paper
> old rags bones saucepans
> waste rubber rope
> string twine kettles irons
> garden rollers fenders.
> please see what you can find.

Most pupils quickly absorbed IT skills. The majority became able independently to select an area for each message, enter text and save their work. Generally, writing required more support.

Poor group dynamics hampered progress. Carly said, 'When other people get it all wrong I get really frustrated.' She wanted to work on her own or with someone in her group level. After a good start, Joleen became bored and frustrated: she resented working with one of the lowest ability boys.

Capable girls were quick to make perceptive observations, empathising with people shown in photographs. Persistent intervention was needed to persuade other pupils to elicit information from these sources. There was great reluctance to make notes in rough. Most children preferred the practical work of making the overlay. Some only needed to be shown once how to locate an area on the overlay editor and type in a message. It was the chore of writing that aroused the greatest distaste. Ricky announced, 'It was exciting. [The best bit was] sticking them on and making the pictures.' Working with Joleen, he had been able to avoid writing anything!

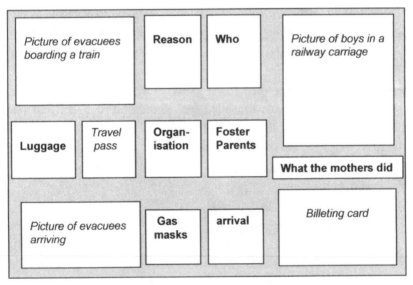

This diagram shows the approximate layout of Simone's overlay, with headings in bold. When a heading is pressed, Simone's writing on that topic is entered on the word processor page.

Notemaking and overlay design

Simone, one of the most able pupils in the class, had produced notes about evacuation. Her notes were not recorded under headings, but were written in continuous prose. For the overlay, her notes had to be organised into separate texts. I suggested that she first list the topics separately. Then she could number the topics and label her notes. Her notes began, 'The reason was it was too dangerous to stay in the city.' She commenced her list: '(1) Reason'. She read her notes, and suggested other headings. Then, Simone thought about her overlay plan. She was very conscious of where the different packets of information were going to go.

Away from the computer, Paul had made the following notes in his rough book:

air raid shelters were verey uncufderble and it wasent nice, at night sometimes you had to go down to the air raid shelter you had to turn of your lights at a surton time so the germans couldent see you they can be sheared by four houses at once and sometimes it flooded

If you never had water you might dehighdrat people tock flasks of water just incase the Germans bombed the water pieps water was verey usefull in case you wanted to clean yourself soe water isent safe to drink

Some of the key points in Paul's notes are identified, together with sources:

Air raid shelters were very uncomfortable.	Agreed in group discussion.
They can be shared by four houses at once.	Noticed from plan in resources pack.
Sometimes they flooded.	I told them that I had read this.
If you never had water you might dehydrate.	Paul's own idea.
People took flasks of water.	I had drawn attention to the air raid leaflet.
The Germans might bomb the water pipes.	I had suggested this.
You might need to clean yourself.	I had asked, 'Why else do we need water?'
Some water isn't safe to drink.	Matthew found this in the air raid leaflet.

While presenting these ideas as continuous prose, Paul has made little attempt to link them. The next stage might be to work on the structure of the finished piece, and then to consider how these separate statements could be linked. When text is retrieved to produce a word-processed report, the emphasis is on structure. In fact, full attention can be given to structural features and linkage, since the material itself has already been written.

However, Paul first had to extract the information from his notes and associate with the images on the overlay. At that juncture, I was involved with another demanding group. In the event, use was not made of some of Paul's notes, because he did not assert himself. His partner took over the activity, and imposed his own ideas.

Using the texts to compile reports

When overlays were complete, the word processing program PenDown was loaded. Most children were quick to appreciate that four or five presses on the overlay would generate an instant report. Ricky realised that text could be added in the word processor: 'If you know more things about the blitz, you let the computer write it in and then you write it in, just after.'

Many errors were spotted for the first time when the texts were displayed in the word processor. When Gary used Ricky's barrage balloon overlay, he pointed out the error in 'The tail were shaped like fins.' Later, I showed the group how to amend the text in the overlay editor. Since the overlay application is running concurrently with the word processor, the editor window may be opened at any time. The file must be saved after making changes.

The visibility of the display contributed in raising awareness of spelling and punctuation. Many similar errors were noted, discussed and corrected. However, the main teaching opportunities which arose were concerned with style and structure appropriate to the genre of the factual report.

Genre and style

Many children had written their texts as captions for the pictures on their overlays. Now, in combining texts to produce a report, they were writing in a different genre. Max noticed that the caption 'This is the Queen Mary...' was out of place. He looked downcast, saying, 'We'll have to write it again.' He cheered up when he realised that this was not in fact necessary. Max, who had been uncooperative, had at least noticed the inappropriate genre.

The more capable and better-motivated pupils gained much practice in reviewing and editing. Vicky's report began, 'These people are coming out of their Anderson shelters.' Vicky inserted and amended text, so that this read, 'After an air raid people came out of their Anderson shelters.' Theresa changed 'This is a gas mask to protect' to 'A gas mask is to protect'.

In one group's overlay file about evacuation, the following text had been stored under the heading 'gas masks':

> They checked their gas mask for damage, one girl's gas mask was cracked, it would've been useless in a gas attack.

This text relates an actual event. Again, there was a need for amendments to link to the preceding sentence, when all texts were assembled into a report.

Pupils who had prepared texts away from the computer needed to make fewer changes. Their texts had been written before the selection of images for the overlay, and therefore had not been composed as captions. The following texts are from Simone's overlay. Each of Simone's texts had been composed after drawing together references from her copious notes:

Gas masks played a very important part in the second world war. They had to be worn everywhere just in case the Germans dropped a poison gas bomb. Gas masks were uncomfortable to wear, the rubber was tight and thick.

Children under 5 were allowed to be evacuated with their mothers. Most mothers were alone as their husbands were in the army, the navy and the royal air force. They worked in factories and built bullets, planes, they made a lot of things.

Structuring reports

A 'report' could be produced in a few presses, but pupils needed to review the result carefully. Where texts had been entered by pressing randomly on the overlay, discontinuity was highly likely. Children read, 'Lawns were changed into vegetable gardens. The tail was shaped like fins.' Gary commented, 'It doesn't make sense because there are two different subjects.'

I explained that we could move the text on the page. Peter suggested putting it at the top, with other text about barrage balloons. Unfortunately, *PenDown*, still used by many primary schools, is outdated in its design. The user must select the text, click at the new position and either call up the edit menu or type Ctrl-V. Gary suggested selecting and dragging the text, but this does not work in *PenDown*.

Ricky learned how to select text and perform Ctrl-X to delete a block. He was able to open the editor window to make a change to an overlay text. He saved the file then, in *PenDown*, selected and deleted the old text, replacing it with the corrected version. Ricky's reading age was below eight years, and he had been assessed as barely achieving at Level 2. Yet I found that he only needed to be shown once how to perform the above tasks. To boost his self-esteem, I asked Ricky to help other groups to edit their texts. Other children, especially the lower ability girls, were much less confident. They were reluctant to try things out for themselves, even where it was a simple matter of deleting unwanted blank lines.

The girls in the highest ability group were all confident computer users. Some developed individual approaches. Naomi constantly went back and forth between the overlay and word processor windows. She added to texts and corrected errors. Areas to press for information were clearly labelled on the paper overlay: *gas masks, how many, who, going, what to take, travelling*. Naomi knew that she should use a different filename for her report, or she would overwrite the overlay file. She saved her report, and copied all the work into Coral's directory on the hard disk, with no intervention whatever from me.

The word processor gave pupils the opportunity to present texts in different ways. Simone patiently experimented with font sizes, and re-aligned the text. She also experimented with columns. She read her

Barrage balloons

Barrage balloons were used to protect the houses from being bombed. Barrage balloons were filled with hydrogen gas. When the balloon was let off it rose 10,000 feet into the air.

There was a vent on the nose of the balloon. It let the air through to inflate the tail. The tail was shaped like fins.

The wires were made of metal and they were very strong. The wires were dangerous because they took wings off planes. The wires done more damage to english planes than to the german planes.

One of the barrage balloons blew up because the enemy were trying to shoot them down.

The enemy tried to shoot the barrage balloons down but the British fired back with their anti air-craft guns.

Ricky's report on barrage balloons. Stored texts were entered by pressing parts of a picture mounted on an A3 overlay. The texts were then re-arranged on the screen.

report carefully to see if any of the texts had been repeated. One text began, 'This is a record card.' Simone wanted to preserve it as a caption, and add a picture to her report. She said that this text should be in a different font 'so people know there's a picture there'.

Having made many amendments at word level, Vicky and Theresa could not suggest how to improve their structure. I asked them to tell me what each paragraph was about. The first was about Anderson shelters, the second about bombing, and the third returned to Anderson shelters. 'Oh – oops!' cried the girls. They wanted to 'swap' the second and third paragraphs. I showed them how to select and move text. At this point, I felt that the overlay keyboards were proving their worth. Paragraphs were quickly generated, but children had to apply careful judgement, to arrange the paragraphs in an appropriate order. They were being encouraged to think in terms of structure.

Lucy explained how she and her partner had structured their report. 'We looked through all the messages. We chose which was the best [introduction]. The first bit's about the rationing books. [Then it tells you] that it carried on after the war.' In the previous chapter, we saw that pupils are normally highly reluctant to experiment with structure while composing with a word processor, because the pressure to attend to surface correction dominates writing activity. Here, pupils were working with texts that had already been written. Even the most reluctant writers realised that they could improve their reports without re-typing anything. They could start a fresh page and press the overlay to display the texts in a different order.

Paul, for example, found writing extremely hard work. His main difficulty lay in organising his thinking about writing. The ease of producing a 'report' from his overlay motivated him to make the effort to add an introductory sentence and change the present to the past tense. The focus was wholly on the stylistic features of the genre. With the writing already done, Paul was able to concentrate his limited energies on improving the structure of his 'report'.

Using the overlay to build a keyword-searchable database

The stored text may be used in any application. *DataCard* is a simple card index database with keyword searching. It normally takes a great deal of time to create a set of cards, and hence is seldom used. Through pressing overlays to enter stored texts, a database containing over fifty 'cards' was created in one afternoon.

Up to six keywords may be stored with each card. To retrieve information, a keyword is selected from a list. Any card containing that keyword is retrieved, and may be displayed and printed. It is also possible to carry out a text search of all cards.

Most children were gratified and relieved to find that, having gone to the trouble of writing the texts, they could now use them for another purpose without having to re-write a single word. They gained experience of another way in which ICT may be used to present and retrieve information. In order to facilitate retrieval, they needed to determine appropriate keywords for their cards.

I explained the function of keywords. If other children are researching this topic, then they need to be able to find cards that might help them.

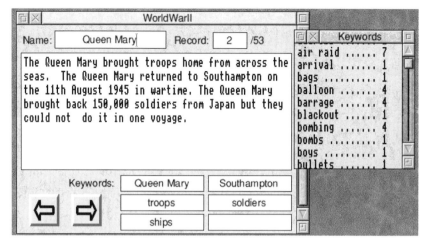

DataCard record card and list of keywords to enable retrieval. The text was entered directly from the overlay keyboard. Pupils then decided appropriate keywords.

The text was entered onto a card, simply by pressing the overlay keyboard. Ricky entered the texts which he had already used in his report, featured above.

I drew attention to the card which began, 'The wires were made of metal and they were very strong.' I asked what the keywords should be. Ricky replied, 'They were strong.' I explained why 'strong' would not be a good keyword, although this was one of the main ideas in the text. Joleen suggested 'damage' and 'planes'. I had to suggest 'barrage balloons'. Children may not have thought of this since it was not present in the text. It is important to know that a keyword need not necessarily be in the text. In the event, pupils suggested improving the text: 'The wires holding the barrage balloons [...]'.

As the database grew, children were able to use keywords to retrieve cards. Ricky clicked on the keyword 'ships' to display other children's work. I asked him to get his own work back and he clicked on 'balloons'. Pupils began to appreciate that keywords were necessary, otherwise nobody would be able to access their cards.

Summary

Pupils in Years 5 and 6 had little difficulty in coping with the demands of the overlay editing software. They were able to select the location on the overlay, enter the text and save their work. Where needed, I was able to show them how to copy texts to a different location.

If examples of work from other classes are to hand, there is a clear advantage. Pupils are able to form an idea of the finished product. This will assist their research, because they will have a better understanding of the type of information that will be needed. This insight should also make writing easier, since the purpose will have been established.

The computer display constitutes a public medium. Awareness of writing for an audience is enhanced, especially once groups are aware that others will make active use of their work. In both cases, pupils were motivated to check for errors and ambiguities and make surface corrections. The need for this extra effort may otherwise have passed unnoticed.

At one school, freeing pupils from other demands proved advantageous. This is only possible if the activity is planned for well in advance. Teachers will need to justify by identifying objectives in other subjects.

Short texts can be written in any order. This helped pupils who found it difficult to draft a sustained piece of reporting. There were many opportunities for children to edit their work. Texts written as captions had to be adapted to serve a different purpose. There appeared to be scope for developing pupils' note making skills. At least one able pupil was motivated to organise her notes under headings, once she had realised that her overlay needed structure.

Children enjoyed making the overlays. Some of the A3 sheets were useful in their own right, showing in picture form some of the information which the children had researched. The products were attractive to other children, and assisted the sharing of groups' research. Accessibility of information was appreciated by users, in particular the linking of relevant information with a point on a map.

Pupils with poor literacy skills found the initial research and writing difficult and burdensome. A high level of support was needed. However, able Year 5 pupils showed much greater independence.

In using overlay texts with a word processor, block editing skills are essential. Pupils must know how to select and delete or move blocks of text. This is an excellent opportunity to teach these skills.

In the word processor, the retrieved text is displayed at the cursor position. Pupils need to check that the cursor is in the right place! However, it is easy to start a fresh page and enter the texts again.

Pupils' dislike of the physical and mental effort of writing discouraged experimentation in different genres. Since the text had already been written, they were freed from the pressures. They could now concentrate on structural and language features in retrieving material to produce a report.

The arrangement would benefit whole-class teaching. Even with a standard monitor, the font may be enlarged so that the text can be clearly seen. The overlay keyboard enables the teacher to display, at a single touch, words, sentences or paragraphs which may be further manipulated on the word processor screen.

Old equipment may be used for this type of work. The Charlton pupils used BBC computers. On newer systems, editor software is considerably more user-friendly and is more likely to be compliant with familiar Windows conventions. More recent editors allow the incorporation of pictures. Children may press the overlay to display a picture, as well as text.

A talking word processor may be used to display overlay text. This appears to offer much potential for further development.

Pupils used their texts to build a keyword searchable database. Keyword identification is a unique ICT skill, and is critical in using CD-ROM and on-line sources. The availability of 'instant text' gave pupils a useful opportunity to engage in this new skill.

CHAPTER 9

INFORMATION RETRIEVAL USING CD-ROM

Multimedia computers with high-speed CD-ROM drives enable rapid retrieval and display of text, graphics, moving images and sound. There is a high level of visual and auditory stimulus. Colourful screen presentation inspires collaborative effort, encouraging fluent readers to pool ideas and share information as they follow cross-referencing links within the material. Interactive multimedia has the potential to engage learners' higher-order thinking capabilities (Dede, 1992) since it requires the skills of hypothesis, problem solving and investigation. However, children's use of CD-ROM is often driven by the demands of a set task, rather than by reflection on individual areas of interest (Oliver and Perzylo, 1994).

CD-ROM offers the potential for a stimulating, highly interactive approach to curriculum delivery. As Greenfield (1984) commented, 'to receive information on the same topic through different media is to learn about the topic from different points of view'. However, the mere availability of CD-ROM in schools may contribute very little. In using any reference source, pupils must be able to access material relevant to purposeful inquiry. On its own, the multimedia encyclopaedia 'does nothing to help with turning the information into knowledge' (Laurillard, 1995).

This chapter draws on published research in reviewing the unique characteristics of CD-ROM. It looks at the ways in which content may be structured, accessed and presented, and considers the information handling skills demanded of pupils. The effect that location within school may have on patterns of use is also considered. A section is devoted to pupils' difficulties with non-fiction texts, an important theme in the case studies.

What are the unique features of CD-ROM?

This chapter looks at pupils' use of CD-ROM in the context of topic-related research. However, there are other growing areas of interest in multimedia publication. A flurry of recent CD-ROMs, aimed chiefly at the home market, focus on core learning skills. While activities such as number recognition, counting and simple arithmetic feature heavily, presentation often takes full advantage of multimedia features. There may even be built-in Internet connection. For example, a five-year-old using Dorling Kindersley's *Jolly Post Office* may connect to the Jolly Postman's web site, simply by clicking on a picture of a telephone to initiate automatic log-on. Children may send in stamp paintings, view the current collection and look at the week's 'winners'. Publishers may, via the Internet, provide support for CD-ROMs through giving managed access to information that is constantly being updated. The switch from CD-ROM to on-line content is seamless and imperceptible.

Many CD-ROMs aim to provide an exploratory environment, with content designed to support topic work. For example, the *Usborne Book of Nature* provides a largely reading-free 'roam' through a range of natural habitats. Children may explore each scene to find animals, which may be 'photographed' and identified using a reference section. One Year 2 teacher thought it was the best software she'd ever used. Staff at another school deplored the lack of a structured guide through the material, and sent back the inspection copy! There are limitations, such as a lack of spoken commentary and the omission of seasonal dif-ferences – crocuses are in bloom while cabbages prosper! Printed books may be used alongside, to compensate for the poorly illustrated reference section.

Despite the drawbacks, there are many ways in which the *Usborne* CD-ROM may be profitably used with younger pupils. Focused investiga-tion, rather than repeated aimless exploration, is more likely to lead to engagement. The teacher's role is critical in negotiating aims. For example, children may set out to find bees, earthworms or slugs. Where are the best places to look?

CD-ROM is a valuable medium for archiving collections of photographs and other images. Lists of keywords and a brief caption may be stored with each image. Keyword searching enables rapid access, but learners must be able to identify keywords in the first place. A lack of focused searching may overwhelm with information.

Each title in the *Photobase* series contains thousands of images. While there is thematic grouping; each theme may be linked to hundreds of pictures. Keyword searching is essential to retrieve a manageable set of images. For example, searching the *Victorians* disc for 'Queen Victoria' produces hundreds of references. If specific information is sought, the user must devise a means of narrowing down the search. This demands subject knowledge. A further keyword may be generated by thinking about important events, places or people in the Queen's life.

In what ways do CD-ROMs differ from books? Readers do not have to cope with continuous text. Navigation can be a hit-and-miss affair, unless one has good knowledge of the specific content and the topic in general. Text and images may be saved on the user's own disc. The transcription of copyright material is, of course, restricted. There is an issue of pupils' ownership of retrieved material. Pupils need to reflect critically on the relevance of what they retrieve, and plan how it will be used. The best results are likely when learners incorporate selections into reworked ideas which are entirely their own (Steadman, Nash and Eraut, 1992).

Some CD-ROMs (for example the *Photobase* series and *British Birds*) are organised in a conventional database structure and demand systematic searching. Many newer publications have friendlier visual interfaces in place of menus, listings and indexes. The top level may feature a simple visual representation such as a picture map, or gallery with doors leading off to theme rooms. In some titles, the interface emulates a collection of objects, immediately imposing a familiar structure on the contents. In *The World of the Vikings*, content is organised into 'evidence boxes'. The six boxes pictured on screen contain images of primary source material, reconstructions and replicas. Children may open them to inspect the contents. When an image is selected, a spoken narrative with further photographs is presented.

In using interactive media, how may the learner be guided and supported? The teacher organises the experience and sets tasks, but can the software partly fulfil this role? In adaptive learning (Laurillard, 1995) the teacher is at hand to guide, offer feedback and give explanations. This is the richest mode of learning, and yet the most expensive. Laurillard identifies an inevitable move towards distance learning. Adaptive media emulate the teacher's role: there is the capability to support different modes of learning. However, pupils must possess information skills: 'the learner expects to have control, and yet a learner does not know enough to be given full control.' In planning the structure of adaptive multimedia, designers must consider what the learner has to do, and how the software in the role of 'teacher' should support the learner. For instance, learners should be kept aware of the goal, and given advice on appropriate ways of approaching the task. There should be freedom to construct one's own approach, and to deviate.

What other features of multimedia support learning? Evaluators of the *Domesday* videodisc were quick to note the potential allure. Primary pupils showed an 'overwhelming interest in pictures rather than text, data or maps' (Hodgkinson, Wild and Bailey, 1991). Pupils are strongly influenced by media messages. The way that information is presented makes a statement about its importance. A teacher told me that, when she provided materials for project research, children paid scant attention to black and white photographs and text sources. Colour images and posters were universally preferred. Video sequences on CD-ROM are rated highest of all.

Sound, including recorded speech, is an important feature. In some titles, children may listen to the text itself, or to a separate commentary. There is much to be gained from encouraging children to listen to the text. Listening to non-fiction material being read aloud enables the child to become familiar with organisational features in a fairly effortless way (Perera, 1986). Listening to non-fiction texts also aids children's writing in the genre (Neate, 1992).

CD-ROM and information skills

What information skills are demanded? Are there new skills which need to be taught? Teachers in the Government funded pilot project *CD-ROMs in Primary Schools* (Wegerif, Collins and Scrimshaw, 1996) found that groups of able pupils were able to use multimedia encyclo-paedias independently. However, children needed to be taught how to plan and conduct research. Pupils need advice on taking notes and on reporting back to others. Otherwise there is a danger that they will simply copy from the screen. Teachers need to be familiar with the content in order to design tasks.

Many teachers have great difficulty in persuading children not to copy verbatim from non-fiction sources (Lunzer and Gardner, 1979). Pupils need to select material in order to re-version within their own work. Tabberer (1987) identifies critical selection as an important ICT skill. Pupils should be taught to reject irrelevant material. They should learn to acknowledge that the information might not be available. Prior knowledge should be made explicit, since this assists in the assimilation of new information. Starting with what the children already know places them in an active role: they own the new knowledge (Lewis and Wray, 1995).

Many children have great difficulty in extracting information from non-fiction texts (Lunzer and Gardner, 1979; Lewis and Wray, op.cit.). They are particularly unsure when it comes to selecting and rejecting material. Even where pupils have been taught to use contents and index pages, they prefer to leaf through sections in linear fashion (Wray, 1995). What are the implications for pupils' use of ICT? Computer-based text is qualitatively different from printed forms (Nanlohy, 1995). It is not presented sequentially: the reader controls the flow. Are there unique skills and pitfalls?

Tabberer (1987) identifies two skills especially relevant to the use of ICT: the generation and use of keywords, and browsing non-linear texts. In generating keywords, the learner firstly needs to become able to think divergently, summoning up sufficient word associations in order to cast a wide net. Many pupils were only able to plan their work once they had had a glimpse of the sources they would be using. 'Browsing' should therefore be encouraged. It is important for pupils to be able to take wrong turnings, so that they may reflect on what could be improved. Teachers should not be too ready to supply answers or solve problems.

The development of keyword identification may be supported in class. Perera (op.cit.) suggests highlighting structural features on acetates overlaid on textbooks. Neate (op.cit.) recommends a similar approach for marking key words which convey meaning. Pupils may take away printed copies of computer texts in order to mark key words and phrases. Later, the keywords that have been generated in this way may be applied in searching for related content. This type of activity also supports the higher-order skill of scanning a text to assess its relevance.

Does location in school affect use?

In the national *CD-ROMs in Primary Schools* project, the location of machines was found to affect the pattern of use (Wegerif, Collins and Scrimshaw, 1996). Where a school has one multimedia computer, it is most likely to be located in the library. This is convenient for pupils' research which draws on books and other resources. Pupils may be trained in downloading text and images to bring back to the classroom. The arrangement contributes in developing wider information skills, especially where there is a library assistant to support pupils' research.

Where there is no support, there are considerable drawbacks. With the CD-ROM machine outside the classroom, teachers are prevented from intervening and monitoring. As schools update and replace ageing computer stock, it will become the norm to have a CD-ROM drive in each classroom. This may lead to more effective teacher-supported use.

Pupils' difficulties with non-fiction texts

How well prepared are pupils to cope with demanding non-fiction texts? Lunzer and Gardner found that, both in primary and secondary schools, pupils' limited reading strategies seriously hindered their effective use of information sources. Pupils needed 'instruction and counselling' in more efficient reading techniques. Teachers rarely read information books aloud, or support children's reading in this genre. There is emphasis on content rather than on reading skills (Neate, op.cit.).

Authors who incorporate swathes of difficult text run the risk of barring pupils who lack higher-order reading skills. Multimedia effects may dominate the presentation to such an extent that children are lured away from the text. As Meek (1991) points out, of what value are the new information technologies without readers? In Meek's view, electronic media will not replace the printed book. Both are complementary in enabling the information needs of the new generation to be met.

If text is too difficult, it is likely to be rejected, given the ease of moving on. Information should be presented as simply and clearly as possible. Prose is often highly condensed, given the space constraints of the screen. The following example is from the Hampshire CD-ROM (HMTC, 1996):

> Although Alresford Pond supplies the main flow of the River Itchen, the true source of the river can be found south of the village of Cheriton. In a wooded hollow beside the lane to Kilmeston lies a quiet pool – the source of the Itchen.

These two sentences each demonstrate a complex construction of subsidiary clauses, which have to be negotiated before reaching the main clause. The style is far removed from that of direct explanatory speech. The passage would be improved if each sentence were to begin with its main clause. There remains the risk of overload through the tight packing of information. The impersonal style of such texts contrasts sharply with the narrative forms familiar to children who enjoy reading stories (Perera, op.cit.).

Study 1: Year 4 pupils use a database of animals

Eight Year 4 pupils, all fluent readers, were introduced to *Dictionary of the Living World*. This CD-ROM, while far from comprehensive, is organised along the lines of many multimedia encyclopaedias with keyword searching and indexing. The pupils, aged 8 and 9, experienced no problems whatever in navigating between records of animals and the index. They quickly learned how to search for a word: as this was usually the name of an animal, there was no undue difficulty.

Initial strategies were centred on locating records with films and sounds. These can be replayed endlessly, enabling children to concentrate on detail, and reflect on their ideas, as they make notes. Much less attention was paid to the text. In fact, all pupils found the advanced level of the text a considerable challenge. Their greatest perceived difficulty concerned making sense of the text. But, as one child pointed out, 'You don't have to go through every word [because] you just look for the one you want.'

This was the Year 4 pupils' first encounter with CD-ROM. After two days dominated by novelty, pupils began to develop considered approaches. Two girls located a film of the mallard. They repeatedly paused to look at still frames, while making notes:

Rebecca   It makes itself look heavy and fast.

Sarah   Let's see the sound. [...] It's noisy and – it sounds like it's underwater – shall we put that?

Rebecca   It sounds screechy – it sounds like it's laughing.

In saying 'Let's see the sound,' Sarah seems to have been aware of a primarily visual medium. Film sequences invariably aroused discussion. Longer sequences offered considerable enhancement. In the following extract, children look at the film of the gorilla. Clare initially makes a cynical judgement of the film's entertainment value, but the whole group is excited by what happens:

Clare   This is a boring thing this – he's not moving – all he's doing is eating his head off. All he's doing is stuffing his mouth with food. He's a greedy prat – he's going back now. [Sharp exclamation, noisy exchanges:] Oh – wow! [...] Look how
he   walks on his hands – like a baby.

Ben   It walks on its knuckles.

The Year 4 pupils made little use of strategy in searching. Due to the nature of text searching, unexpected records were sometimes retrieved. For example, a search for 'zebra' retrieved the iguana, due to the presence of the word 'zebra' in the text. There was, however, no reflection on this, and children were quite content to study the iguana instead.

Searching the CD-ROM may sometimes be a more direct process than locating the correct book. A child wanted to research the scorpion. He was aware that it is not a mammal, nor an insect. He wasn't sure where to look on the library shelf, but he was able to go to the CD-ROM and find it straight away. He needed help from me to find the scorpion in a book. Although it had been hard to locate, the book was more informative.

I asked, 'If you want facts about an animal, where is the best place to look?' To my astonishment, a pupil pointed to the BBC computer and replied, 'On there.' Despite its lack of sophistication, children had preferred using the *Mammals* tabular database to obtain facts. This was solely due to its consistency. Provided that a particular mammal was in the file, children knew that details of its size, diet and habitat would be present. Due to the uniformity of the record structure, children knew exactly where to look for what they wanted. I observed Rebecca waiting with her finger on the screen at the expected place, while her search was in progress.

Children's use of retrieved information

Individual work on paper was frequently copied verbatim from sources. This was less likely when pupils composed directly on screen, largely due to the fact that they were working with a partner.

> The rhinoceros is a timid creature. It lives in Africa and Asia.The black rhinoceros is quite rare. Two horns are present on the muzzle, the first about 25 cm [10 in] long and the second set futher back hardly noticeable.The rhinoceros likes to live in the zoo but do you think he would prefer living in the wild? The Sumatran rhinoceros is very hairy. On the computer we saw the Indian rhinoceros. It had a scaley body. Rhinos eat grass and leaves.

This writing is a collage of related fragments from different sources. It incorporates blatant copying from the CD-ROM, with errors introduced by the pupils (as often happens, due to low engagement in the task). However, they include their own ideas and facts gleaned from other sources, as shown below:

Two horns are present...	copied from CD-ROM
The rhinoceros likes...	children's own idea which they discussed with me

The Sumatran rhinoceros ...	observation from a picture in a book
On the computer ...	direct reporting of experience
Rhinos eat...	a fact retrieved from a computer database

Improvements in factual writing need to be developed over time, but there appear to be distinct advantages in working in small groups as content is negotiated. The teacher has a vital part to play in shaping and directing children's thinking. Pupils benefit from the opportunity to relate their discoveries. The talk which invariably accompanies viewing of video sequences throws up ideas which may provide starting points for writing.

Children agreed that they could find more things in books. 'The Living World' is a broad theme, well represented in the school library. Even so, all expressed a preference for using the CD-ROM. Simon preferred writing on paper, but liked looking things up on the computer. Rebecca commented, 'You can see the animals move on the computer and you can't in the books.'

Many points for teaching and learning can arise from even a short encounter with the disc. Young children benefit from the focus provided by judicious teacher intervention. With thirty or more children in the class, the teacher cannot observe or intervene in each child's exploration. Teachers may prefer to structure tasks, which may be negotiated in advance through class discussion. Follow-up may then take place with groups as the opportunity arises, or more formally when the whole class reconvenes.

There is a need for a balance between children's self-directed exploration and the pursuit of negotiated goals. While children enjoy unrestricted use of the resource, there is a need for a deeper focus on some aspects, to maximise learning benefit. The teacher needs to plan for particular outcomes, structuring the children's tasks.

Since text takes a relatively tiny proportion of disc space, there seems no reason why there should not be a choice of text level. The level could be set in advance by the teacher or controlled directly by the learner. Additional information could be displayed at the click of a button. There are very few titles which offer this type of differentiation. *Creepy*

Crawlies offers two text levels, but the content in the lower level is unfortunately over-simplified.

Study 2: Pupils in Years 5 and 6 use CD-ROM to support topic-related research

Gleaning information from different media

Pupils in a mixed Year 5/6 class used the *Usborne Book of Nature* (see page 132). They had already been taught to download and insert images into their own word-processed work. To some, the whole point of the activity appeared to be to learn ICT techniques. A pupil proudly explained how the graphic had been 'dropped' into the document.

Scope for genuine investigation seemed limited. Later, I found that groups had simply copied lists of facts from the CD-ROM. Two girls explained that the aim was to 'look around' and choose your 'favourite' picture, then make a 'fact sheet'. They opted to search for fish that looked attractive or had interesting habits. The eel was rejected because it 'didn't have very pretty colours'.

On this CD-ROM, the quality of some hand-drawn pictures is poor. Children failed to match a butterfly to an illustration in a published field guide. They were adamant that they trusted the CD-ROM picture rather than the illustration in the book. I was told, 'The computer has more information – it's more accurate'. One pupil thought that the designers of the CD-ROM were more likely to have seen the butterfly.

The level of information on the Usborne disc, appropriate for Years 2 and 3, offered insufficient challenge to these older pupils. Other CD-ROMs appeared to offer more potential for engagement, through presenting information in different ways. In *Creepy Crawlies*, short video sequences, still pictures, differentiated text and independent spoken commentaries are available. Here, Year 5 pupils watch the earthworm film:

Liam   Oh! It's quite fast. It uses it to slither with its body movement.

Rosie   [Hushed voice] Woah! Look!

Charly   It pulls things – there – either to drag it down or to help it up.

[The worm is pulling a leaf.] It's dragging it down!

RosieOh – gosh -

Charly   That's the egg! It was coming out of the egg! Really! Yes!

The film was viewed several more times.

Liam   Wow! That's just amazing! They *have* got mouths.

RosieIt goes all big. It goes all wide.

[The worm moves through a tunnel.]

Liam   It stretches and it hangs on to something and it pulls the rest
of [its body] up. It just hunches together.

I showed the group how to pause and move frame by frame. They wanted
to look closely at the hatching. Then, they reviewed the worm pulling at the
leaf.

Liam   We've got to find out what that's for. It eats it, dunn'it?

I suggested they now read the text and listen to the spoken commentary
which contains additional information. They read that the earthworm
moves by means of muscle contractions, using stiff bristles to grip. I asked
what the commentary told us that we had not known.

RosieIn a garden you can get over one thousand worms.

Liam   Well, I heard that in Australia or somewhere you get type of
worms that are over ten foot.

I asked the group what they thought were the most important things to
include in writing a report on earthworms. 'Movement' was suggested, but
nothing else. When I asked what good is done by earthworms, Rosie
replied, 'They keep the garden clean.' Liam added, 'They drag pieces of
leaves and stuff which gives nutrients to the soil, to help things grow.'

How had pupils gleaned this information? *Creepy Crawlies* differs from the
talking story format (Chapter 7), in that texts and commentary are not
identical. There are supplementary facts in the commentary. Given the
emphasis on listening in the English curriculum, this is a welcome resource.
Using headphones, children may listen repeatedly. Teachers may ask
questions such as, 'What does the picture show? What did you discover
from the film? What did you find out by reading? What other interesting
facts did you hear?'

Searching a CD-ROM database

The next title used by the pupils was *British Birds*. Again, information is presented in a variety of media, including video, photographs and recordings of bird song and calls.

Records for each species are stored in a tabular database. *Fields* include colour, length, habitat and residential status. The possible categories for each field can be cycled, rather like a rotating barrel. In searching for a particular species, as many fields as possible have to be set to the desired match and 'held'. For example, I recalled flocks of large, noisy birds that I used to see in the depths of winter. I had genuinely forgotten what they were called. I held *winter visitor* and a small number of records were retrieved, including fieldfares.

It is not possible to search for an individual species by entering its name. There is a quick way to cycle through the letters of the alphabet, but I chose not to reveal this to children. The CD-ROM presents an excellent opportunity to apply what is already known about a species in order to retrieve its record.

There are problems. If all you know about your bird is that it is 'brown', 103 records are retrieved! One group wanted to find the magpie by searching for birds of a certain length, but the magpie's length was wrongly estimated initially. I suggested holding the attributes *black* and *farmland*, and this sufficed. In a published identification guide, children found the magpie straight away. They were keen to repeat the search, because they had found the magpie's overall length in the book.

Alison, a capable pupil in Year 6, explained how she and Maddy retrieved the robin. 'We went to the colour of it, then we went to *resident*, then we did the size, and then – it lives in a town, and there were six matches, so we quickly found it.' The girls had entered *brown*, *resident*, *10-19 cm* and *urban* to narrow the sample down to six records.

Pupils viewed the film, then suggested looking in books to find out more. Throughout the session, they paid no attention to strident calls from treetops outside the classroom. They were far more interested in the sounds on the disk! I had to draw attention to the commotion outside. I was told that blackbirds and starlings lived in the trees around the school.

The blackbird was found, by searching for *black, resident, 20-29 cm.* Both the song and alarm call were played. Children recognised the latter instantly. In great excitement, they took my tape recorder outside to record the calls of the blackbirds in the trees.

The next step was to investigate the functions of song and alarm calls. There are hypertext-style links within the text. Pupils clicked the word *call.* The following was displayed:

> Sounds which are simpler than songs are referred to as calls. They each perform a single function such as contact within the flock or between young and parents, or to convey a message such as alarm at a predator.

Yet again, pupils were confronted with adult level text. They did well to pick out two of the three reasons for alarm calls. I encouraged children firstly to recap, with me or with each other, then to take notes. To minimise time at the computer, I asked them simply to write whatever key words they would need as reminders when drafting their report, with the addition of any new vocabulary and difficult spellings.

For example, Maddy wrote 'alarm call'. She recapped, 'He does it [...] to warn the other birds that there's predators around.' She then wrote down 'predators'. Her notes read:

> Family thrushes
> description
> female – brown pale breast dark speckles
> male – black bright yellow bill
> Live in towns, country, gardens, parks
> song – attract females – territory
> alarm call – predators

Her next task, away from the computer, was to develop her notes into a draft report which she finished later that day.

The system of searching by attributes is quite unusual. Most reference CD-ROMs feature keyword searching, as in the next example. The pupils' next project was to research famous bridges and design and make models. *The Photobase Landscapes* disc proved a useful resource. A text search for *bridges* produced only two pictures. The caption of each picture contains the word 'bridges'. I drew attention to this, and pupils realised what had happened.

Keywords, as well as captions, are stored with the images. Keyword searching is faster and there is the advantage that a list of keywords is displayed. The keyword search for *Bridge* returned a large number of matches. Narrowing down (AND) was called for, and we looked at other keyword categories. The pair had a particular interest in the Sydney Harbour Bridge: this was found by specifying *Bridge* AND *Australia*.[1]

The *Finding Out* pack (NCET, 1996c) was developed in response to teachers' requests for curriculum packs which present specific inquiries. A worksheet from the NCET pack provided an easy introduction to the *Kingfisher Micropaedia*. The aim of the sheet is to enable children to gain a feel for the way the information is organised, and for retrieval strategies. Some queries demanded nothing more than entering a topic such as 'Niagara Falls' into a search box. The question 'Which is the longest river in North America?' called for a narrowing-down strategy, searching in two steps.

Year 6 pupils praised *Kingfisher's* ease of use. They found the text easy to read but were critical of picture quality. Generally, they found answers quickly. A book 'takes hours – you have to look for deserts, then for the word you want – instead of just clicking'.

The question 'Do all volcanoes look the same?' was tackled. Pupils retrieved a long list of references. The list was arranged alphabetically, with volcanoes right at the bottom. The pupils found text relevant to the question very quickly:

> Some volcanoes are gently sloping mountains, other volcanoes are steep-sided mountains with large holes at the top. These are called cone volcanoes. They are the kind that explode.

Children did not want to read any more of the text on volcanoes. Generally, there was no continued engagement once they had found the answer to the question on the worksheet. In contrast, when the same pupils looked at bridges, there was sustained interest in matters of construction, differences in design of old and new bridges, and the question of how load was supported. The worksheet exercise contributed to confidence and ICT capability. However, set questions do not often lead to sustained inquiry. Teachers need to identify starting points in children's own interests, and in ongoing classroom activity.

Another factor was the closed nature of some of the questions. It does not appear to take much to persuade children that the task is to find the 'right answer'. Worksheets may model the style so effectively that there is an immediate impact on their topic research. When I asked pupils to prepare their own ideas for research, they produced lists exclusively of closed questions.

Summary

Multimedia features such as sounds and video clips arouse intense interest, stimulating discussion. Spoken commentaries enable children to listen for information. Unlike a human speaker, the 'voice' may be paused, stopped or played repeatedly.

The quality of text is critical. Even if the text is spoken, pupils are not assisted if sentences are densely packed and poorly constructed to begin with.

Browsing is an essential element, but there needs to be a balance with more focused interaction. Provided the teacher is familiar with organisation and content, s/he can set structured tasks. The teacher must bear in mind what the learner has to do, and ensure there is adequate support.

Teachers should consider how material downloaded from CD-ROM might be used. Wholesale plundering and verbatim copying are unwelcome. In fact, when copying, pupils are less cognitively engaged and errors frequently creep in as a result. Selection is an important skill. An approach should be developed where pupils rework the selections into a coherent whole, combining with their own ideas.

Notemaking is an important skill. Pupils found it helpful to write down and link together key ideas and vocabulary. This discouraged copying and minimised time at the computer.

Advance planning is essential if children are to benefit from the opportunity to carry out CD-ROM based research. If the teaching of ICT skills is viewed as an end in itself, children are less likely to engage in the content. CD-ROM is most effectively used alongside other resources.

The presence of CD-ROM in the school library emphasises that it is a resource to be used alongside books and other collections. However, there are drawbacks where no support is available. Located in the classroom, the teacher is able to intervene and monitor. The importance of teacher intervention in raising questions and focusing inquiries must be stressed.

There are advantages in group work, but it is impossible for the teacher to be constantly present. Whole class discussion enables joint planning of inquiries, communication of findings, review of what has been learned. A large screen display will be a considerable advantage.

Pupils should be taught to appraise critically the sources they use. Children may accord unwarranted status to the new technology. For example, pupils insisted that information stored on CD-ROM was more accurate than that in a book. In one case, pupils were more interested in listening to birds on the computer than real birds outside!

Published materials provide a convenient basis for teaching retrieval skills and strategies. They may also model approaches to recording information. The sheets are not an end in themselves. Children's own interests and questions related to on-going work in class are far more likely to lead to sustained inquiry than single closed queries or one-off worksheet tasks.

Note

1. Logical searching is discussed in more detail in Chapter 11.

CHAPTER 10

MULTIMEDIA AUTHORING

What are authoring tools?

ICT provides an important means of enabling children to record and communicate their observations and findings. Perhaps the most versatile option is to use a multimedia authoring application. This tool enables the creation of interlinked pages incorporating text, graphics and/or sound. A picture, word or special graphic may be clicked to display another page.

Page design and overall structure is fully under the control of the author. Anything from simple sequencing of pages to a complex hierarchy or web is possible. Recently, authoring tools have become much easier to use. In the case of *Textease*, teachers who upgrade to the multimedia version do not have to master an entirely new program with different conventions. This is largely true, too, for Microsoft *Word* users who learn to use *PowerPoint* for multimedia presentations.

As with any ICT-supported design activity, some advance planning is essential. Clear layout is important. What is the most effective way to structure and present information? Should the pages involve an element of interaction? Questions may be asked, and multiple choices given, each choice displaying a different message.

The illustrated page on page 150 was produced with *Textease*. This elementary counting activity is hardly an outstandingly original application of ICT. However, the screen demonstrates the interactive possibilities of teacher-authored multimedia. When the child clicks a

A page from an interactive presentation by first year student teachers.

number, an appropriate message is 'spoken' by the built-in synthesiser. When the correct answer is clicked, a fresh page appears. Students with no prior experience created the set of five linked screens during a two-hour workshop session.

The teacher may set up a structure which enables individual contributions to be linked together. The presentation may provide scaffolding, giving younger children a supportive framework on which to record their ideas. Scaffolding may be provided through speech, or through questions asking children to record their own impressions and findings on the page.

There are many approaches to planning and design. The 'title page' may offer a menu of topics, a picture, ground plan or map. In *Farm*, produced by a Year 2 class for the Horizon project (HMTC, 1993) the 'title screen' is a picture map. Clicking on a map feature leads to informative pages featuring children's pictures and writing composed directly on screen.

The first authoring packages were complex and difficult to learn. While menus and dialogue boxes largely overcame the need to learn a high-level programming language, authors still needed to grapple with a range of specialised functions. While these powerful tools warrant their place in the professional developer's repertoire, simpler software adequately serves the needs of younger pupils.

The advantage of using a familiar word processor with built-in multimedia toolkit is that pupils are not faced with learning to use a new piece of software. Pages are designed in much the same way as any other writing task. There are some special considerations. Because the work will be viewed on-screen rather than in printed format, it may be preferable to set the page size to A5 landscape. Children do not then have to scroll up and down to view the whole page. Also, pupils need to consider where to place *links* to other pages. Special graphics, often called *buttons*, may be dragged onto the page. However, it is possible to link any frame containing text or graphics. When a link is created, the child needs to give the name (i.e. the saved filename) of the page to be displayed.

Multimedia authoring allows graphics to be used in exciting and original ways. The cost of digital cameras and scanners has fallen sharply. These are a worthwhile investment, and a good-quality colour scanner forms a valuable resource for the whole school. A collection of wildlife pictures, from drawings or photographs by children, may be used to create a simple electronic book. The creatures are classified into groups, and the title page features a menu leading to the categories. On each page, the children may add captions and commentary. As well as a simple branching structure, pages may be linked sequentially.

It is worth using the best available computer and display. Two or three scanned colour images in Acorn *sprite* or Windows *bitmap* (BMP) format can fill a floppy disc. For the same reason, sound recording is unrealistic unless pupils are able to store work on the network server or hard drive. It goes without saying that careful disc management is a priority. Where pupils have their own work directories, they should be trained to delete files they no longer need.

How does multimedia support learning?

Heppell (1993) suggests three multimedia modes of activity:

- narrative, involving watching and listening;
- interactive, involving browsing, exploration, navigation, making choices;
- participative: as 'interactive', with opportunities to originate and present.

Many published products fall into the first two categories. There is controlled navigation, and choice is restricted. In the participative mode, the learner is enabled to design and create multimedia resources. Interactive published multimedia was reviewed in the last chapter: this chapter focuses on the participative mode.

Is multimedia authoring worthwhile?

What are the advantages of presenting teaching and learning material in interactive format? Jessel and Hurst (1997) have observed the playful aspects of children's interaction with multimedia presentations. Attention is often held for long periods. Exploration is rapid, and children become adept at reading clues, for example detecting where links to other screens are likely to be hidden. Children may not stop to 'read' a picture, but the links themselves convey information as they establish relationships within the information.

Can teachers actually find the time to become involved in multimedia authoring? The Horizon project (HMTC, 1993) was set up to support teachers and pupils in planning and creating multimedia presentations and interactive learning materials. A CD-ROM was produced, featuring the work of the participants. Evidence showed that it was important to have the right hardware tools at the start. Very few teachers had prior experience of equipment such as scanners and digital cameras. To many, the idea of combining text and pictures on the word processor screen was still very new. Multimedia enhancement was a considerable step.

In one case, the project 'involved every computer in the school and many hours of extra-curricular activity'. In another primary school, a teacher was released for one day per week throughout the year, enabling the project to be completed within school time. The head teacher considered that this was money well spent, since, as a result, all computers were in full use. Children acquired confidence and learned a great deal.

Do all pupils benefit equally? One teacher felt that multimedia authoring was ideally suited to Year 6 girls who liked everything to be meticulously tidy. These pupils stressed the importance of preparation: 'Plan your outline, how many chapters and what's in them – it's definitely easier to work from a plan.' Planning sheets were stored in loose-leaf binders. The boys in the class had ideas, but lacked the patience to work in this way. Girls prepared work at home, and came into school early to use the computers.

The Horizon teaching materials show a high degree of professional finish. Teachers were highly motivated, but many felt that they could not have undertaken the work without the support of the project team. The quality of outcomes is varied. Some Horizon materials are purely instructional and others, though interactive, are little more than electronic worksheets. As McCraw and Meyer (1995) found in a study of American teachers, the use of the computer reflects the teaching style.

The Horizon report is candid in regard to technical hitches, support needs and the scale of investment of teachers' personal time. One teacher, who considered herself 'hooked', worked 'ten to twelve hours a day' over her Easter break. Another claimed to have spent over a hundred hours of his own time in polishing the presentation. Was it worth it? It is difficult to assess in advance the time scale for a multimedia project. While teachers were willing to give personal time, the threat to other professional responsibilities and commitments must be regarded with some concern.

Fernández (1995) reports the experiences of a group of US teachers who authored presentations on various themes, to use in class. Scanned pictures, video sequences and animation were used in addition to text, graphics and sound. Teachers had been able to adapt material to students' needs, eliminating the unnecessary material often found in textbooks. However, production had proved time-consuming, demanding effort, personal discipline and motivation.

Fernández concludes that, if pupils are to work on a similar project, the likeliest benefit is that they will become more familiar with the topic material. In planning a design, a high level of thinking is demanded. Authors are proud of the finished result. However, the focus may be too narrow. Larger concepts and themes may not be covered. Given too wide a focus, the task may be overwhelming.

It is now possible for teachers with basic WP skills to produce high quality printed teaching and learning materials. Are there any advantages in spending weeks authoring on-screen multimedia? To investigate, I prepared an application on the theme of life in the bush in Southern Africa, to use with Year 6 pupils in a Geography topic. A number of scanned photographs were featured. It took two weeks to produce twenty-four pages. I prepared a printed version, with contents page and index, for comparison.

The screen version contained blank frames on certain pages, where children could respond to questions or add comments and observations. The on-screen version could be seen by up to four children at one time. Individuals preferred to read the book. One boy was very keen to take the book away on his own.

Children were able to use an alphabetical index quickly and efficiently. The majority were able to locate information more quickly in the book. Surprisingly, they preferred reading from the screen version. Pupils maintained that text in frames[1] was easier to read than normal text in books. Frames make it clear where a section of text begins and ends. It is easier to pick out a relevant chunk of text. Quality of screen display is a critical factor.

One child commented, 'It takes time – it's still fun, but the book's quicker.' They were very much taken with the 'talking' frames. They appreciated being able to write on, then print, the page. In practice, most children were reluctant to stop the exploration and write, even where the group had discussed what might be added to the page.

There was more discussion about text on the screen than in the printed version. Children only pointed things out to me when they were reading the screen, which again demonstrates the public nature of the medium. One girl called out, 'Have you seen this yet?'

Links between sections should be planned carefully. Otherwise, users may become 'lost' and waste time in trying to get back to the starting point. There must always be a route back. The conventional broad 'chapter' structure was not ideal. An improved design would offer a list of sub-topics, with direct links to appropriate material. Text searching could not be relied upon to locate information, since text has to be matched exactly.

One pair successfully found the answer to a question, because they had earlier spotted a reference near the end of the book. The computer group took some time to locate the same information. The book users had been able to employ a physical landmark. There is no sense of 'near the end' with the computer presentation, because of its non-serial organisation. However, routes can be memorised and retraced. For example, children remembered how to get to certain screens from the title page.

Overall, there was no evidence of more effective learning from either version. Print and computer versions appeared to have their own characteristic advantages. There may be an improvement over print materials where computer-based presentations are designed to be more interactive (White, 1995).

It had been impossible in the time available to incorporate a range of interactive features. Faster drive or network access, higher capacity storage and improved authoring tools will enable more use of graphics and sound, and the potential for interaction may be more fully exploited. Multimedia authoring brings selection and presentation under the teacher's full editorial control. However, few teachers are likely to feel that they can justify the weeks of effort that researching, designing and writing even a modest application may demand. This issue is raised again in Chapter 14, in the context of Internet-based collaborative work.

Authors should note children's difficulties in reading densely packed, demanding texts on CD-ROM. We saw in Chapter 9 that pupils may need a great deal of support in extracting key ideas. Clear pointers may assist in 'signposting' the text. Incorporating an interactive element may help. For example, a presentation on local history may include a page which begins, 'The River Itchen helped trading in Winchester in three ways.' The reader needs to click on three 'buttons' in turn, to display the sentences one by one.

Multimedia authoring by pupils

As suggested in Fernández' study quoted above, there may be advantages for pupils in the direct creation of their own presentations, in that the process may lead to high-level thinking and deeper engagement in the topic theme. Aspects of a broad topic may be individually researched by groups. Is this type of work feasible and, most importantly, can it be justified, given pressure of time?

The Acorn application *Genesis* was used in the following studies.[2] The user creates a series of numbered pages, the first of which is called the *title page*. On each page, frames are dragged out to the required size. Each frame may contain text or a graphic image, or it may store a sound which will be replayed when clicked.

Buttons may be placed on the page, enabling actions such as displaying the next page or returning to the title page. Links may be established between any frame and any page. The route does not have to be linear. It is therefore possible to create a simple hypertext system, in which conventional linear routes are replaced by a network of connections, enabling conceptual links between related ideas.

However user-friendly the software, a systematic, well-organised approach is essential. A short account by Gain (1994) of multimedia authoring with Year 7 pupils stresses the importance of prior planning. With teacher support, a flowchart was developed, and responsibility for pages delegated to groups.

My initial experiences suggested that pupils as young as nine years old were able to grasp the concept of linking pages. Groups were able to create an application of up to ten pages featuring text and graphics, given background teacher support. A nine year old girl commented, 'We are using the computer to put all our work together.' This strongly suggests a parallel with the 'topic folders' created by primary pupils.

In 1990, I worked with eight members of a Year 6 class engaged in a study of Victorian England. Two Acorn computers were available. The class teacher had asked the group to research the lives of famous Victorians. Children worked in pairs. While four children were occupied in research and notemaking, one pair worked directly on the *Genesis* page, while the other two pupils prepared text on a word processor.

In the summer of 1996, I spent a week with thirteen pupils, all Year 5 members of a mixed-age class in a small rural school. The Year 5 pupils were studying Ancient Greece. I was responsible for teaching the children throughout the week, which was wholly devoted to the authoring project. A small room had been equipped with five computers. Pupils organised themselves into groups of two or three.

The dates are significant. The Year 5 pupils had all used published multimedia in school, and had encountered CD-ROM reference materials on computers at home (or in friends' homes). However, they had no experience of planning a presentation. The Year 6 pupils had no prior experience of multimedia whatever. It proved difficult for the Year 6 groups to organise the information they had gathered into a structured format. Despite this, two Year 6 pupils were able to create new pages, import text and link frames to pages with no help from me, after one session.

Initially, the main challenge arose from the demands of researching the topic. The process did not appear to differ in any way from research for topic folders. However, the introduction of ICT necessitated planning and design at the outset. What models were in evidence?

Two members of the Year 6 'Victorians' group found a lengthy encyclopaedia entry on Charles Dickens. They did not know where to start. I encouraged them to think of important questions that someone might ask, such as 'Why is Dickens famous?' I suggested that they scan through the text. What were the main topics? They found three: Dickens' life, novels and characters. Later, the pupils planned their title page, with links to the three topics.

No-one else suggested a structured format. The pupils might just as well have been working on their topic folders. After all, the task mainly consisted of writing, from the children's point of view. Other children planned simple sequences of pages, as in a book. One pair decided on a standard layout for each page, consisting of one text frame and one picture.

Once the pupils began working with *Genesis*, visual presentation became particularly important. Much time was devoted to surface details, such as choosing colours for pages and experimenting with text fonts and sizes. I was told that it was important that colours should 'match', and that the information should stand out. Pupils were rightly critical of fonts which they found difficult to read.

Clarity and visual impact are essential elements of effective communication. The opportunity to experiment with effects, and review changes, was beneficial. Combinations of text and background colours were carefully considered. Pupils rejected the use of multiple colours on one page. I was told that people would not enjoy reading 'rowdy' pages. The use of colour in guiding the reader was also considered. One group agreed that 'headings' should be a uniform colour, so that people could see where to click the mouse.

The choice of appropriate visual format is an important communication skill. However, in the absence of teacher intervention, tinkering with design may account for rather too much effort. Individuals were prepared to spend a great deal of time experimenting with colour combinations and moving frames around, even after the design had been agreed by the group. Considerably less attention was paid to correcting and improving the content.

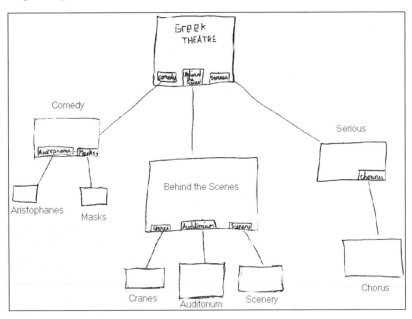

Structural plan for a presentation by two Year 5 boys.
I have added the typed labels.

In contrast, the Year 5 pupils were able to plan, in advance, relatively complex hierarchical structures on paper. They seemed to have a very strong idea of the 'title' or 'home' page as the top level, leading to lower levels of increasing detail. The teacher commented that pupils had often seen her draw flow diagrams on the board as the class discussed a new topic. They appeared to be particularly influenced by their use of a published presentation, even though each child had had no more than three 20-minute sessions on this.

One group used their prior knowledge of the topic in planning their presentation on Greek Theatre. The title page led directly to three topics: *Comedy, Behind the Scenes* and *Serious*. Each of these screens led to sub-topics, as shown in the boys' plan. The class teacher was intrigued by the choice of Greek Theatre. She was not aware that pupils had this level of knowledge, but had noted that, while using books in the classroom, children would often go off at a tangent and look with great interest at other topics. The two boys worked entirely independently in constructing this plan.

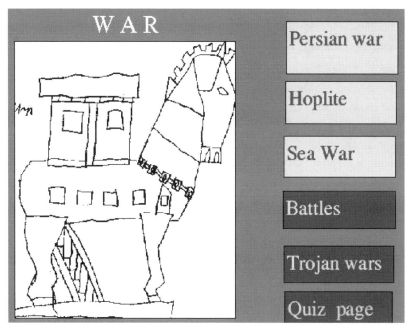

Title screen of a presentation on war in Ancient Greece.

As the presentation took shape, the pupils explained how it worked. From the title page, *Comedy* could be selected, followed by *Masks*. To look at another *Comedy* sub-topic, I was told to 'go back up to Comedy, and you can go down to the one you want because you're at the main screen.' The idea of moving 'up' and 'down' between adjacent layers seemed to be well understood.

Another group planned a presentation on war, featuring a quiz. Again, the structure was planned in advance, and the title screen with six frames was sketched. One boy told me that important words would be explained, 'like in a program'.

The 'Gods' group enthusiastically began to plan their presentation. Nathan explained: 'We're going to put every god in a box and [...] if they're like the god of wine, you put a wine glass next to it. [...] There'll be a symbol for each god.' Other children suggested a shield for Ares, and a musical note for Apollo.

For example, clicking on the bow and arrow selects Artemis. As the page is displayed, music performed on chiming instruments is heard as the pupils chant 'Artemis!' The music was recorded using an Oak Recorder, and added to the presentation as a final touch. On the Artemis page, a prominent 'home' button has been incorporated to lead back to the title page.

Unexpected problems caused delays, but pupils were always prepared to try something out for themselves. They knew how to obtain menus, and often saw for themselves what they needed to do (e.g. 'Create page'). However, I was regularly called upon to help with linking pages, a difficult feature in *Genesis*. Over several days, most children began to pick up this skill.

Even so, two Year 5 pupils successfully linked their first page back to the title page, before I had had a chance to show them what to do. The process involves clicking within the frame, and dragging a link 'tool' onto the page below. Two windows, containing the two pages, must be arranged on the screen so that both the frame and the page to be linked to can be seen. These 10-year-olds appear to have made an intuitive response. A typical adult reaction would be, 'What on earth am I supposed to do now?'

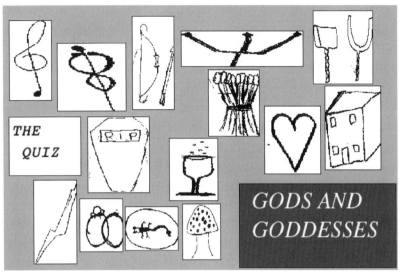

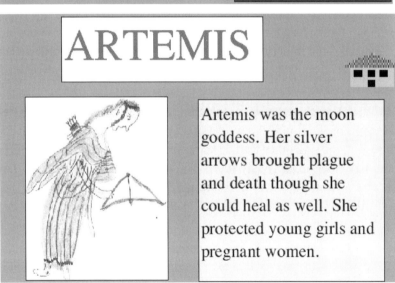

Title screen and page about the Goddess Artemis, from a Year 5 presentation on Greek gods.

Year 5 groups took choice of colour just as seriously as the Year 6 pupils in the previous study. Time was wasted as individuals decided which combinations they liked. However, the 'Gods' group had a rationale for colours. On Ares' page, grey was used to symbolise swords, and red to represent blood. At Zeus' page, I was told, 'Background's light blue and text white. Blue for the sky and white for the clouds.' I found the text rather difficult to read!

Year 5 children were strongly aware of ways in which others might use their applications. One pupil explained, 'If you've got some worksheets to fill in, you can go back and you can keep on flicking through the pages like a book.' The quiz page featured didactic instructions: 'Label the Greek Hoplite's equipment right here.' Holly wanted to add, 'Go to the quiz last'. She wished to make sure that users read all the pages before attempting questions. The Year 6 pupils, on the other hand, lacked previous exposure to multimedia. They wrote solely for their own and for the teacher's attention, as they would do when working on individual topic folders. I suggest that children are strongly influenced by other ICT applications, and are receptive to models for presenting their own work.

The Year 5 teacher commented that it is extremely difficult to organise this type of work into the week, since children need to devote much time to it, missing other work. She makes every effort to integrate ICT and has data logging apparatus set up semi-permanently in the classroom. She finds that, in contrast, data logging fits in well into the busy classroom routine as children may use it when they have a few spare moments.

In the Year 6 class, a small group of pupils were able to continue multi-media work in the weeks after my visit through taking advantage of odd moments when the computer was free. The Year 6 teacher did not feel that she had sufficient confidence to support further work. However, she made time available for children to work independently.

Three Year 6 pupils, Oliver, Peter and Tim, researched and wrote a presentation in the form of a World War II newspaper. I helped them start the first page on one of my visits to the school, but did not see them again for five weeks. During this time they worked unaided: none of the staff were able to use *Genesis*. In break times and spare moments they had completed four pages and now wanted to link them together. They knew how to do this, but did not know how to access the pages they had saved.

They had adopted a consistent format for each page. A text frame was accompanied by an illustration. Below the picture, frames were positioned, containing the words *Back* and *More*, to link to adjacent pages. The pictures had been drawn using a simple painting program, and were monochrome for authenticity. The Times Roman font had been an obvious choice.

I observed the group make a fifth page. There were agreed roles, and an established procedure. Tim was the operator, while Peter and Oliver took turns to tell Tim what to write. Oliver was by far the most knowledgeable. For example, he told the others, 'When France was captured it was really the start of the war [...] The only reason Britain didn't send aid to the Spanish Civil War was that they didn't want to offend Adolf Hitler.' Oliver, exclusively, drew the pictures.

They had decided that their paper needed a page about Russia. They studied the columns of a facsimile contemporary broadsheet belonging to Peter. Oliver found a 'brilliant' start. Peter was anxious about literal copying, but agreed that they could start with that. The page, entitled 'The Red Army's Revenge', appeared to contain a verbatim transcription. To many teachers, the validity of such work is diminished because it has been copied. However, the boys employed a critical approach to text selection and editing. As Heppell (1993) has pointed out, transcription is highly likely where pupils use non-attributable electronic sources. There are cases where clarity and cohesion, quality of research, presentation and organisation should be rewarded, even though the work is not original.

From a long paragraph, Oliver made cuts, leaving out sentences which described earlier actions of the Red Army. He appeared to concentrate his selection on events that were about to happen. The results made sense, with no loss of continuity through Oliver's cuts:

> Strengthened and re-equipped, the Red Army was now to show its fighting ability in a winter offensive. It was going to attack across the Dnieper to regain Hitler's greatest territorial prize, the Ukraine.

Peter's role was to check for errors, and ensure authenticity. He urged the others to adopt what he called the 'point of view – so they're going to try to do it'. This led to editing. With Tim, he debated whether it was better to write 'is to show', 'is now to show' or 'now is to show'.

Completed pages were saved and printed. Much satisfaction and pleasure was gained from this. Peter commented, 'If you had a piece of paper and you did it with pencil, it could just go wrong, but with this you can just shift it around until it's perfect.' In the teacher's view, the pupils were engaged beneficially in problem solving. She commented:

> If the children were asked to write collaboratively, there would be just as much discussion as if they were using the computer, with regard to the ideas and content. But there would be less interest in the production. A child would not be interested in sitting and watching another child writing or cutting and pasting an assemblage of work. There is more sustained concentration using the computer, they are using a new tool. They have to cope with the demands, they are problem solving. It takes them longer. This may be a benefit, as they have more opportunity to review and discuss the text.

> They would not normally co-operate so well. Oliver finds it difficult to work with another person, they split over the Victorian dolls' house they wired up. Tim is also normally unreliable, he gets angry. Peter doesn't normally work well in a group because his superior attitude is not accepted. Here they do work better than in any other situation. They respect each other's skills.

The positive outcomes noted by the teacher could be claimed to be more general advantages of ICT. A desktop publishing package could have been used to achieve the same printed results. However, the experience presented a unique problem-solving opportunity, as the teacher pointed out.

The Year 6 teacher looked for evidence that pupils' written work had been influenced in some way by multimedia authoring. She noted that children did not rush off to organise their loose-leaf topic folders into sections, but expected that they would be able to do this if it were set as a task. In writing about science experiments, children drew 'frames' containing drawings, lists of apparatus and so forth. This type of layout became very popular. Even work planned in rough books was written within frames. One girl actually adopted different 'fonts' in her hand-writing!

Summary

It is a challenge for 10 and 11 year old children to produce a design based on information structure and needs of the readership. Much depends on prior experience, such as the teacher's use of flow charts in introducing a new topic. Pupils will readily adopt a format that they have seen in another presentation. They should be encouraged to evaluate the effectiveness of their design. This may influence their future work.

The medium invites attention to presentation. Children are highly motivated to experiment with page design. Pupils appeared seriously concerned to achieve a clear visual impact. They have become aware of the importance of visual aspects of communication. However, teacher intervention may be necessary to ensure that the content of written communication is also subjected to such thorough review.

Pupils need knowledge of the subject, to be capable of organising themes and sub-themes into a network or hierarchical structure. This leads to deeper engagement in the subject, and may be one of the most significant benefits of multimedia authoring.

Where pupils had not previously encountered multimedia, approaches to research and writing did not differ from normal work in topic folders. Children with previous experience of multimedia incorporated interactive features, such as a quiz.

Multimedia authoring enables teachers to produce learning materials with a high level of professional finish. The investment of time is a major consideration. Weeks, or even months, of effort are demanded if full coverage of a theme is to be attempted.

Notes

1. In *Genesis*, as with many authoring and desktop publishing applications, a 'frame' or box is dragged out. The cursor is then positioned in the frame. Typed text is bounded by the frame. A border is optional.

2. *Genesis* is no longer the first choice for pupils' work, in view of its complexity. However, it is similar in approach to other authoring tools.

CHAPTER 11

THE TABULAR DATABASE AS A TOOL FOR INQUIRY

Chapter 6 showed one example of pupils creating and using a database to support learning in Mathematics. This chapter looks in depth at the stages of planning, creating, amending and interrogating a database, and identifies the demands on teachers and learners. While there may be starting points in data collected by pupils themselves, computer data handling applications are sophisticated and complex. It is vital that teachers understand the advantages and limitations, in order to judge whether the tool is appropriate for a given task.

There are many ways of using computers to store, manipulate and present data. The term database may refer to any organised collection of information. Most database software in schools embodies a two-dimensional tabular structure. In the *tabular* structure, each column represents a *field*, each horizontal row a *record*. Each record contains information about an individual *entity*. Tabular structures, and other database models, are discussed in more detail by Underwood and Underwood (1990).

A series of records in a computer database is analogous to a box file of cards or forms. A familiar example is the library card index. Each record contains information such as *title*, *author* and *classification*. The data on each record is organised identically. In other words, the same *headings*, or field names, appear on each record.

length

food

speed

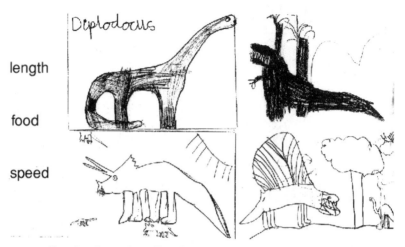

Overlay for a data file of dinosaurs by 6 and 7 year olds.

A simple database of dinosaurs was created by Year 2 pupils using *List Explorer*, a BBC program from the 1980s. Records of four dinosaurs may be accessed directly by pressing a picture on an overlay keyboard (see Chapters 7 and 8). Alternatively, children may press a heading, then select from a search menu. Searching enables answers to questions such as, 'Were any of the dinosaurs more than 20 metres long?' 'Which dinosaurs ate meat?'

The structure of this simple database is best envisaged as a table. The table and its contents are shown below:

Name	Length (m)	Food	Speed
Diplodocus	26	plants	slow
Tyrannosaurus	14	meat	fast
Triceratops	9	plants	slow
Dimetrodon	3	meat	fast

List Explorer appears, like the dinosaurs, to have suffered extinction. However, the concept of accessing structured information through pictures lives on in classroom multimedia presentations (Chapter 10). This type of work is entirely consonant with the IT curriculum. At Level 2, pupils should 'use IT to sort and classify information and to present their findings' (DfE, 1995b). Indeed, the creation of a simple data file in non-fiction writing composition in Year 1, Term 3 constitutes the only explicit reference to ICT at Key Stage 1 in the Literacy Framework (DfEE, 1998a).

The IT Orders refer to data handling processes rather than specific database skills. At Key Stage 2, pupils should be taught to 'use IT equipment and software to organise, reorganise and analyse ideas and information'. At Level 3, pupils use IT to 'access stored information, following straightforward lines of enquiry'. At Level 4, pupils 'add to, amend and interrogate information that has been stored. They understand the need for care in framing questions when collecting, accessing and interrogating information.'

Broad progression has been identified, from using an existing database to creating a new structure (Hunter, 1985). There is an intermediate stage, where pupils build a database using a content-free structure which has been designed by the teacher. The National Curriculum reflects this progression in that inquiry involving searching, sorting and graphing precedes file creation. Through adding to and amending an existing file, pupils acquire the skills that they will need in creating a database at a later stage.

It is pointless to teach data handling skills in isolation. Purposeful, successful use relies upon pupils' developing mastery of the processes of critical inquiry. In order to make effective use of the computer to support investigation, learners need to be able to plan and review questions and strategies, interpret outcomes and make use of information. Teachers need to plan and provide opportunities for children to apply data handling skills in active, purposeful investigation.

When is it appropriate to use a database? What are the aims of the inquiry? Most teachers find data handling highly problematic. Without experience, it is exceedingly difficult to identify suitable curriculum contexts and plan for learning outcomes. There is a limited range of applications, in any case. The tabular structure imposes significant constraints on the way information may be stored. Where a large, consistently structured body of information lends itself to database treatment, relationships and patterns otherwise impossible to detect may become evident.

Pupils need some working knowledge of the way information is stored in the file, in order to access what is there. A computer data file cannot be handled physically. To show pupils how data is organised, Ross (1984) and Heaney (1986) used wallcharts before introducing the computer. Pupils suggested questions, which led to examination of the tabulated data. Ross described how a child would run a finger down a column, looking for records containing a particular entry. By the time the computer was introduced, children already had a critical appreciation of how tabular representation could enhance information retrieval.

Large quantities of data may be explored and analysed by pupils. A Year 6 class compiled a database from local sources on victims of a pit disaster (Powell, 1990). An overall profile was gained from plotting the co-ordinates of victims' addresses. Pupils gained an immediate impression of the impact of the disaster on the community. Furner (1987) described pupils' research into ships built or rebuilt at Woolwich dockyard. Nearly two hundred records, spanning three centuries, were entered into a file. Investigation enabled children's writing to be developed beyond mere statement of facts. Pupils were able to appraise the significance of findings, and suggest tentative explanations. In other cases, pupils using census data lacked understanding of the structure, and had no clear purpose (Galpin and Schilling, 1988). Many teachers lacked confidence, found the software user-unfriendly, or were unable to grasp the structure.

Banks (1985) reported the use of tabular databases in children's science investigations: 'The purpose of our activities is no longer restricted to enhancing children's observation and measurement skills [...]. We now have the opportunity to develop the additional skills of looking for relationships and forming hypotheses which can be tested by experiment.' Ross (1989) described how his pupils created a database to investigate strength of conkers. Attributes had been measured, and tests conducted with a 'destructor' which pupils had designed. They discovered a negative correlation between age and strength. Given the large amounts of data collected by the pupils, this connection would not otherwise have been apparent. The discovery challenged the popular belief that seasoned conkers are stronger.

Does database use enhance the development of inquiry skills? Eraut (1991) argued that problem-solving processes become more explicit, and hence more easily integrated into the curriculum. Carter and Monaco (1987) pointed out the need for higher-order reading skills, readiness to reflect, understanding of information structure together with a questioning, systematic approach. While concepts underlying database use were adequately grasped, the chief obstacle was pupils' lack of inclination to reflect. Yet, as Quee (1991) stated, 'It is the children's own questions which give purpose and direction to an investigation.'

File creation

The curriculum does not require database creation to be taught until Key Stage 3. However, there are important advantages in involving the whole class, under the teacher's direction, in the processes of planning an inquiry and constructing a database. Pupils need to understand database structure in order to interrogate successfully (Spavold, 1989). This is best achieved through active involvement in discussing what questions to pursue, and in exploring possible models for the file.

Much of the work of creating a new database takes place away from the computer. Firstly, pupils identify and articulate a problem. Secondly, they brainstorm, then prioritise, questions related to the problem. Once the pupils have collected the information, it must be organised according to categories. Which attributes, or properties, are relevant to the inquiry? In many instances, the existence of patterns and relationships is initially only speculative.

A system of criteria for classification may need to be developed to organise the data. Consistency is essential, though not always easy to achieve (Underwood and Underwood, 1990). When pupils gathered data on 'hair colour', a variety of descriptions were used. To the computer, each entry was unique. It was impossible to use the file to answer simple questions such as 'Are there more children with fair hair than brown hair?' Pupils realised the need to group people with *similar* hair colour into a single category. This case mirrors a serious dilemma faced by professional users. In standardising to suit the computer application, much original richness of detail is lost (Mawdsley et al., 1990).

It is important to bear in mind that fields themselves are abstractions. A good choice of fields for a data file of mammals would include *habitat* and *diet*, for example. Children have to recognise that it is *habitat* and not 'tropical forest' or 'desert' that constitutes the field! Creation of the file requires specification of generalised attributes, at a higher level in the hierarchy. Lions inhabit grassland; cats live on land; every mammal has a habitat. Galpin and Schilling (1988) noted the difficulties children encounter in making the necessary abstractions.

In a survey, the critical planning stage is in questionnaire design. Fields may derive directly from questions asked, or tests carried out, by the pupils. It must be possible for the information yielded by the survey to be mapped out as a simple table, with columns and rows. A Year 7 class carried out a survey to find what facilities younger children wanted in the new playground. Pupils asked, 'What playground markings would you like?' The varied range of responses could not be tabulated. A question for each playground marking was needed, with a 'yes/no' response. The questionnaire was redesigned.

Later, one group looked at their batch of twelve completed questionnaires. For each type of playground marking, they decided to count the number of positive responses. Michelle made columns on a sheet, writing down the totals. It took nearly five minutes for all to be counted, and the 'favourite' marking was announced. The teacher asked how the computer might help. Michelle replied, 'We could ask the computer the same questions about all hundred people.'

The group then spent several more minutes checking through their sample. This was not a waste of time; rather, it was of value for the children to gain a feel for the structure and the nature of the data, and the type of questions they might ask later. Pupils were beginning to appreciate why we use computers to handle data.

A Year 4 class undertook a survey of children's journeys to school. Questions were suggested by the children. Children had to consider whether the answer would provide the information needed. Where two versions of one question were suggested, children agreed that the second would yield more information:

Do your friends take you to school?
Who takes you to school?

The initial emphasis was on what it might be interesting to know about individuals. Then, children realised that they could ask questions about the data as a whole. One boy suggested that we could find 'how many come by car and buses, we can see which is the most popular'. Some pupils speculated about likely relationships within the data. It was suggested that older children would be more likely to walk to school. These ideas could be investigated using the completed file. I therefore encouraged children to write them down.

Since the software allowed *multiple choice* fields, pupils needed to think of categories for the response. One child suggested the question:

How do you travel to school? car, bus, bike, walk.

Children liked this format: 'It shows you the ways you can come to school and you can just tick them off.' Multiple choice fields greatly speed up data entry and overcome problems caused by inconsistent spelling. However, it is easier for an assertive child to dominate by directing the task. Eraut (1993) found greater collaboration where non-routine tasks demand the focused attention of everyone in the group. Children did not appear to see the entry of text as a chore.

As data is entered, there is a need to review. Is the data accurate? Have we entered everything that we need? Many children enjoy checking records for consistency and accuracy. Bryan, aged 10, told others that they needed to put something 'comparative'. Spavold (1989) noted the leadership role adopted by children who most thoroughly understood the operation of the system, and who had the best mental map of file structure.

At this level, are children able to conceptualise database structure? Their understanding is likely to be operational, derived from conventions which they have encountered (Smith, 1997). In other words, they form ideas of 'what works'. Abstract models of database structure are exceedingly unlikely in children of this age group. However, pupils are able to suggest possible applications, and questions that might be asked. One Year 6 class suggested musical instruments, sea life and planets as potential themes.

Database applications are inappropriate in many contexts, due to the limitations of the tabular model. It may be difficult to evaluate whether the computer can support the inquiry at all. Survey data, particularly from tallies, may not fit the tabular structure. Mr Howell's Year 4 class conducted a series of traffic counts. Children were keen to suggest questions: Were there more lorries at certain times? What were peak times for cars? Did the numbers of passengers vary throughout the day?

Mr Howell envisaged records entitled 'cars', 'lorries', etc. There would be fields for different periods during the day: each would contain the number of sightings. Since the software only permitted frequency graphs, it was impossible to compare sightings for particular periods, since each unique number entered would be counted as *one occurrence* of that number. Counts of numbers of passengers could not be accommodated. After an abortive attempt to create a file, Mr Howell asked the class to produce graphs by hand.

Gareth, a student on teaching practice, planned a survey of minibeasts. He wanted children to tally the numbers of different creatures found in metre square areas, in contrasting locations around the school. The counts were to be repeated for several days. The children would then be able to investigate daily differences, due to weather. They would also be able to compare habitats. Unfortunately, the data model is three-dimensional. Since there are three variables, the data cannot be organised in rows and columns.

Problems arise where there is insufficient information, even though there may be no fault in the structure itself. Miss Childs planned for her Year 5 class to make a database of castles. All seemed to go well at first. Pupils agreed fields, such as 'location', 'type', 'date' and 'wars' (in which the castle had been besieged). The children were highly motivated to research their castles. Unfortunately, there were large gaps in what they were able to find out. History books gave details of unique features. There was no consistency in the information. With only four records complete, the data file was abandoned.

Miss Childs' experience convinced her that the tabular database is a poor vehicle for the collage of facts and fragments assembled by children in the course of their research. As Marshall (1991) has argued, creation of a database to launch book-based research imposes an 'unfortunate constraint' on what pupils might discover. However, it is valid for children to wish to compare details such as construction dates and types of castles. If pupils cannot find this information, then the books, rather than the inquiry, are at fault. Authors of information books and CD-ROMs should exercise consistency in answering *general* questions children might ask about a topic (Neate, 1992). For example, children may well ask, 'When was this castle built?' Is this key question answered, for each castle? If so, the use of reference sources in compiling a database need not be ruled out.

Data handling software now available in schools has been designed to make file creation and data entry as easy as possible. Form design may be as simple as using an elementary word processing program. User-friendly software does not reduce the need to plan and prepare in advance. There is a greater risk that children will fail to distinguish structure and data. It is helpful to look at the growing tabular display during data entry. Children need to know how the column headings relate to the information which they gathered initially.

Editing the file

The need to amend or *edit* the file nearly always arises, especially where children have entered data themselves. Editing may prove time-consuming and laborious. However, the process involves problem solving, and often makes demands on formal thinking skills. Social benefits emerge as changes are negotiated. Conference between groups over proposed changes may take place. The development of communication and listening skills is supported as children articulate their points of view to others.

Pupils found that graphs were the easiest way to highlight problems, since any departures from expected groupings or patterns could be clearly seen. They enjoyed 'trouble-shooting', and began to appreciate the importance of accuracy and consistency. In other contexts, pupils were sometimes unaware that human error had caused unexpected results. Logical explanations were sought, and there were attempts to attribute errors to the computer. Children found it hard to accept that there could be errors in published files! They appeared to have more faith in IT sources than in published books, believing that the former were more up to date.

Searching

In principle, the computer retrieves records through a process of matching, in response to a *query* formulated by the user. In practice, the precise method of searching varies from one application to another. Current software in primary schools is menu-driven, avoiding the need to compile a complex sentence using the search language. My examples use a general form which varies in certain applications. However, the three-part format is consistent.

For example, to retrieve all records of children aged 10, the following query is entered at the search menu:

Age / equal to / 10

The first part is the *field name*. Here, the computer is instructed to check the data stored in the 'Age' column, in much the same way as the child running a finger down the wallchart of data.

The second part of the query is the *search condition*. For numeric fields the search conditions *equal to, not equal to, less than, greater than* are normally available. Otherwise, comparison is carried out by matching text. Examples of text search conditions are: *the same as, not the same as, includes, does not include.*

The third part of the query is the value, or text, to be matched.

A *multiple search* involving more than one comparison may be possible. This enables the inquirer to narrow down or add to the sample. For example, we may ask, 'Which ten year olds play football?' This may simply involve the application of two searches in succession:

Age / equal to / 10
Sport / includes / football

Extending the inquiry in this way *narrows down* the sample, eliminating all ten year olds who do not play football.

The query 'Which children are ten years old OR play football?' has a different outcome. Depending on the software, OR may be available as a search option. In this case, the sample is widened. All ten year olds and footballers (of any age) will be selected.

Simple queries

In text searches, *includes* (contains) is often a better option than *equal to*, since the latter demands an exact match with field contents. Year 5 pupils were able to judge when to use this strategy. In searching for people with dogs, Neil, a 10 year old of below average attainment, realised that 'dog' (not 'a dog' nor 'dogs') would achieve the match:

Pets / includes / dog

Neil was responding to another group member's suggestion that they enter the *kind of* animal they were searching for. There is an important social dimension in computer-based group activity (Light and Blaye, 1990). Hoyles et al. (1991) argue that the group 'shapes the behaviour of its members by throwing up lines of development and ways of reasoning which can be understood but not constructed by an individual alone'.

It is possible to search for records where a particular text string is not included in the specified field. However, Bezanilla and Ogborn (1992) have reported 13-14 year olds' great difficulties with negative search sentences. Primary pupils make little use of negative conditions. Even so, a group of 10 year olds found out how to eliminate a subset of records. I was told: 'You say what you want to exclude, like sea mammals, then it will give you the other ones.'

Children were readily able to use mathematical relations such as *equal to, less than*. Marc, aged 10, explored a database of mammals. He looked at a histogram of 'overall length'. He noticed that there were creatures in the range 0-3 cm. To find these, he entered the search:

Length / less than / 4

Josephine, aged 11, used a file of characters in a computer simulation. She wanted to find adults in the age group 35 to 39. With great care, she carried out two searches in succession, to narrow down the sample:

Age / less than / 40
Age / greater than / 34

Not all pupils grasped this strategy. A Year 6 class compiled a database of performance times. They had devised a stiff endurance test which involved hanging from wall bars! A histogram showed two records in the highest range, 200 to 219 seconds. To identify the two children, one group entered the search:

Arm hang / greater than / 200

To pupils' surprise, only one record was matched. Going back to the source data, they found that the lower of the two times was exactly 200 seconds. However, they still could not correct the search. Practice in the use of mathematical relations, with examples from the context, may be needed to support retrieval.

Complex queries

The language of multiple searches involves Boolean logic. Pupils may make successful use of multiple search techniques, provided there is match between the natural language of the question and the logical expression. Queries such as 'Which children go swimming and play football?' cause little difficulty. The framing of the question implies searching for the first attribute and then the second.

Logical OR presents problems, as its exclusive and inclusive senses are often confused. The sense of 'Will the new baby be a boy or a girl?' is clearly exclusive, ruling out the possibility of both. However, the statement 'You may use a pencil or a crayon' implies that you may indeed use both. This *inclusive* sense of OR is used in databases, but is much harder for children to understand (Bezanilla and Ogborn, 1992). If we search a database for children who swim OR play football, the results will contain records of swimmers, footballers *and* children who do both. A further problem is that 'and' is used in natural language in an additive sense. If we wish to search for paintings by Rembrandt and Monet, we must use OR. There cannot possibly be a painting by Rembrandt and Monet!

Searching following complex lines of inquiry is not required until Key Stage 3. However, many of the apparently straightforward inquiries suggested by primary pupils contain more than one step: 'Do any of the children who live in Sheffield Road walk to school?' 'Did it always rain on cloudy days in March?' Teachers must judge when it is appropriate for pupils to engage in a multi-part inquiry. Much depends on pupils' understanding of the file structure, and prior experience of working on similar problems with adults and peers.

Underwood and Underwood (1990) reported children's consistent difficulties in this area. However, I observed ten year olds apply an OR search to a published database of mammals. Bryan recalled, 'I did a complex search for buffalo and bison. In America they'd be bison, and in Africa they're buffalo [...] so we said "contains buffalo or bison". If we'd said "buffalo" it would only have given us the water buffalo.'

When Nicola wanted to search for deer *and* antelope, she suggested that it might be an OR search. In this case, 'and' suggests the wrong search! Nicola was unable to provide any reasoning to support her choice. She thought that OR would work because she had seen other children doing it. She had presumed, correctly, that this procedure could be extended to extract any two types of mammal. Tasks which seemingly demand abstract reasoning may be accomplished through application of rules and procedures specific to the context. In any novel situation, conventions, rules and expectations are constructed through classroom interactions (Walkerdine, 1982).

There are important differences in the logical function and everyday meaning of the two principal Boolean operators. If we ask, 'How many cat and dog owners are there in this class?' the logical answer is 'None'. The logical set *cat and dog* is empty: nothing can be both a cat and a dog! We have to search for cat OR dog.

What if the question had been asked, 'Who has a cat *and* a dog?' Here, narrowing-down is implied. Fewer people are likely to have both animals, than dogs or cats alone. In this case, a special difficulty arises because the field must be searched twice. To find who has a dog and a cat, (ii) below is correct. Placing 'and' in the text to be matched, as in (i), is a common error. Read aloud, (i) and (ii) seem to mean more or less the same. The outcomes of the searches may be quite different:

  (i) Pets / includes / dog and cat
  (ii) Pets / includes / dog AND Pets / includes / cat

Laura emphatically urged others in her group not to enter (i). She did not explain, but supported another child's suggestion to use (ii). This incident reveals the emerging formal thinking ability of a capable 11 year old, aided by the scaffolding of group interaction. From her experience of searching the file, Laura had been able to make the distinction between the functional parts of the search query.

Aidan, a 10 year old of low ability, was unresponsive at the searching stage and gave no indication that he actually understood what was happening. However, he was delighted when, on further narrowing down the search to find who had a dog, a cat and a bird, two records were found, including his own. He clearly understood *why* his record had been retrieved. The value of the 'Ourselves' theme was demonstrated. Although the findings were of little import, and could have been achieved simply by asking the class, the personal closeness of the data assisted children in coping with the formal logic of the system. Underwood and Underwood (1990) commented on the performance gains made by less able children following work with a computer data file, where they were 'exposed to discovery learning with clear structure which proved very beneficial to them' (p.91).

Sorting

Records may be sorted, in ascending or descending order, on any selected field. Sorting is simple to do, and it is easy to see the effect when records are displayed. However, the strategic value of sorting in database inquiry is often overlooked. There is direct mapping to a certain type of query: 'Which is the largest / smallest?' Unfortunately, the framing of the question suggests a search, especially when the child is asked, '*Find* the largest / smallest.' On many occasions, pupils have attempted to estimate the highest (or lowest) value, then searched the file. This has invariably involved extra work!

Pupils should be shown how to print selected fields, to enable comparison of sorted lists. They need reminding when sorting is appropriate, as the language we use tends to suggest searching. Children are often told that the database can be 'searched' for information. It is hardly surprising that minds become set on impulsive search strategies.

Graphing tools

Graphing tools display a profile of the contents of any database field. Patterns and trends may be revealed; errors in the data may be glaringly apparent! Graphical tools have the advantage of enabling children to apply mathematical skills and knowledge (often taught in isolation) to some purpose. Through interactions with the teacher and within the group, opportunities to use mathematical language arise.

Frequency bar graphs, histograms and pie charts are most familiar. Their value in children's database inquiry is in answering questions such as 'Which is the commonest?' 'Which happened most often?' However, the ease of production causes many teachers to overlook the difficulties children experience in interpretation. Frequency graphs have caused particular problems, yet are ubiquitous in classroom data handling.

Graph formats, and the distinction between discrete and continuous data, were discussed in Chapter 4. Given the automatic nature of computer chart construction, it is important for teachers to discuss with pupils what the computer actually does. For example, children may display a bar chart for 'sports', to find which is the most popular. For each child who plays football, one is added to the 'football' set. The computer thus 'counts' how many children play football, how many children go swimming, and so on.

Although frequency charts do not reveal individual record details, they provide a useful profile of the data as a whole. Tendencies and patterns often become apparent through graphical displays. Graphs are also of great value in drawing attention to errors and inconsistencies. Children are able to investigate relationships within the data, particularly with the help of scattergraphs, in which the contents of one field are plotted against values stored in another. An example featured in Chapter 4. Since one data file can yield many graphs in different formats, the emphasis is on interpretation. However, children need sufficient experience of plotting graphs by hand, otherwise they will lack the imagery necessary for interpretation.

Bar charts and frequency histograms

If children lack experience of the construction of frequency bar graphs and histograms, they are highly likely to encounter difficulties in interpretation. The highest bar will suggest the biggest, rather than the commonest. For example, a Year 6 class had created a file of weather data, including midday temperature. 11 year olds of high ability were convinced that the tallest bar represented the hottest day, rather than the mode (i.e. the most frequently recorded temperature). Children have powerful mental models derived from other experiences which support such interpretation (Smith, 1997). A typical instance featured in Chapter 4.

On the other hand, frequency bar charts relating to non-numeric categories such as 'male/female', 'yes/no' and months of birth were readily understood. Problems arise with numeric data such as height or temperature. Talking through what children already know about the data is helpful.

A group of Year 6 pupils displayed a histogram of children's heights. They believed that the highest bar represented the tallest person. The teacher intervened, to remind them of earlier work. A coin had repeatedly been rolled through a maze with four outlets. Pupils had drawn a frequency bar chart of outcomes. The group recalled that they had plotted the number of times the coin had appeared at each exit. It suddenly dawned on one child that the height chart showed 'numbers of people'. There was great relief and delight at this point, and correct interpretation followed.

A Year 5 group looked at a frequency histogram of people's ages. Most were convinced that the tallest bar showed the oldest people. Bryan said, 'That shows who was the most of the same age, not who's the oldest!' There was some dispute over this. Then Susie, looking at a bar of one unit's height, drew her finger across the screen to the y-axis. She said, 'You look on that one there – and it's about one whole person.' This language, describing the one-to-one correspondence of the pictogram format, derives from experience lower down the school. Again, the child has to recall past learning in order to interpret the computer graph.

Pie charts

The manual construction of a pie chart is a laborious task. The computer is able to produce pie charts readily. Children have the advantage of being able to see the same data presented in pie and bar chart format. Younger pupils have been able to make qualitative interpretations. A teacher of a Year 2 class was surprised that children were able to identify the 'slices' on a computer pie chart, and talk about what the biggest slice showed. Across the age range, children generally experience few difficulties with qualitative interpretation. Quantitative interpretation is another matter.

In order to interpret the chart quantitatively, children must possess a clear grasp of the unity which the whole pie represents. The 'pie' is notionally the whole set of records. Sub-sets are shown as fractional parts of the whole. In the frequency bar graph, the height of the bar shows the number of records represented. With the pie chart, the child must make the connection between a *fraction* (the part of the whole sample) and an *integer* (the number of records represented). This seems a significant cognitive leap.

The percentage fraction may be given, but this does not always appear to help. In one case, the largest 'slice' represented 54% of the sample. When I asked, 'About how much is that?' capable 10 year olds could not answer. I then asked, 'It's just over 50 per cent – what is that?' A child did eventually suggest one half. Rounding of values may cause difficulties. A 'slice' representing three records in a total sample of 29 was labelled as 10%. Year 6 pupils of above average ability found this exceedingly hard to grasp.

At Level 4, pupils should be able to recognise 'approximate proportions of a whole and use simple fractions and percentages to describe these' (DfE, 1995b). In other words, most children in Year 6 should be able to make a close estimate, at least by identifying 'slices' as fractions. I found it helpful to use 'mini-files' containing 8 or 12 records, since these yielded pie charts with halves, quarters and other familiar fractions. Children were able to apply intuitive understanding in interpreting these charts. Due to a lack of mathematical language, however, they were frequently unable to share their understanding. While language is not essential to operational thought, lack of it seriously hinders communication. Children were thus less able to contribute to each other's learning as they had done in other information retrieval activities.

Summary

A database is more than a receptacle for collected facts. File creation adds value, provided that structure is well-planned to accommodate the data and to serve the aims of the investigation. Interrogation of the completed database may permit the discovery of new information, as well as enabling retrieval of what is already known.

Structure may be based on classificatory analysis, and/or hypothesised connections and relationships. Understanding of file structure and nature of the data is needed for successful retrieval. Highly differentiated data must be grouped into categories, otherwise groups cannot be compared.

Outcomes depend on the accuracy and scope of the file contents. Inaccurate data will lead to distorted representation. Teachers should note that generalisations can only be made if the records represent a valid statistical sample. Findings about an ad-hoc collection cannot be claimed to represent a wider truth.

Pupils' first interactions with the completed data file may involve the tracing and correction of errors and inaccuracies. Many errors become evident when graphs are displayed. Error tracing and correction can take time, but may involve the application of a number of data handling skills. Higher order thinking is often demanded in accounting for strange results.

Having learned from experience about the effects of errors in the file, pupils become aware of the need to check data on entry. Consistent categorisation is essential.

In searching text fields, pupils often find that use of *includes* leads to greater success. Mathematical relations in search expressions are generally well understood. However, children may need support when using greater *than / less than* to retrieve a range of values.

10 and 11 year olds are able to carry out multi-part inquiries provided that they can associate the language of the question with a particular search. The use of inclusive OR is especially difficult: it is unlikely that children at this level will be able to reason when it is appropriate. However, rules of thumb are acquired, and passed on to other children. In this way, pupils may successfully carry out multiple searches without recourse to formal thinking.

Although sorting is conceptually easy, its strategic value is often over-looked. Sorting provides the quickest route to answering questions of the type 'Which is largest / smallest?' Children should be shown how to print sorted lists for comparison.

Computer graphs are attractive, and easy to produce. These facts often lead teachers to overlook the difficulties children experience in inter-pretation. In frequency histograms, the highest bar may suggest the tallest, or strongest, rather than the commonest. Children need to be able to relate the representation to the context.

Across the age range, children were able to cope with qualitative interpretation of pie charts. Quantitative interpretation is far more problematic. Children are able to identify 'the most', and so forth, but find it difficult to relate to a fraction of a sample in a quantitative sense.

CHAPTER 12

DATA LOGGING

Using the computer to store and display sensor data

In Chapters 4 and 11, we looked at children's use of computer graphs to represent statistical information. Data had already been collected by pupils, and entered into a graphing program or database. Through using sensors with a data logging device connected to the computer, variables such as temperature or light level may be monitored. Data loggers take accurate readings at regular intervals, allowing continuous graphing over time.

In *real time* graphing, data is displayed directly, usually in line graph format (as on a heart monitor). Some sensing devices have a digital display, giving spot readings. Other options depend on the software used to communicate with the logging device and manipulate data. For example, *Junior Insight* is able to display bars, which rise and fall as values increase and decrease. If the window is dragged out to cover the screen, the whole class may easily see the display. This provides a useful introduction, especially for younger pupils. One teacher has used the light sensor in this way with Year 2, as part of an investigation of light sources. The advantage of the line graph is that it shows change over time. This is a more abstract form of representation. Pupils must learn to interpret graphical features, such as gradient.

It is also possible to measure data away from the computer. A battery-powered data logger may be taken out of doors. Later, the device is connected to the computer. The stored data is 'fetched' and displayed graphically.

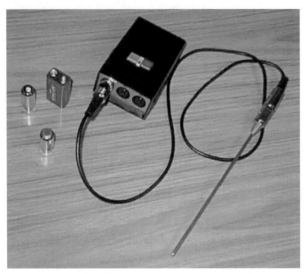

A Log-IT is shown with light and sound sensors. A stainless steel temperature probe is attached to an extension lead.

The system used in the following studies was the Log-IT Junior pack[1]. The standard primary pack contains three sensors for temperature, light and sound. Up to three sensors, fixed directly into DIN sockets on the Log-IT, may be used at once. Additionally, pupils used a set of three heavy-duty stainless steel temperature probes, with extension leads. These accessories enabled children to investigate the cooling of hot water in insulated containers. The extension leads also proved useful where sensors had to be located a small distance apart, as in the propagator experiment which follows.

Software is also needed, to enable communication with the logging device and to display the data graphically. In the following studies, *Junior Insight* was used. It is not essential to set options beforehand, other than specifying that the Log-IT is to be connected. The software detects automatically which sensors are connected, and scales axes appropriately. The *Junior Insight* menu features options such as setting the time span for continuous monitoring. If the Log-IT is used *remotely* (i.e. away from the computer), the x-axis will be scaled automatically to show the time span. The only restriction is battery life. I have heard of one case where pupils monitored temperature variation in a wormery for an entire month!

Interpretation of line graphs may present unexpected difficulties. Pupils may be distracted by pronounced features such as a sudden sharp rise, causing them to neglect the rest of the graph (Preece, 1983). It is of great help to be able to watch features being formed in real time. Pupils controlling, say, a light source are able to interact directly with the display and cause the line to rise or fall. The linear plot also shows whether changes are gradual or sudden. However, correct interpretation should not be taken for granted. In the first of the studies which follow, pupils' difficulties led to the development of practical teaching strategies.

The data logger carries out accurate, fully automatic monitoring over a long period if required. The computer is able to collect and manipulate large quantities of readings (Rogers, 1994). Line graphs provide a qualitative profile of the data; pupils are freed from laborious manual construction.

What are appropriate contexts for data logging? An excellent starting point for teachers is *The IT in Primary Science Book* by Roger Frost (Frost, 1993). The book contains a number of practical ideas for investigation. Many of the activities are appropriate for younger children. As these activities demonstrate, it is not always necessary to obtain graphical displays to monitor change. For example, there is an investigation of the sound-proofing qualities of different materials. A steady sound source such as a buzzer or bell is recommended; it is only necessary to take single readings. Digital readings may be displayed directly on the screen or on the data logger's LCD display. However, where change takes place over time, line graphs are of value in profiling the change.

Predictions, and the use of one's own senses in making initial judgements, are important in Frost's investigations. For example, children may first sort various sound sources into order of volume, according to their own judgement. Since the sound sensor is calibrated to a numerical scale, it is necessary to decide what is 'loud' and 'very loud'. Children should first make a sound level scale which corresponds to the range of the sensor, and mark this to show 'quiet', 'loud' and 'very loud'. Children should compare their qualitative judgements with the sensor's output.

In the IT Curriculum (DfE, 1995b) there is a requirement for pupils to learn to use IT to 'monitor external events'. The Science curriculum requires the use of tables, charts and graphs to 'present results', leading to comparison and identification of trends and patterns. How transparent are these images to children? What impact does real-time display, on a computer screen, of data obtained through sensor measurements have on children's ability to interpret line graphs?

In many instances in the classroom, graphical presentation is the end point of pupils' investigation. Pratt (1995) called this 'passive graphing'. Pupils were not actively making use of computer graphs in furthering investigation. In 'active graphing', there is emphasis on reflection and interpretation. Graphs should be generated at an early stage, and employed to inform planning and decision-making. Friedler and McFarlane (1995) studied the use of portable computers for data logging in investigative science. In particular, they examined the effect of real-time line graphs on pupils' understanding. The dynamic nature of the growth of the display with time helps pupils' understanding of this abstract form and development of graphing skills.

Introducing data logging to a Year 6 class

The following studies both took place in Year 6 classes, but there were significant differences in the settings. In the first study I worked with fifteen pupils at an urban primary school. Most pupils were achieving at, or just below, the national expectation. In statutory assessment at the end of the year, eleven (73%) gained Level 4 in two or three subjects. Only one child achieved a Level 5 for Mathematics. Four children (27%) obtained Level 3 in all subjects

A portable computer was set up, with a small ink-jet printer, in a small area adjacent to the classroom. The Acorn computer proved not to be as 'portable' as I had hoped, due to the failure of its rechargeable batteries. However, there are advantages in using even a mains-powered compact machine for this type of work: it does not dominate the work area, and can quickly be moved aside.

Children worked in mixed-ability, mixed-gender groups of four or five. I took one group at a time, which allowed a high level of interaction and monitoring. This is, needless to say, a practical impossibility for the class teacher during normal teaching time. In practice, many teachers have set up data logging equipment for pupils to use independently, and I have heard that this works well (page 162).

I first introduced the light sensor to groups. Without exception, the pupils were enthralled by the Log-IT and its accessories. Several children asked where it could be bought, as they wanted one for Christmas! Among the objects investigated by the children were small torches, a range of pea bulbs in holders with batteries, and a set of flashing LEDs.

Children investigated what happened when light sources were moved towards and away from the sensor. Problems were caused by bright sunshine. I quickly adapted a cardboard packing box, opening the flaps at either end so that light source and sensor (on extension lead) could be placed inside. A Log-IT was connected directly to the computer to display a real-time line graph.

Initial explanations were tentative. Children knew that the flashing of the light caused the 'spikes'. Some were not at all sure that the peaks showed when the lights were on. At this stage, 'hands-on' exploration was vitally important, allowing children to test their tentative ideas through exploring cause and effect:

Sara   It's measuring dark and light!

Mark   Can it go right down to the bottom, if you cover it completely   up?

HS   Try! [...] If you leave the torch on, what will happen?

Mark   It will go up and stay up and carry on going along.

HS   Well done! And what will happen if you make a short flash?

Shaun   It'll go up like that and then go straight back down.

Next, I asked a child to manipulate a light source inside the box. From the display, the rest of the group attempted to give an account of what was happening. One group watched the graph being formed as Alan moved his hand in front of the torch. Pupils assumed correctly that he was doing this at regular intervals. I asked how they knew, and a child said, 'The peaks are all roughly the same height.' In other words, height rather than spacing was critical. To develop understanding of the x-axis as a time line, I took Alan aside and asked him to repeat this pattern:

Flash once (i.e. quickly turn the light on and off)
Wait five seconds
Flash twice
Wait five seconds before starting again

Pupils identified the two rapid flashes on the graph, but I felt that some were still unsure. Helpful links could be made with time lines in history and performance of graphic scores in music. On these representations, closely spaced events are close together in time. To extend their experience, I introduced the sound sensor to investigate drumbeats. I asked the pupils to explain what they saw on the display:

HS	Why didn't it go right down between the hits?
Patrick	If I leave it too long there's no sound at all, and it will go right the way down.
Michael	If he hit it fast instead of slowly it wouldn't have a chance to go down.
HS	Hit the drum and let's *listen* to what happens.
Ch.	It echoes! It vibrates.

Some children were able to compare changes over time. Where a 'slope' had been made by turning slowly out of the light, I was told, 'If it was quicker it would have shot right down.' I was told that 'thick' peaks meant that the torch had been left on for a long time. One pupil promptly read the x-axis, saying that the torch had been left on for twenty seconds.

When I felt that pupils had gained a sound understanding of graph features, I showed them how to take remote readings and display the data. All that is necessary is to disconnect the Log-IT and fit sensors and battery. Pressing the green button twice starts recording: pressing the green followed by the red button stops the process. Up to four sets of data may be recorded, and the computer recognises the most recent as '1'. All pupils quickly learned how to 'record' remotely with the Log-IT, connect to the computer and instruct *Junior Insight* to 'fetch' the data. No differential according to ability was in evidence. Graphs were printed and pupils were asked to label the features.

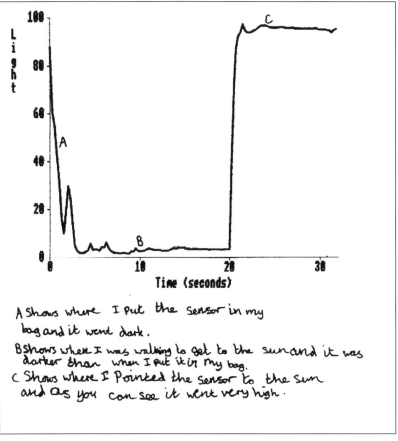

A Shows where I put the sensor in my bag and it went dark.

B Shows where I was walking to get to the sun and it was darker than when I put it in my bag.

C Shows where I Pointed the sensor to the sun and as you can see it went very high.

Junior Insight graph of changing light level.

In the first instance, children experimented by recording light levels in dark and bright places. Joanna insisted repeatedly that the darkest place was at the top of the 'hill'. There was much value in talking through graphs such as the one illustrated. Kim, after some hesitation, agreed that James must have 'turned' quickly into the sunlight. She said, pointing to the pronounced corner, 'There's a sharp turning round.' She had given the right interpretation, but she seems to have been prompted by a pictorial feature, rather than the sudden change in gradient.

The significance of the gradient is not obvious to children and the graphs can be highly deceptive. One group displayed data collected out of doors using a Log-IT. They were convinced that a long, almost vertical line, caused by a rapid change in light level, showed a *slow* change. Pupils may interpret line graphs as paths or trails, laid down at a constant speed. I was told, 'I reckon he done it slowly because it's quite a long line.' When I asked what would happen if the light were dimmed, I was told, 'It'll go straight down but slowly.'

At this point, I set up the cardboard box again to make real-time graphs. Patrick observed that the line 'slanted quite a lot' when the light source was withdrawn slowly. I encouraged the group to look at the x-axis. One noticed that, when the light is switched off, the line 'lands in the same place as before.' Shortly afterwards, group members correctly interpreted a sharp drop as a rapid change.

Pupils, once again, need practical experience followed by teacher-led discussion. The teacher aims to develop understanding through giving pupils opportunities to communicate and explain what they have observed. The language to describe and explain graph features is being developed. The ease of graphing enables children to gain experience of the actual formation, in real time, of graphs showing change over time.

To check understanding, children talked through their printed graphs before writing what the features showed. Trevor told me, 'I think that bit's where we pointed it up to the sun and then I put it up the drainpipe, and then I think when I pointed it up to the sun again, that's there, and then I pointed it to the ground.'

In writing about their graphs, several pupils commented on pictorial features. Joanna remarked, 'It's like a cliff!' When it comes to interpretation, it's important that pupils understand what these features mean. Some identified patterns, showing that they were forming a concept of the growth of the graph with time. Kate wrote below her 'wavy' graph:

> This is when I was holding my data logar in the drain and moving it round in a sequence. I think the repet partern was good and made a good efect.

Another opportunity for speaking arose when I asked children how they thought they could make a really interesting graph with the Log-IT. Joanna said that she would 'find a dark place and put the sensor into the dark place and keep it there for a while, then I'd find a very light place where the sun is.' The graph would look 'like really dark, sort of like down, and light, going up.' I was pleased, since Joanna had initially thought that high peaks represented darkness.

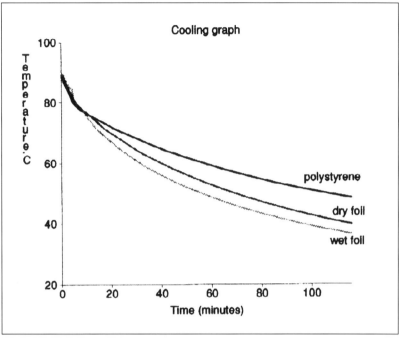

Graph from sensor data, showing the cooling of hot water in three identical cans with different insulating arrangements.

One group used a Log-IT fitted with three stainless steel temperature probes to investigate insulating properties. Three tin cans were prepared: one was placed in a box and surrounded with polystyrene chips, one was wrapped in bubble packaging, and one encased in aluminium foil. Logging was carried out over 90 minutes. The resulting line graph was displayed.

Pupils showed good understanding of why materials such as aluminium foil and bubble packaging were effective insulators. There was no reflection on why curves were steepest at the outset. Only Stephanie, the most cognitively able child in the class, showed some understanding that heat is lost more quickly from hotter water. This of course is what accounts for the curved profile of the cooling graph.

Stephanie remarked, 'It's like when you have a Cup-a-Soup, if it's too hot you pour it into a cold mug and it cools down.' I asked, 'What other ways could you cool Cup-a-Soup down?' Suggestions were made (stirring, blowing, simply leaving it for a while) and a fair test was devised.

Pupils suggested ideas for further experiments. One group wanted to boil water, inserting probes at the top and near the base. I was told that 'it will be hotter at the top, because the heat rises.' With the Log-IT, 'you can compare the differences.' Trevor thought that the rising steam would be hotter than the water itself, 'because heat rises'. Both assertions were tested using a Log-IT fitted with three temperature probes, but no evidence in favour was obtained. Children suggested that heat is carried upward by the steam, but is lost to the surrounding air.

Investigating through data logging

The second Year 6 study focuses on development past the introductory stage. The setting was markedly different from that of the previous class. I worked with twenty-one pupils: seven (33%) had achieved Level 5 in all SATs. Only one pupil had a majority of Level 3 results. All others had consistently achieved Level 4, or two 4s and one 5. While many of these pupils are ready for Key Stage 3, the study shows some of the opportunities for extending able pupils. However, unexpected difficulties came to light in written recording. There are implications for preparing pupils lower down the school.

The school is situated in a rural community where residential property is at a premium. Children are highly motivated academically and benefit from a supportive environment in the home. Most children have access to computers at home. The class teacher feels that technology is a weak area, since parents tend not to attach much status to practical work. She therefore places high priority on Design and Technology.

I had been invited to work with the class in the context of a Design and Technology project. Children had designed and made propagators for seedlings. The main challenge had been to design and construct a framework covered with heavy-duty polythene. Doors or hatches were added to some designs. Data logging enabled the propagators to be tested out of doors. Did temperature rise in sunlight? Was warmth retained when the sun went in? Was there any variation in the effectiveness of different designs?[2]

Children had no difficulty whatever in relating to the display, whether produced in real time or from logged data. Features caused by rapid or slow change were correctly identified and explained. There was no confusion of steep drops with lengthy time intervals. I was told, 'It goes vrmm – straight down like that.' The introductory activities discussed earlier in this chapter were inappropriate. I began to feel that the pupils would not be adequately challenged if we lingered at this stage.

During a particularly noisy indoor playtime, a sound sensor was set up. Pupils had recently looked at information about sound levels and health. Decibels were eagerly read from the graph. The average noise level was estimated, and there were resolutions to be quieter in future! I introduced the [standard] temperature sensor. Changes can be effected in the normal classroom environment by rubbing hands together, or plunging the sensor into a cup of cold water. These changes are small. To examine the detail, the y-axis must be re-scaled.

The light and sound sensors readily provided illustration of sudden, sharp change. The temperature sensor portrayed gradual change. Children had no difficulty with this. They understood that the temperature sensor requires time to adjust to the surroundings. A pupil observed, 'It took time to take up heat. We can tell because it's not so steep.' Another pointed out, 'If you turn the torch on and off, you can do it quite rapidly, but with temperature, it has to have time to level.'

Pupils noted that the line dropped down more rapidly in the cold water 'because it's a big drop in temperature'. It levels off 'because it's getting to the temperature of the water'. These experiences are valuable in developing early intuitive understanding. The concepts underlying measurement and representation of changes in rate are highly abstract, and it is unlikely that pupils will develop formal understanding for some time to come.

A data logger with light and temperature sensor was placed inside a propagator. Recording began and the apparatus was left for an hour. The mixed weather conditions were ideal. Brilliant sunshine soon gave way to cloud. The change was readily apparent on the line graph.

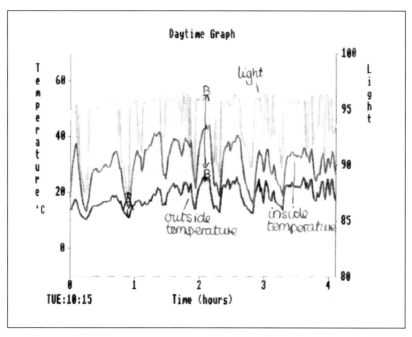

This graph shows temperature changes inside and outside a propagator, together with fluctuations in light level.

I asked one group to predict what would happen, and explain. Francesca thought it would be slightly warmer inside the greenhouse, because 'it's got covering and protection'. I asked what was warming the air in the propagator. Claire replied, 'The covering is keeping the warm air in.' The group found that the difference between inside and outside temperatures was greater in sunlight. The teacher used this observation to challenge the notion of some children that 'heat from the air outside' had entered the propagator. While they were aware that heat is trapped, no-one actually suggested that the sun warms surfaces in the propagator. Since nearly all children had encyclopaedias (CD-ROM or books) at home, the teacher asked the class to research the 'greenhouse effect' for homework.

I asked whether the temperature rose the moment the sun came out. The group agreed the temperature rose gradually. Pupils noticed that peaks and troughs were never quite together. They estimated that temperature peaked about two minutes after the light level had gained its highest reading. The cursor was dragged across the display, enabling this interval to be measured accurately.

The pupils suggested using a second temperature sensor, to monitor conditions outside the propagator. Niall wanted to repeat the experiment with a second *light* sensor. He expected that light levels would be lower outside the propagator. He was convinced that the curved polythene roof 'magnifies' the light. Bad weather prevented other children from testing out of doors. Instead, a reading lamp was set up in the classroom. A large sheet of black paper was used to simulate a cloud. This enabled children to control when the 'sun' went in.

In the indoor test a 'double-glazed' propagator, with a double layer of polythene, retained heat for longer. The differences in temperature were slight but consistently maintained: it would have been impossible to record with sufficient accuracy using a conventional thermometer.

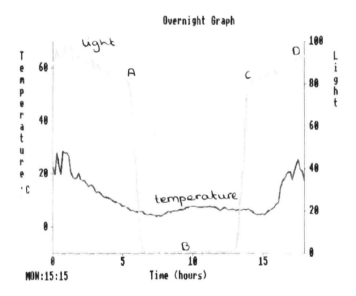

Light and temperature changes have been monitored overnight.

At the end of the day, in fine weather, children placed a temperature sensor and a light sensor inside a propagator. Recording commenced, and the apparatus was left out of doors overnight. There was considerable excitement next morning when data was 'fetched' from the Log-IT. Children consulted a daily paper to find sunrise and sunset times. Julia recorded on her graph, shown above:

A: This is where the sun went down 6.5 hours later (2145)

B This is the middle of the night.

C This is when it became light 13 hours later (0415)

D This is where the sun got higher.

Pupils' own investigations

Children were asked to think about things that they could investigate themselves with the Log-IT equipment. One group wanted to investigate the sound insulation properties of materials. A child was to speak through a piece of material, with the sound sensor on the other side. The whole class debated what was needed for a fair test:

Peter   You get the same person saying it in the same tone.

Francesca   Use the same amount – the same size piece of whatever.

Ben   Have the thing in front of you the same distance away from your mouth when you say it.

Francesca   Make sure the sensor's the same distance away.

One group investigated which colour tissue paper let through the most light. The paper was folded and used to cover a flash lamp lens. Measurement took place in a dark cupboard. Quantitative measurements were noted down but there were problems in matching readings to colours because children had not written down the order in which they had carried out the tests!

Another group wanted to see whether percussion instruments could make sounds in water. They hit the instrument then put it in water 'while it was still playing'. A pupil wrote, 'We had a bowl of water, we had some chime bars, some bells and a triangle. [...] In the water there was some sound with the triangle, you could hear a tiny bit.' Other groups' reports simply described what they had done.

This type of pupil-directed investigation needs much further development. What are the aims? Why use the logging equipment? What will the data tell us? Miss Johnson noted that none of the ideas had involved change over time. They were all concerned with instant comparisons, and the data could just as easily have been transferred onto a block graph.

Miss Johnson commented, 'They just wanted to measure "How noisy is it here? How noisy is it there?" without thinking about a period of time. It's obviously a concept which requires a great amount of development of their thinking. I still think there's a perception among the children that you do block graphs in the infants, and you do line graphs in the juniors. As you get older you learn to do these things. [Children don't appreciate] that they're about different things entirely.'

Interpreting the evidence

The IT skills were quickly mastered by these pupils. IT challenges are outweighed by other demands, such as the skills of identifying and focusing questions, designing an experiment, recording, analysing and interpreting data. In interpreting the evidence, some pupils had difficulties in identifying precisely what the graphs had showed.

For example, the most pronounced feature of the propagator graph was the way it revealed the relationship between light level and temperature. Children agreed that when the sun came out, it caused the temperature to rise. The class teacher drew attention to the graph as evidence. She asked, 'How do we know that?'

Niall and Ben were among the few who explained graph features in their reports. Niall wrote, 'The graph shows that the light always rises before the temperature.' He labelled an example on the graph. Ben did likewise, writing, 'This shows that the light came up first, but it took time for the temperature to rise.'

Gemma wrote, 'I think this experiment was very successful, because it shows how good the propagator works.' She provided a key for the graph and labelled one point, 'This is when the temperature inside is close to the temperature outside. We think this is when the clouds went over.' Other children's reports were mainly descriptive. Claire wrote, 'We found out the propagator kept the heat in. She did not say *how* we know. She summarised rather weakly, 'We found out what we were trying to find out.' Claire, like Gemma, had achieved Level 5 in all SATs.

Miss Johnson thought that the children were having problems in selecting appropriate vocabulary and articulating their interpretations. This was apparent in both verbal and written statements. I noted that the girls were more inclined to be descriptive while the boys, with one exception, were more prepared to look at features of the graph and give a quantitative interpretation.

Children are trained over many years to write statements such as 'This graph shows that ...'. Confronted with a new type of graphical display, they must first identify and account for the *features*, since they form the basis of interpretation. Teachers need to prepare pupils to explain the important graphical features on which we base our interpretation.

There are many ways in which the pupils' investigations could be developed, given time. For example, a humidity sensor would enable further testing of the propagator's effectiveness. What would happen if pupils put a black sheet over the propagator? Could they set up propagators in different circumstances? They could make comparisons with commercial products.

Summary

Line graphs of change over time provide an immediate profile of events. Sudden and gradual changes may be distinguished. Details are shown that would be missed with manual recording. Most Year 6 pupils quickly learn to interpret 'high' and 'low' features. Younger and less able pupils may need much practical experience before reaching this level. Practical experience of producing real-time graphs, followed by teacher-led discussion, is invaluable in consolidating understanding.

Width and horizontal spacing, showing duration and time intervals, are less readily interpreted than height of features. Pupils were misled by long vertical drops and pronounced corners. Some may have problems in reconciling their understanding of two-dimensional space with this representation, in which the horizontal dimension is *time*.

A large number of examples may be generated. However, the advantage is lost if reflection is not encouraged. Pupils benefit from opportunities to discuss features with each other, and with the teacher. It is particularly important that children learn to identify correctly the features of the graph, and account for these changes in considering the evidence.

Children should be taught to appreciate why we use ICT in measurement. The computer enables large amounts of data to be stored and displayed in graphical form, thus enabling profiling of change over time. But we also need to judge when digital sensors are an unnecessary sophistication. For example, we can trust our senses in making simple comparisons. Inexpensive testers will display spot readings, if that is all that is required. Teachers should provide all these experiences, and discuss the choice of measuring device.

The equipment was relatively easy to set up, and children quickly learned to use it. The small size of the portable computer was an advantage. There was space on the tabletop for other apparatus.

Printed graphs were useful for work away from the computer. Unfortunately, it was difficult to read plotted values with any accuracy. This is easy to do on screen, simply by moving the cursor. This is not a great disadvantage at Key Stage 2, since most interpretation is qualitative. It would be an advantage for older pupils engaged in quantitative analysis to save the work onto laptop computers, which can be taken away from the experiment.

Notes

1. Please see the Appendix for full product details.
2. A humidity sensor is supplied for the Log-IT. Unfortunately, none was available at the time of this study.

CHAPTER 13

APPROACHES TO CONTROL
TECHNOLOGY

This short chapter introduces Control Technology in the context of work with floor robots and turtles, discussed in Chapter 3. It presents an approach which builds on this work, in extending pupils' programming to incorporate the use of sensors.

Control systems – supermarket doors and security lights with proximity sensors, motorway fog warnings and burglar alarms – are pervasive in everyday life and most of us now take them for granted. Sophisticated as they may appear, these control systems embody the same basic principles. An action or set of actions is carried out when information is received from one or more sensors. Children will know of many examples, such as the driveway lights which are switched on automatically as you walk down the street. These systems incorporate a heat sensor, timer and light sensor (the light only comes on in the dark).

In the Key Stage 2 IT Programme of Study, pupils are taught to 'create, test, modify and store sequences of instructions to control events'. At Level 3, pupils are expected to 'control equipment to achieve specific outcomes by giving a series of instructions'. At Level 4, pupils are able to control events 'in a pre-determined manner'.

An important step is embedded in these terse statements. At Level 3, many pupils will be at the stage of building and testing sequences a step at a time. By Level 4, children should be able to plan in advance, through envisaging steps leading to an outcome. Much depends on opportunities to develop and practise control skills, with guidance and support. The teacher, above all, should be concerned that pupils use control commands correctly and that they plan in advance. This may involve, for example, drawing a simple flowchart showing the sequence of events one step at a time.

Control technology is open-ended and there are potential contexts in more than one subject. In the Science programmes of study, there are references to control in *Experimental and Investigative Science* and *Physical Processes.* In Design and Technology, computer control may be integrated in the design of a product. The aim is to operate the model in a predetermined way at the press of a switch (or signal from a sensor). For example, children may construct the façade of a 'castle' using Corriflute. A 'drawbridge' powered by a technical Lego motor may be raised when 'intruders' step on a pressure pad.

In *Information Technology and the use of language* (SCAA, 1996b) links are made between the learning of IT skills and linguistic development. The accurate, precise manner in which commands must be given to the system 'develops children's awareness of how language is used for different purposes'. Children's experience of specialist language in producing outcomes is also widened.

It is important to ensure that control work takes place in a relevant context. There is no point in teaching control programming skills in isolation. Starting points should be simple, and related to pupils' experience. This is easier to achieve than may at first seem, given children's familiarity with automated toys and household gadgets, barriers and warning systems, and so forth. Simple models (for instance, with a single light or motor, single sensor and simple sequence of actions) will enable full coverage of the IT requirement.

There is no need to dive immediately into complex modelling of cranes on turntables, fairground rides or pelican crossings. Harm may have been done by enthusiastic Inset tutors who have demonstrated sophisticated working models (in all likelihood, made by secondary pupils). The natural response of most primary teachers is, 'I / my children could not possibly make that.' The difficulties of analysing the problem and programming the solution may be significant. Much work is needed if children are to internalise the command language and work independently on a wider variety of problems (Stephenson, 1997). However, control technology offers an excellent opportunity to challenge the thinking of highly capable and gifted pupils. There are benefits in other domains. As Stephenson says, control 'provides children with a procedural way of working that mirrors and complements similar processes across the curriculum.'

Progression

In Chapter 3, we saw how children may progress from simple control, giving a single step at a time, to the programming of sequences of instructions. In driving the Roamer or Pixie, the foundations are being laid for control programming using a Logo-like language.

From Reception through to entry into Key Stage 3, the progression is as follows:

- Simple switch or button control
- Single commands, to have immediate effect
- Sequence of commands, still with direct effect
- Simple procedures, or named sets of instructions to carry out specific action(s)
- Incorporating sensors, so that the procedure is only carried out if the sensor detects an event
- Writing, testing, debugging and refining procedures to carry out a planned series of events.

A good example of early control activities is shown in the BBC-TV NCET *Learning Zone* broadcast on IT in the primary curriculum, first shown in January 1996. Reception children use a variety of toys as they investigate how things move. From simple toys which have to be pushed to make them go, children progress to using handsets and infra-red control. They progress to commanding a floor robot in single steps, as illustrated in Chapter 3. An important advance takes place when children become able to quantify – in other words, attach a value to a command. Moving from the Pixie to the Roamer takes pupils through this progression. Instead of pressing the 'forward' arrow three times, the child now enters 'Forward 3'. Later, as we saw in Chapter 3, pupils become able to devise and enter a short sequence of commands, before pressing 'Go'.

If pupils have already worked with floor robots and Logo, they will have had an excellent preparation for the Key Stage 2 curriculum. Here, they progress to incorporating sensors to monitor what is happening in the immediate vicinity. They also learn to construct procedures which enable a system to carry out actions in response to sensor information.

Process skills, such as analysing a problem and breaking down into steps, are also important in control. As in Logo, it is most helpful to think procedurally. *A procedure* is a unit of actions (page 39). For example, the child may say, 'I want the motor to start when the pressure pad is touched. Then the motor must stop as soon as the drawbridge is closed.' The procedure is simply the sequence of commands to carry out this action. The system is instructed to wait until the sensor is on. Then the motor is switched on. A second sensor is positioned to detect when the drawbridge is shut. As soon as this happens, the motor is switched off.

Each procedure is given a name. Once the procedure has been entered and stored, the child only has to type the name to activate the sequence of commands. This is exactly the same as the use of the procedure SQUARE to draw squares, in Chapter 3.

Children begin to appreciate the need for accuracy, not just in what they type into the computer, but in the initial breakdown of the problem. This is why it is important to work through in advance what exactly is to happen, step by step.

Developing control with the Roamer

The Roamer control interface extends the use of equipment already familiar from Key Stage 1. While the full control pack with lights, motors and sensors is relatively costly, it is considerably cheaper than buying an additional computer. The control elements of the Programme of Study up to Level 5 may be fully covered. The advantage of using the Roamer lies in its simplicity and familiarity. There are relatively few new commands for children to learn. The emphasis is on the process skills of breaking down a problem, planning, testing and reworking.

The model in the photograph has been constructed using technical Lego. The base has been mounted onto the Roamer with Blu-tack. For the best operation, the wheel should be horizontal. Pupils should ensure there is a collar under the rotor arm.

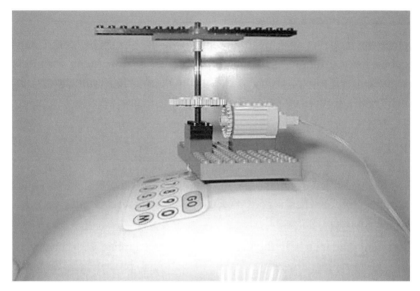

The Roamer is turned into a helicopter. The model, constructed from technical Lego, is powered and controlled by means of the Roamer control interface.

The control interface is securely fixed below the Roamer. There are three pairs of red and green terminals (Outputs 1, 2 and 3). The Lego motor leads are connected to one of these pairs. The 'T' button on the Roamer's control panel refers to 'Output'. The command T 1, for example, means 'instruct Output 1'. There may well be some confusion at first, because the numbers 1 and 2 are also used to indicate 'Off' and 'On'.

If we assume that the motor is connected to Output 1, the command for turning the output on (strictly speaking, to a *high* state) is:

T 1 2

The motor will only work while something else is happening. It must be combined with a Wait instruction, or a command to move. The motor will stop when the command has been carried out.

It is always advisable to test a model before putting complicated instructions into the Roamer! Here is a simple test which may be run as many times as you like by pressing GO repeatedly:

CM CM (clear previous commands)

T 1 2 (set Output 1 high: in other words, turn it on!)

W 1 (wait approximately one second)

Once the model is working, children may devise scenarios for the 'helicopter'. For example, it may be programmed to stop, hover for a few seconds, then move off in a different direction. The command to turn the motor off mid-sequence is:

T 1 1

Roamer accessories include sensors such as buffers, light and sound detectors and a simple push switch. Sensors detect events or changes in the Roamer's environment (as, for example, when the Roamer collides with a chair, or when it goes dark). One sensor at a time may be fitted to the Roamer.

Detailed guidance is in the illustrated booklet supplied with the sensor kit. In principle, the approach is to define a procedure telling the Roamer what to do when the sensor detects an event. Anything is possible: it may be that the Roamer turns 180 degrees, plays a tune, or both!

For example, with a buffer fitted, the Roamer can be sent off on a long journey (Forward 10 should suffice). When the buffer hits the wall, the procedure is carried out automatically. The Roamer turns, plays a tune (or whatever it has been told to do), and continues to complete the Forward command.

With the sound sensor fitted, the Roamer will respond to a loud noise. Since everything is done through single key presses, the commands are simple to enter. The teacher should take pupils through the steps carefully at the outset. Support materials may be helpful for reference. 'Expert' pupils may be able to solve problems if the teacher is busy. The work is absorbing and highly motivating, which aids discipline. Pupils who disrupt or dominate group work risk having to wait until all other children have had their turn.

Controlling using a command language

Control boxes with sockets for motors, sensors and low-voltage outputs allow progression into using command language. At first, pupils use the computer as a simple switch. Through entering commands one by one, they are still employing direct control. The next stage is to plan and write a set of instructions. This is where the computer comes into its own. Once entered, tested, modified and stored, a control program may be run repeatedly.

Pupils will have experienced direct physical control in many other contexts. For example, they will have carried out experiments with various types of electrical circuit incorporating a battery, switch and light. They will almost certainly have played with toys which respond to different stimuli (direct collisions, noises, radio control). Extending this experience through control technology is an important aspect of the IT curriculum, since pupils come closer to appreciating the unique contribution of the microprocessor to the modern environment.

At Level 5 of the IT Programme of Study, pupils are taught to 'create sets of instructions to control events'. They become 'sensitive to the need for precision in framing and sequencing instructions'. Using control software such as *CoCo*,[1] lights and other low-voltage devices may be switched on and off directly, by clicking with the mouse on the control panel window. The next step in the progression is to enter single commands. Pupils first connect the light to Output 1, then type the instruction SWITCH ON 1 (case doesn't matter). At this stage, the pupils are still giving direct control. There is no automation: the light will stay on until someone types SWITCH OFF 1.

Sequences of instructions may be stored, to be carried out later. Pupils now progress to planning, building and testing simple sets of instructions or procedures. The computer may 'run' a procedure repeatedly, or only in certain conditions. For example, we may want a fully automatic lighthouse to repeat its flashing pattern over and over again, but only while it is dark. This is an important step in developing pupils' awareness of how, and why, we use programmable devices. In *CoCo*, a sequence may be 'built' step by step using the BUILD command.

The teacher may wish initially to model the process for the benefit of the group or whole class. In the following illustration, pupils have constructed a lighthouse. A basic bulb holder is fitted with a 6v bulb and connected to the appropriate jack. The jack is pushed into Output 1. To program a simple flashing sequence, type:

BUILD LIGHT

In *CoCo*, this opens a new window, the Procedure window. In this window, type:

SWITCH ON 1
WAIT 1
SWITCH OFF 1
WAIT 1

The 'OK' button is clicked to enter the whole sequence. An important observation to make at this stage is that nothing happens! All we have done is to store the sequence. To *run* the procedure, we simply enter its name. In *CoCo*'s 'dialogue box', type LIGHT to run the procedure. Children should be immediately aware that this is not a useful procedure because the light only flashes once! Again, it is worth pausing to reflect on what we now need the computer to do.

The procedure now has to be modified. Enter the command:

CHANGE LIGHT

Press Enter to insert a blank line right at the top. On the top line, type:

REPEAT FOREVER

Below the list of instructions, type:

END REPEAT

Click OK and type LIGHT to run the procedure again. This time, it will run literally forever – at least until the computer is switched off! Press the Escape key (Esc) to stop it running.

At this stage, pupils will be ready to make and test their own sequences. The teacher has a dilemma in that the process of amending procedures is fraught with potential problems. In *CoCo*, it is not possible to insert text, then press *Enter* to split the line. A new line must be made first. Hopefully, new versions of control software will offer word processor style editing.

Once the basic procedure is working, there are many possibilities for differentiation and extension. Various flashing sequences may be devised, with timed long and short intervals. Children may be aware that real lighthouses have unique patterns, to enable identification. Pupils may incorporate a buzzer, plugged into Output 2, as a fog warning. Be advised that the buzzers supplied with control packs make a piercing noise!

At this stage, the IT may dominate, but it is important to encourage pupils to review the design of their model. A humble torch bulb may not give quite the effect that was wanted, but how may we contrive a brighter beam? There is no point in casting light over land, so a reflector may be designed to throw all of the light towards the shipping. Later, data logging kit (Chapter 12) may be used to measure the light from each lighthouse.

When pupils are ready, the teacher may ask, 'What do we need the computer to do, to make the lighthouse come on automatically?' There is no point in wasting power during the day. We want the lighthouse to come on only when it goes dark. The teacher introduces the light sensor. This is connected into Input 1. The light sensor is incorporated by changing the procedure and adding this command, on a fresh line made at the very top:

WAIT UNTIL INPUT 1 IS OFF

Now, we run the procedure again by typing LIGHT. The lighthouse will not come on until it goes dark. If a child puts her hand over the sensor, that will suffice. When she removes her hand, the lighthouse will continue to flash. To make the lighthouse fully automatic, the command REPEAT FOREVER is changed to:

REPEAT UNTIL INPUT 1 IS ON

The lighthouse now responds to light and darkness, and may be controlled by covering and uncovering the light sensor. Extension work may follow. For example, pupils design a burglar alarm which is triggered when someone steps on a pressure pad. A simple flat 'pressure pad' switch is usually included in control packs. If not, pupils may design and make their own, using foil-covered card bent over so that contact is made when modest pressure is applied.

This time, of course, the alarm system needs to WAIT UNTIL INPUT 1 IS ON. Residents may want the buzzing and flashing to continue as the burglar intrudes deeper into the house. Children therefore need to decide how to stop the alarm. It may stop after a fixed number of repeats, or a separate switch may be implemented. At all stages, it is vital first to have a clear mental picture of the sequence of events. This should then be written down. A simple flow chart serves well:

Alarm is set
Burglar breaks in, steps on pad
Buzzer sounds for three seconds
Voice says, "Get out of my house!"
This is repeated 10 times
Alarm stops

The pupils decide to call the procedure BURGLAR. They type the command BUILD BURGLAR and then, in the procedure window:

WAIT UNTIL INPUT 1 IS ON
REPEAT 10
SWITCH ON 1
WAIT 3
SWITCH OFF 1
SAY GET OUT OF MY HOUSE
END REPEAT

Alternatively, the alarm continues until the police arrive. They press a separate switch outside the house, which is connected to Input 2:

WAIT UNTIL INPUT 1 IS ON
REPEAT UNTIL INPUT 2 IS ON
SWITCH ON 1
WAIT 3
SWITCH OFF 1
SAY GET OUT OF MY HOUSE
END REPEAT

There is no need at this level to introduce any further programming concepts. The essential skills lie in being able to plan for an outcome, if necessary tackling the problem stage by stage. Taking each stage separately, pupils record each step in the sequence. Only then should the sequence be translated into computer language. For example, the alarm pattern (repeated buzzes alternated by synthetic speech) may be constructed and trialled first. Then the pupils consider incorporating the sensor and switch.

It is a waste of time to plunge in at the keyboard with a trial-and-error approach. No professional programmer would explore a problem in that way! The teacher has an important part to play in modelling the process initially, and in encouraging pupils to talk through their plans. However careful the preparation, programs rarely work first time. It may be necessary to go step by step through what the pupils have instructed the computer to do. It is important that pupils learn to account for what actually happens.

The ICT Framework for Key Stages 1 and 2 (QCA, 1998) gives further guidance on resourcing. Many teachers find the range of switches and sensors supplied with control kits quite bewildering. Simple starting points, such as those explained above, help in demystifying the process. The Roamer control pack effectively bridges the gap between simple Roamer activities at one extreme, and programming a control interface using *CoCo* at the other.

Note

1. The examples here are for *CoCo* (Commotion Control). The same principles apply in other control software, although the precise framing of instructions may differ. Please consult the user guide!

CHAPTER 14

THE INTERNET IN
PRIMARY SCHOOLS

Many readers will now be connected at school, as a direct result of the first phase of the National Grid for Learning. The NGfL, which has a four-year timescale, is linked to the Government's standards agenda. There will be a particular emphasis on literacy and numeracy. A training programme is included, and there is a specific aim to promote links between home and school, and with governors. There is also a drive to facilitate school administration through electronic communications.

There are regional differences. Some local authorities, particularly unitary authorities within a small geographical area, are setting up high-speed *intranets* with permanent high bandwidth connections. Many networks are now fully in place, giving schools unlimited, free access to services managed by the LEA, including filtered access to the wider Internet. In rural regions, high-speed digital connection for small primary schools is far less likely in the short term. Many will be reliant on standard telephone connection for the foreseeable future.

What will the Grid offer primary schools? At more than one recent presentation, civil servants have referred glowingly to all the 'super' worksheets and lesson plans that will flood into schools. But the Grid is more than a 'digital hose pipe pumping content' into classrooms (Heppell, 1997). It creates a community of learners and co-learners, able to share the outcomes of their learning. A major issue will be differentiating between curriculum resources which are ready for immediate take-up, and those such as pupils' email and video conferencing which require planning, development and co-ordination. This chapter looks at starting points available now to outright beginners, and the longer-term challenge of engaging in collaborative ventures using email, sometimes across great distances.

Unfortunately, there is no space here to advise on important matters such as the choice of service provider and mode of connection. These issues are amply covered in the free booklet *Connecting Schools, Networking People* (BECTa, 1998). The booklet presents advice on planning a school ICT development programme within the brief of the local authority's ICT Development Plan. Technical aspects, including networking and types of connection, are clearly explained, with details of costing. There are profiles of pupil projects involving email and video conferencing. Other issues covered include safety, security and staff development. The booklet draws on the considerable body of research evidence gathered under the Education Departments' Superhighways Initiative (EDSI, 1997).

The provision of access, equipment and basic training is not enough. The development of the Grid must be driven by a clear understanding of the potential of new communications technologies in promoting effective teaching and learning. It is not simply a matter of teaching pupils to use the Internet. Teachers must be in a position to judge for themselves how ICT can best help them meet professional objectives.

Curriculum resources have been published by a range of organisations including public services, businesses, museums, independent charities, higher education institutions, Internet service providers and schools themselves. Children may publish their own work for a global audience, and communicate with others using email. Distance and time zones are immaterial. As an increasing number of homes have on-line access, the Internet offers an important means of linking school, home and the local community.

After basic initial training, teachers will quickly find many resources ready for take-up. There are CD-ROMs which link directly to the Web. Pupils' email, publishing of pupils' work and video links are in need of development. Schools must determine objectives, and staff training should be delivered before classroom introduction. The first priority is to connect schools so that teachers can develop awareness and confidence, and begin to make their own judgements about practical issues, opportunities and benefits.

Internet safety is an important issue. Where a local authority intranet is in place, filtering of objectionable material may be carried out automatically. BT's *CampusWorld*, while permitting full Internet access, has a 'walled garden' option allowing users to sample only educational content. The Internet Watch Foundation advocates a system of rating at source, arguing that authors will take responsibility for rating their own content, as clients will otherwise avoid their sites (IWF, 1998). As one American teacher wrote, 'The Internet is a reflection of our society. In real life, we can choose to ignore or pretend that certain elements of society don't exist. On the Internet, it is another matter.'

The scope, magnitude and diversity of the Internet is only fully appreciated through searching on-line. A *search engine* maintains an index of millions of pages, incorporating billions of words and phrases. Some serve the needs of specialist groups. *Yahooligans* is for children, and only permits access to approved sites. Most engines index the entire Web and it will not take long for the user with the purest of intentions to stumble across some of the less savoury aspects. Unless it is narrowly focused, a search may return a quite unmanageable list of pages.

The first year of NGfL will give primary schools the opportunity to explore logistics. Siting is an important issue. Unless a hub is installed to distribute access throughout the school, connection will be in a single location such as the library. In the long term, a school may plan an area dedicated to ICT, where networked machines will share on-line access.

Outcomes greatly depend upon how computer tasks are integrated into classroom activity. Some schools are able to afford additional staffing. For example, a full-time technician may be jointly responsible for library resources and Internet access. Others have successfully recruited and trained volunteer parents. In the absence of adult support, children will be required to manage their own searching, selection of material and downloading onto disk. However, it must be recognised that filtered services do not remove all risk of accessing undesirable material. Internet safety must be addressed in the school's ICT policy.

Towards the end of this chapter, we look directly at children's use of the Internet in researching their own selected area of interest. Can pupils use the Web with minimal support? What information handling skills are demanded? Can pupils identify what is relevant, and select what they need? How accessible is the content? What are the unique features of the medium, and implications for learning? The small study sheds some light on these important questions.

Starting points

The Virtual Teachers' Centre was launched in January 1998 as a proto-type for the Grid. The objective is to offer quality assured materials to support teaching and learning. At the time of writing (September 1998), the VTC appears static, with little discernible development over the summer months, other than the addition of the Standards Database. In contrast, school and local authority NGfL sites have begun to proli-ferate. The latter give a much better impression of the developing Grid as a connected learning community. They offer a better starting point to teachers going on line for the first time.

Curriculum resources have been specially commissioned by the major educational providers such as *CampusWorld* and RM *Internet for Learning*. A selection is freely available to non-subscribers. An excel-lent starting point is *Argosphere*, maintained by ArgoNet, a specialist educational service provider. Users have to register, but there is no charge and access is immediate. Learning activities are grouped in age-related categories, for children aged three upwards. There is a high level of interactivity and themes are diverse. The interface resembles a good-quality multimedia CD-ROM, and there is virtually no difference over a fast Internet connection.

School websites

The most fully developed sites often portray a unique character. There is a sense of purpose and joint achievement in celebrating of the life of the school. Inevitably, most sites are the effort of one person, but contributions are featured from all the classes in the school. There is an expectation that all teachers will use the pages and contribute ideas.

A typical feature of a school website, along with the usual prospectus information and welcome from the head teacher, is a page of *bookmarks* to curriculum-related resources for primary children and parents, to support Web use at home. At many schools, pupils are encouraged to use the computer in the library for self-directed research. Curriculum links to topics, by year group, are set up in advance on the website. One example is at Fryern Junior School in Hampshire. This site, of well over two hundred pages, has been authored and maintained using an Acorn computer[1].

A high level of interactivity distinguishes Sutton-on-Sea Primary School's website. Extensive use has been made of *Test Maker*, a free utility from Argosphere, in presenting a range of interactive activities. In the 'Weather Station', records sent in from schools are stored in a database. This may be searched by anyone who visits the site. Records may be selected by temperature, type of weather, wind direction and so forth. Teachers who wish to contribute have a choice of two levels of weather report form. When data is sent a page is returned with the 'report' written out. The new record is automatically added to the database.

Manor County Primary School in Oxfordshire features 'Pond Watch', which ran from March to July 1998. Each week, groups of children observed events in and around the pond, such as the rescue of a frog stuck in a drain, the development of tadpoles and the arrival at school of spring lambs in a box. There are rich descriptions such as that of the frog 'sitting on an escaped crisp packet'. Each page features colour photographs taken by children. The worth of the digital camera is amply demonstrated.

A school's website has potential for fostering home-school links, and providing information about the local community. Sutton-on-Sea has a section for parents, giving advice on issues such as bullying and helping with reading and maths. Parents may also read information about helping in school. The site also has a 'chat' area reserved for former pupils.

LEA Advisory Services are making use of their websites to showcase special developments, such as Barking and Dagenham's Aboriginal Art project. Advisory teams also use the Web to publicise courses, and to promote effective teaching through policy and curriculum guidelines.

Birmingham, for example, has an extensive Mathematics site, covering both primary and secondary phases. Free resources include Mathematics games from other cultures and a collection of problem-solving activities for KS1. 'Butterflies', or little things that make a difference, are suggestions from teachers for enhancing and enlivening Mathematics lessons.

Kent's NGfL site features resources from the Environmental Education Centre in Canterbury. For example, there is a 'big book' about a family of swans. Given a data projector or television screen, big books on-line may be shared with children in much the same way as the printed equivalent, with the additional advantage of interactivity. In the Kent example, each page of the book contains a simple question. The answer is shown when the question mark is clicked. Underlined words may be clicked to display more detailed definitions for older children. Teachers may print out materials for using the Kent resources in the Literacy Hour.

The screen shows a 'big book' from the Kent NGfL website.

A school may use allocated space on the Service Provider's server for its own pages, each of which will have an URL (unique resource locator) and be accessible anywhere in the world. If a school is to develop its own site, there needs to be someone at hand with the skills and spare time to create pages. Much will continue to depend on enthusiastic endeavour. There should be no pressure on IT co-ordinators to undertake this work as they already have enough to do! In many areas, NGfL funding has bolstered local advisory services. Technical advice and support will be of considerable benefit to teachers who wish to publish curriculum materials or children's work.

Collaborative projects and email

Cych (1996) found that key features of a successful email project include 'a specific focus and a clear purpose, a definite time span and a well-established timetable of events'. One way to become involved is to join an appropriate *listserver*.[2] All messages posted to a selected list are automatically forwarded to all subscribers (there is no subscription charge). You may wish pupils in your class to respond to a request. Alternatively, you may post a request, offering to publish your results, as did this American teacher:

> My second grade class wants to know what kinds of snakes live in other communities. The students plan to correspond via E-mail with all respondents. We will graph the responses. At the end of six weeks we will post our results to the list. We would like to know what kind of snakes are in your community, if they are poisonous or if there are none at all.

Many postings are in response to threads initiated by the list owner or a fellow subscriber. For instance, a number of current postings on the *uk-schools* list are on the theme of the Literacy Hour. Etiquette should always be observed: for instance, a reply should be directed to the individual rather than the whole list, unless the content is of general interest. It need not take a great deal of time to respond to a genuine request. Pupils may find that their efforts are greatly appreciated. An American teacher wrote to thank all her respondents:

> I requested messages for my special education classroom, not knowing how much we would benefit from the activity. I taught my children to respond with brief thankyou messages, but in case we missed someone personally, thanks to all of you who responded. It seems some people had low expectations of my students, but not any more. Our classroom map is spotted with sticky tabs all over the United States and 15 other countries. Small – small world.

The above postings appeared on Kidsphere, a popular list which will generate up to 80 messages a day! A better starting point is the *Times Educational Supplement Internet Staffroom*, which describes itself as 'an open forum for all in education'. The TES on-line edition is free, and the *Staffroom* page features clear guidelines for contributors. It is necessary to visit the page to read contributions, since they are not automatically emailed as in the case of a list. One well-managed list is *uk-schools*[3]. The owners monitor other global lists, and post selected requests for participation.

Schools and teachers' groups may also use their websites to publish project outcomes. The Apple Project (October 1997) aimed to teach writing skills and poetry appreciation. The invitation was open to teachers of 6-7 year olds, to a limit of twenty-five classes. Each contribution was published, with one illustration from each class. Sample poetry formats, such as cinquains, apology poems and couplets, were posted in advance. The project pages also contain feedback from participants and visitors, with links to related resources. Even though the project is over, children's work may remain on the Web for an indefinite period. The 'apple' poems, in various formats, may be used to stimulate writing on virtually any theme.

It is not difficult to organise an email project, particularly if tasks are planned in advance. It may be helpful to ask colleagues if there are times when their own computers are free. Any word processing software may be used to prepare email, as work can be saved and subsequently cut and pasted into the email editor, off-line. One or two pupils may be trained as 'experts', and they may 'cascade' their skills to others. It may only take a few seconds to send the full contents of the email 'outbox'.

Sutton-on-Sea Primary School hosts *Kids Chat*, a list for children. Postings are strictly moderated, and there are themes with an emphasis on fun and children's interests. As well as writing letters, pupils gain experience in responding to the views of others in the chosen thread. There is a 'Gossip' area, where children can write about anything at all, for practice. Participating schools may select a monthly topic. There is a sample of past postings on the schools' website.

'Learning circles' are electronic communities, typically composed of around eight classrooms. Pupils and teachers collaborate on jointly negotiated, curriculum-related projects. The service provider is responsible for overall guidance, technical support and project co-ordination. Children research a topic and pass on their findings to other members of the circle. Riel (1990) noted the high levels of motivation and collaboration among pupils. Relationships change as teachers become learners alongside their pupils as the class participates in joint investigations. The teacher cannot predict the course of events, since much depends on what other participants do. Teachers in the circle learned from one another, as advice on organising the classroom for this type of work was passed round. Teachers rated their own learning as one of the most satisfying outcomes, and self-esteem increased[4].

Examples include investigations of climate and weather patterns, and the effects on peoples' lives. Pupils researched the traditions and history of their own communities. They became involved in analysing and evaluating the information they received. Reports were written jointly and published electronically. The hallmarks of authentic learning, including inquiry-based research and the opportunity to present outcomes to an audience, were all present. Riel (1992) found that writing improved through the need to make details explicit, due to the physical distance separating writer and reader. Furthermore, recipients may have no idea of any special difficulties affecting the writer.

In collaborative projects on-line, pupils synthesise their own findings from the contributions of others. Children in schools some distance apart may collaborate on writing, sending successive drafts via email. Riel's observations (1989) suggested that children may gain more from editing others' writing than from routinely correcting their own. They were prepared to be more critical than when teamed with a classmate in the role of 'response partner'.

Large-scale collaborative ventures, many involving European partners, are currently taking place as part of UKNetYear. Private sector funding and sponsorship underpin initiatives such as Tesco's SchoolNet 2000. Curriculum projects jointly researched by participating schools will form part of the Millennium Dome Web site. Support will be provided by regionally-based advisory teachers, and training facilities will be set up in Tesco stores.

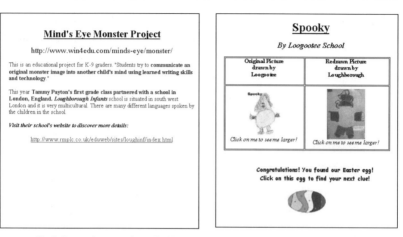

Collaborative project linking a London infants' school with a school in the US.

Pupils researching on-line: what are the issues?

As with any other research task, teachers need to plan carefully. Clearly defined tasks should be negotiated with pupils. The problem of disorientation (Collis, 1991) is exacerbated on the Internet since a single link may summon material originating from a source anywhere in the world. The route to the sought information may not be transparent. There is a serious risk of cognitive overload as one is exposed to a volume of information greatly exceeding that demanded by the inquiry.

The critical issue of Internet safety has already been mentioned. Filtering by service providers may deal with the worst cases, but the fact remains that the great bulk of material is quite irrelevant to learners' needs. If children are to search the Web under supervision, they need to be taught information handling skills and strategies. A critical skill lies in being able to identify and reject material irrelevant to the inquiry.

Is there a risk that children may come to regard possession of information, on paper or disc, as a substitute for actual knowledge? There is no value in children downloading quantities of information without engagement in the content. There is no intrinsic way in which information accessed electronically is converted into knowledge (Laurillard, 1995). The use of such material in informing and in contributing to pupils' presentation can only be developed in the context of wider classroom activity.

Reading level is an important concern. Many Web sites have been developed for a specialist audience with access to a common technical vocabulary. A good example for younger readers is In *Search of Giant Squid* at the Smithsonian Museum of Natural History. Each page deals with one question, and is presented in a clear, direct style, without superfluous additions. A high standard of graphic design clarifies structure and contributes visual impact.

Is searching the Internet to support research the most desirable use? In the BBC Internet Project (Durbin and Wright, 1995), teachers highlighted concerns at being confronted by a 'plethora of information' and were fearful of 'not having got it all'. There are parallels in the *CD-ROMs in Primary Schools* project where teachers found themselves under considerable pressure to ensure a positive learning experience in a short time (Wegerif et al., 1996). There were limited opportunities, since teachers wanted every child in the school to use the single machine.

The volume of information has increased to such an extent that simple searching cannot be relied upon to find anything of relevance. If teachers are really determined to provide experience of full Internet searching, they should note that highly specified text searches such as 'Cadbury World' or 'Hubble Space Telescope' are more likely to retrieve a list of sites with a high degree of relevance. An alternative approach is to use 'Treasure Hunts' which give children experience of locating pages and scanning them for specific information, without exposing them to the frustrations and risks of the entire Web. Good examples are available at the BECTa site.

For teachers intent on searching the full Internet, familiarity with binary logic (Chapter 11) is useful, though not essential. Some search engines simplify the process, with 'buttons' to click for the type of search. The buttons in *Lycos* are:

> All the words (AND)
> Any word (OR)
> The exact phrase

There may simply be a box in which to enter the search, with no apparent choices. Generally, AND results (all search words present) are presented first, followed by OR. If the precise phase is sought, it is usually enclosed in double quotes, e.g. "Natural History Museum". Some search engines are case specific by default. To avoid wasting precious time, it is really worth displaying, printing and reading any Help pages beforehand.

The ability to select relevant material from a lengthy list of titles is a critical skill. Although navigational tools are easy to use, 'resource discovery is the issue' (Addyman, 1994). A pupil researching Hajj located hundreds of pages, many of which were purely commercial, such as advertisements for bargain flights to Mecca. A search for information on symbolic dress worn by Sikhs (kangha, kara, karpan) was successful, due to the highly specific nature of the search. Needless to say, the level of retrieved texts may be well above the pupils, further reducing the scope for independent research.

Nevertheless, some successful searching has been carried out by pupils. Unusual animals provide a safe starting point. Children who searched for 'Jumping Spiders' located an Australian primary school site, where pupils had published their research. It was rewarding to discover informative, illustrated pages written by other children. In writing for their peers, children may do a better job than many adults!

Some teachers will have high expectations of the Web as a treasure trove of resources for lesson preparation. However, tracking down relevant material may prove disconcertingly difficult. How, for example, may one go about locating material on the Ancient Greeks? Using *Lycos*, a search for 'Ancient Greece' yielded over 11,000 matches (August 1998). Adverts for educational videos featured prominently. Repeating the search for 'Ancient Greeks' matched 1800 sites. Some highly relevant material, much of it authored by teachers, was found. The first ten matches included the well-known website of All Souls JMI School in Westminster, which has a guide to the Greek exhibits in the British Museum.

Pupils researching this topic may alternatively use an educational collection such as the BBC Learning Station. The search "Ancient Greece" (in quotes) located one site of high relevance. The US based collection, *Berit's Best Sites for Children*, also yielded a small, manageable selection of reviewed, highly appropriate sites. The children's search engine, *Yahooligans*, reported 21 matches, but several sites were included twice in the list. Both Berit and *Yahooligans* proved exceptionally easy to search, with no need for logical expressions, menu selections or punctuation.

A further strategy is to use an international guide such as *Museums Around the World.* There is a direct route to the National Archaeological Museum in Athens; there is also a link to a virtual tour of the Acropolis. The text level is advanced, but pupils may navigate these pages which contain many photographs of exhibits and ancient sites.

The Web has not superseded books, libraries and other means of finding out. Children in a Hampshire school knew that their village has a connection with Benjamin Franklin. Researching this connection proved a good test of the Internet as an information source. Many Franklin sites were found, but they were unhelpful in the context. Franklin's autobiography was located, but it would not download. I found the answer within two minutes in the local Public Library. Franklin frequently stayed with the Shipley family in Twyford and wrote his autobiography there.

In Chapter 9, we saw how 10 year olds responded to a CD-ROM video clip showing an earthworm pulling at a leaf. There was no explanation in the text, and children wondered whether earthworms actually eat leaves. They consulted books in the library, but to no avail. The school did not have Internet connection, so I pursued the question at home. All I could find was advice on stocking wormeries. It occurred to me that a class wormery would indeed provide the most memorable means of finding out! Eventually, I dug up the answer in the CD-ROM encyclopaedia *Information Finder*: 'Earthworms feed on dead plant material that is found in the soil.'[5] If the teacher prepares for this type of question in advance, s/he may usefully model the processes of finding out using electronic sources in the presence of the whole class.

The Galileo Mission on the Web

In this section, we see how Year 6 pupils encountered NASA's Galileo mission to Jupiter. Since the school was not on line, I arranged for a group of pupils to visit King Alfred's College. Following discussion with the pupils, the class teacher passed children's suggested topics to me. In advance, I searched for relevant sites and prepared a folder of bookmarks. NASA was the most popular choice among boys, followed by Manchester United. Girls were particularly interested in wildlife, with 'space' a second choice. This was hardly surprising, since new images from Galileo had featured on TV news the previous day.

The Galileo spacecraft was launched from the space shuttle in October 1989. It was not aimed directly at Jupiter. In fly-pasts of Venus and Earth (twice) it gained velocity through gravity assists. En route to Jupiter, photographs were taken and studies made of the Earth, Moon and Venus. The first close encounter with an asteroid was achieved, and an asteroid with a moon was discovered. As Galileo orbited Jupiter, a probe separated from the spacecraft. In December 1995, the probe entered Jupiter's atmosphere and transmitted data for over fifty minutes before succumbing to the hostile environment. Galileo continues to transmit spectacular images as it continues its close encounters with Jupiter's moons (August 1998).

NASA makes extensive use of the Web to communicate its work to educational users and the general public. The extent of NASA's presence on the Web has led to a complex network of interconnected pages. The inherently open yet highly elaborate structure presents navigational problems. In following a link, the impression of one small step may be illusory: the reader may be taking a giant leap into another research team's site. There are difficulties in reconstructing routes (which a teacher may well want to do, if something useful has been found).

It is exceedingly difficult to form a mental map of the NASA sites, even after numerous visits. In any case, content and links may be transformed overnight. As one team advises, 'This page is constantly growing and changing.' This is a unique feature of on-line media. The first edition of a book may soon be revised, but hard copies of the original still exist. The same applies to CD-ROM: an updated version may be released, but the copy that you have cannot be changed in any way.

Given the interest in the latest Galileo images, I decided to bookmark the Project Galileo home page and make a start with this. Given this start, pupils who had not used the Internet before rapidly acquired basic navigation skills. They selected a link which took them directly to the new Ganymede images. The discovery aroused much excitement. Later, pupils told me that they had found that Ganymede is Jupiter's largest moon. They were particularly excited to note how blurred Voyager's 1979 images appear in comparison.

In their eagerness, children were less prepared to read the text, and decisions about where to go next. Two boys evaluated the NASA pages. Adam declared that a page with detailed explanatory text was more useful than a page full of links. (This was despite general unwillingness to read the text!) Tim had a quite different view of what is good information. The most important thing was to be able to get to the facts. 'You don't need all the details,' he said. 'You can just click on [these links] for whatever you want to know.' This is an example of the 'exploratory talk' that takes place as learners get to grips with the nature of the resource (Mercer, 1994). The problem is to identify the type of information which best serves the dictated need.

To my surprise, Adam suggested that a page posted six months previously was out of date. I have never known Year 6 pupils to pay any attention to the date of publication of a printed book. Adam seemed prepared to reject information for lack of topicality. This is a common response among Web users. If a site has not been updated for several months, its perceived value is diminished. Teachers who maintain school web pages should take note. Regular updating (even if changes are minimal) is necessary to extend shelf life.

When a page of heavily technical data was displayed, Tim commented, 'It's what the scientists want to know.' The boys realised that pages such as 'Amazing Facts' are intended for the general public. Exploring a large website aimed at a varied readership will complement the Literacy Strategy (DfEE, 1998), where Year 6 pupils are expected to comment critically on the features of various non-fiction texts.

I felt some concern that the boys were content to save pages to disk, rather than read them. However, they had succeeded in discovering the date of launch and duration of Galileo's mission, and found that Ganymede is Jupiter's largest moon. They had learned that Galileo is in orbit around the planet. They were aware of the value to scientists of the mission, having noted the blurred Voyager photographs. Later, pupils were eager to discuss the duration of space travel.

Two girls had opted to look at nature parks and zoos. From a prepared list of bookmarks, Sara chose Sea World and Busch Gardens in Florida, for the good reason that she had been there. From the *Animal Bytes Database*, the girls were able to access large colour images and listings of facts with supporting text. Later, they joined the boys to look at the Ganymede pictures.

Sara had Internet access at home, and appeared to be the most knowledgeable about ICT. However, as the pupils chatted during a break, the boys were heard to denigrate the girls' interest in 'zoos' and 'nature'. This annoyed the girls, and they defended their choice. Gender typing has been evident in other contexts where pupils have been allowed to research personal interests. At another school, a dominant boy insisted on searching for motorcycles, despite protests from girls in the group. Of course individual children will express different interests. But teachers will need to monitor groups carefully, reminding pupils that it is quite unacceptable to criticise others' preferences.

What was gained from this first experience (for most of the pupils) of the Web? The boys achieved their objective of getting the Ganymede pictures. Expecting them to find out more about the mission would have been quite unrealistic. It is best to avoid poorly focused instructions such as 'get some detailed information' (about what?). Activity should be carefully planned by the teacher, who should ensure that pupils understand the information need. Otherwise, they may rapidly become frustrated.

The difficulty of some texts (admittedly not written for children) caused problems. I noted at the time that the opacity of the material made it difficult for me, as teacher, to formulate appropriate questions to engage the pupils. Lacking prior knowledge, I could not absorb the content at a glance. Pages where information is presented in small chunks are the most helpful. Texts should be written in a clear, explanatory style. There should be clear signposts within the text, enabling readers to detect the main idea (Armbruster and Anderson, 1988).

A key issue beyond the scope of this small study is how children make use of downloaded material. There is a need for further research and development in classroom contexts. Given the opportunity to combine information from different sources, in varying forms, pupils' higher order thinking skills are developed (Robinson, 1994). The user has access to masses of non-attributable text (Nanlohy, 1995). It is possible to download material and re-present it, scarcely contributing an original word.

A brief summary of outcomes

The Grid – or the wider Internet on which it is based – is relevant to all phases of education. Given a fast connection with minimal on-line charges, interactive resources for young children may be explored in the library or classroom. Well-managed school and LEA sites provide a safe, pupil-friendly, interactive environment.

The Web provides opportunities for independent research by older pupils. However, teachers need to create a supportive environment with an emphasis on purposeful use. Preparatory and follow-up activities should be planned for, as well as opportunities for guided exploration. Pupils need to appreciate that it is not enough simply to plunder files from the Web. Thought needs to be given to the off-line use of printed and saved material. Safety must be given priority.

Pupils readily acquire navigational skills, but the plethora of sources presents problems. Searching can be time-consuming and frustrating. Only the most specific searches are fruitful. There is no guarantee of success. Information skills are of critical importance given the realities of information overload and the quantity of irrelevant material.

Sites of relevance to the curriculum should be selected for quality and accessibility, and bookmarked. It is preferable to explore one source in full rather than to dip into numerous sites.

Teachers must be in a position to judge when use of the Internet is appropriate. When might other media – books, newspapers, CD-ROM, video – be a better means to find out? On-line research may complement the use of other media, as when pupils visit a website to follow up interests aroused by TV news.

It is easy to overlook the potential of email in the rush to explore on-line multimedia. Email projects enable pupils to share research, or work together on a joint publication, with distance no object. There are a number of starting points, from moderated 'chat rooms' to organised projects.

All staff should be expected to participate in developing the use of the Internet in school. While it is likely that one or two teachers will lead the way initially, it is everyone's joint responsibility to support their efforts and learn from them.

As local authorities implement the early phases of the Grid, head teachers will need to give careful consideration to aspirations and objectives. As with any educational change, teachers must be convinced of the relevance. The risks are:

- Overloading with materials of indifferent quality and relevance
- Inadequate planning at school level
- Unforeseen costs and delays in getting schools on line
- Training which concentrates on technical issues, rather than teaching and learning.
- Failure to differentiate resources which are ready for take up from those which require development.

The Grid is already an important source of professional support and development. As more services become available on-line, the distinction between the various forms of teacher education and professional development becomes blurred (Collis, 1994). In embracing the new technologies, schools must shift away from isolated application to integration of ICT in curriculum subjects.

There is no reason why the new ICT should not stand alongside the more established and familiar computer-based tools. I hope that this book has provided fresh insights into older applications, while highlighting the new opportunities and their potential for teaching and learning. The contribution of ICT to effective learning depends, above all else, on teachers' creativity and imagination in using new and established applications to support learning across the curriculum. As teachers become able to use ICT to create their own curriculum resources, the time invested in learning to use the technology will have realised its full value.

On-line references

All Souls JMI School, Westminster: http://www.rmplc.co.uk/eduweb/sites/allsouls/index.html

Amazing Picture Machine: http://www.ncrtec.org/picture.htm

Apple poems: http://members.aol.com/Apples2nd/index.html

Argosphere: http://www.argosphere.net

Barking and Dagenham's Aboriginal Art project: http://www.bardaglea.org.uk/aboriginal/home.html

BBC Learning Station: http://db.bbc.co.uk/education-webguide/pkg_ main.p_home

BECTa Internet information sheet: http://www.becta.org.uk/info-sheets/internet.html

BECTa Treasure Hunts http://www.becta.org.uk/thunt/

Berit's Best Sites for Children: http://db.cochran.com/db_HTML: theopage.db/

Birmingham Mathematics: http://www.visitweb.com/maths

Fryern Junior School: http://www.rmplc.co.uk/eduweb/sites/fryern/ index.html

In search of Giant Squid: http://seawifs.gsfc.nasa.gov/squid.html

Kent NGfL website: http://www. kent.gov.uk/ngfl

Loogootee Elementary School: http://www.siec.k12.in.us/~west/

Lycos: http://www.lycos.co.uk

Manor County Primary School: http://www.rmplc.co.uk/eduweb/sites/ manorlh

Project Galileo: http://www.jpl.nasa.gov/galileo

Sea World / Busch Gardens: http://www.seaworld.org

Starchild: http://heasarc.gsfc.nasa.gov/docs/StarChild/StarChild.html

Sutton-on-Sea Primary School: http://www.sutton.lincs.sch.uk

Times Educational Supplement: http://www.tes.co.uk

Worm World: http://www.yucky.com/worm/

Yahooligans: http://www.yahooligans.com

Notes

1. Ian Taylor at Fryern Juniors wrote these pages directly in HTML, using !Edit, a rudimentary text editor. A range of higher-level authoring tools are available, making the task little different to writing a normal page. An optional extension to Textease (Chapters 7, 10) automatically converts a word-processed page, graphics and all, into HTML. (Hypertext Markup Language is an international standard for electronic publications.)

2. Libby Black's web page offering advice on US listservers and collaborative projects is at: *http://bvsd.k12.co.us/curriculum/inet/partners.html*

3. This highly recommended list for UK teachers has a Web page with full joining details and an archive of postings at http://www.mailbase.ac.uk/lists-u-z/uk-schools/

4. For a fuller review of Learning Circles and other aspects of electronic communications, see Davis (1997).

5. A second search located the New Jersey *Worm World* site, a humorous yet highly informative resource which featured the answer to our question and much more.

6. *Starchild* is NASA's site for elementary schools. There are two levels of text. Level 1 is more appropriate for young readers, although some explanations are rather complex.

Appendix

Details of suppliers

Textease:
Softease Ltd, The Old Courthouse, St Peters Church, Derby DE1 9DR

Living Books:
TAG Developments, 25 Pelham Road, Gravesend, Kent DA11 0HU
www.tagdev.co.uk

Tizzy's Toybox, Oxford Reading Tree Talking Stories:
Sherston Ltd., Angel House, Sherston, Malmesbury, Wilts SN16 OLH

Flossy the Frog, A Mouse in Holland:
4Mation, 14 Castle Park Road, Barnstaple, Devon EX32 8PA

MyWorld, MyWorld2:
SEMERC, Broadbent Road, Watersheddings, Oldham OL1 4LB

Roamer:
Valiant Technology, Valiant House, 3 Grange Mills, Weir Road, London SW12 0NE

LogIT:
Griffin & George, Bishop Meadow Road, Loughborough, Leicestershire LE11 5RG

Kingfisher Micropaedia, Creepy Crawlies:
Media Design Interactive,
Alexander House, Station Road, Aldershot, Hants GU11 1BG

Junior PinPoint, Junior Insight:
Longman Logotron
124 Cambridge Science Park, Milton Road, Cambridge CB4 4ZS

British Birds:
Interactive Learning Productions, North Street Court, North Street East, Newcastle, NE1 8HD

Mighty Maths Carnival Countdown:
Multimax Ltd, Gloucester House, Station Road, Sturton, Brigg, South Humberside DN20 9DW

Bibliography

Addyman, T. (1994) 'The Internet: international information highway'. *New Library World*, 95(1115), 4-9.

Ainley, J. (1996) *Enriching Primary Mathematics with IT.* London: Hodder and Stoughton.

Armbruster, B.B. and Anderson, T.H. (1988) 'Learning from Textbooks' in Eraut, M. (Ed.) *International Encyclopaedia of Educational Technology.* Oxford: Pergamon.

Ball, D. (1990) 'What is the role of IT within the National Mathematics curriculum?' *Journal of Computer Assisted Learning*, 6, 239-245.

Banks, D. (1985) 'Weatherwise'. *Primary Teaching and Micros*, September 1985, 16-17.

Becker, H.J. (1985) 'How schools use microcomputers: results from a national survey' in Chen, M. and Paisley, W. (Eds.) *Children and Microcomputers: Research on the Newest Medium.* Beverly Hills, CA: Sage.

BECTa (British Educational Communications and Technology Agency) (1998) *Connecting Schools, Networking People.* Coventry: BECTa

Beynon, J. (1993) 'Technological literacy: where do we go from here?' *Journal of Information Technology for Teacher Education*, 2(1), 7-35.

Bezanilla, M.J. and Ogborn, J. (1992) 'Logical sentences and searches'. *Journal of Computer Assisted Learning*, 8, 37-48.

Blake, Y. (1989) 'Word processing with Infants: stimulating and developing knowledge of the writing process using word processors'. *Microscope* 28, Newman College/ Micros and Primary Education.

Blythe, K. (1990) *Children Learning With Logo.* Coventry: National Council for Educational Technology.

Broad, A. (1997) 'Using Pixies in the Key Stage 1 classroom'. *Microscope Early Years Special, 38-39.* Newman College/Micros and Primary Education.

Carr, J. (1996) 'From Living Books to writing books', *Hexagon* 29, Wheatley: Oxfordshire Computer Education Unit. http://www.rmplc.co.uk/eduweb/sites/oxceu/ hexagon/29/livbooks.html

Carter, C. and Monaco, J. (1987) *Learning Information Technology Skills.* Library and Information Research Report 54. London: British Library.

Chalkley, T.W. and Nicholas, D. (1997) 'Teachers' use of information technology: observations of primary school classroom practice'. *Aslib Proceedings* 49(4), 97-107.

Clements, D.H. and Sarama, J. (1997) 'Computers support algebraic thinking'. *Teaching Children Mathematics,* Feb. 1997, 320-325.

Cobden, D. and Longley, M. (1996) *Fun with Spreadsheets.* Dorset County Council.

Collis, B. (1991) 'The evaluation of electronic books'. *Education and Training Technology International,* 28(4), 355-363.

Collis, B. (1994) 'A reflection on the relationship between technology and teacher education: synergy or separate entities?' *Journal of Information Technology for Teacher Education,* 3(1).

Cullen, P. (1995) *Reports on using Roamer in the classroom: case study materials.* Leicester: University of Leicester School of Education.

Cych, L. (1996) 'Santa comes alive with e-mail'. *Times Educational Supplement,* September 13 1996.

Darby, R. et al. (1997) 'Reading on screen: exploring issues in reading for information with CD-ROM'. *English in Education* 31(2), 34-44.

Davis, N. (1997) 'Communications and new learning opportunities' in Somekh, B. and Davis, N. (Eds.) *Using Information Technology Effectively in Teaching and Learning: Studies in Pre-service and In-service Teacher Education.* London: Routledge.

Davis, N., Desforges, C., Jessel, J., Somekh, B., Taylor, C. and Vaughan, G. (1997) 'Can quality in learning be enhanced through the use of IT?' in Somekh, B. and Davis, N. (Eds.) *Using Information Technology Effectively in Teaching and Learning: Studies in Pre-service and In-service Teacher Education.* London: Routledge.

Dede, C.J. (1992) 'The future of multimedia: bridging to virtual worlds'. *Educational Technology* 32(5), 54-60

DES (Department for Education and Science) (1988) *Report of the Committee of Inquiry into the teaching of the English Language* (the Kingman Report). London: Her Majesty's Stationery Office.

DfE (Department for Education) (1995a) Statistical Bulletin Issue Number 3/95.

DfE (Department for Education) (1995b) *Key Stages 1 and 2 of the National Curriculum.* London: Her Majesty's Stationery Office.

DfEE (Department for Education and Employment) (1998a) *The National Literacy Strategy: a Framework for Teaching.* London: DfEE

DfEE (Department for Education and Employment) (1998b) *The implementation of the National Numeracy Strategy, Final Report of the Numeracy Task Force.* London: DfEE.

Derewianka, B. (1990) *Exploring How Texts Work.* Rozelle, New South Wales: Primary English Teaching Association.

Durbin, C. and Wright, J. (1995) *BBC/NCET Internet Project: Report summary.* NCET/ BBC Education.

EDSI (1997) *Education Departments' Superhighways Initiative: Report Summary* at http://vtc.ngfl.gov.uk/reference/edsi/

Elliott, A. (1995) *Pedagogical issues and computer supported learning in early childhood.* Paper presented at the World Conference Computers in Education, Birmingham, July 1995.

Eraut, M. (1991) 'The information society – a challenge for education policies? Policy options and implementations strategies' in Eraut, M. (Ed.) *Education and the Information Society,* 164-231. London: Cassell.

Eraut, M. (1993) *Grouping policies for computer-based work,* paper presented at the British Educational Research Association annual conference. Liverpool, September 1993.

Eraut, M. and Hoyles, C. (1989) 'Group work and computers'. *Journal of Computer Assisted Learning,* 5(1), 12-24.

Fern·ndez, M.T. (1995) 'Teachers as authors: HyperCard projects for the classroom' in Willis, D.A., Robin, B. and Willis, J. (Eds.) *Proceedings of SITE95:* sixth annual conference of the Society for Information Technology and Teacher Education. San Antonio, Texas, March 1995.

Friedler, Y. and McFarlane, A.E. (1995) *Data logging with portable computers: a study of the impact on graphing skills in primary and secondary pupils.* Paper presented at the World Conference Computers in Education, Birmingham, July 1995.

Frost, R. (1993) *The IT in Primary Science Book.* Hatfield, Herts.: Association for Science Education.

Fullan, M. (1991) *The New Meaning of Educational Change.* New York: Teachers' College Press.

Furner, M. (1987) 'Information retrieval and ship construction at Woolwich Dockyard'. *Primary Teaching Studies* 2(2), Polytechnic of North London: PNL Press.

Gain, J. (1994) 'Introducing multimedia authoring', *Microscope Multimedia Special,* 26-27. Newman College/Micros and Primary Education.

Galpin, B. and Schilling, M. (1988) *Computers, Topic Work and Young Children: Learning to use Information in the Primary Classroom.* Library and Information Research Report 68, British Library Board.

Goldstein, G. (1997) *IT in English Schools: a commentary on inspection findings 1995-6.* OFSTED/NCET

Gomersall, M. (1994) 'Keyboard clues: primary history and the concept keyboard'. *Microscope* 43, 10-12. Newman College/Micros and Primary Education.

Green, D. and Graham, A. (Eds.) (1994) *Practical Guides: Data Handling.* Leamington Spa: Scholastic Publications for the Mathematical Association.

Greenfield, P.M. (1984) *Mind and Media: the Effects of Television, Video Games and Computers.* Harvard University Press.

Hargreaves, L., Comber, C. and Galton, M. (1996) 'The National Curriculum: can small schools deliver? Confidence and competence levels of teachers in small rural primary schools'. *British Educational Research Journal,* 22(1), 89-99.

Heaney, P. (1986) 'Information Skills in the Primary School'. *Greater Manchester Primary Contact,* 4(1), 68-78.

Heppell, S. (1993) 'Teacher education, learning and the information generation: the progression and evolution of educational computing against a background of change'. *Journal of Information Technology for Teacher Education,* 2(2): 229-237.

Heppell, S. (1997) *Issues for a future curriculum*. SCAA conference, Information Technology, Communications and the Future Curriculum.

Hertfordshire Education Services (1997) *Making IT Manageable: Creating a scheme of work for IT from Early Years through Key Stages 1 and 2*. Wheathampstead: Hertfordshire Education Services.

HMI (1994) *Information Technology in Schools*, evaluation of the ITIS Initiative. London: Her Majesty's Stationery Office.

HMTC (1993) *The Horizon Report*. Portsmouth: Hampshire Microtechnology Centre.

Hodgkinson, K., Wild, P. and Bailey, C. (1991) 'Interactive video in one primary school: comments on the value of the Domesday discs'. *Computer Education*, 68, 2-4.

Hoyles, C., Sutherland, R., Healy, L. (1991) 'Children talking in computer environments: new insights into the role of discussion in mathematics teaching' in Durkin, K. and Shire, B. (Eds.) *Language and Mathematical Education*. Buckingham: Open University Press.

Hunter, B. (1985) 'Problem solving with databases'. *The Computing Teacher*, 12, 20-27.

IWF (Internet Watch Foundation) (1998) *Rating and filtering Internet content: a United Kingdom perspective*. Cambridge: IWF.

Jarvis, C. (1997) 'The Write Touch'. *Hexagon* 34. Wheatley: Oxfordshire Computer Education Unit. http://www.rmplc.co.uk/eduweb/sites/oxceu/hexagon/34/writouch.html

Jessel, J. (1997) 'Children writing words and building thoughts: does the word processor really help?' in Somekh, B. and Davis, N. (Eds.) *Using Information Technology Effectively in Teaching and Learning: Studies in Pre-Service and In-Service Teacher Education*. London: Routledge.

Jessel, J. and Hurst, V. (1997) 'Children exploring the Queen's House in hypertext' in Somekh, B. and Davis, N. (Eds.) *Using Information Technology Effectively in Teaching and Learning: Studies in Pre-Service and In-Service Teacher Education*. London: Routledge.

Joy, A.M. (1994) *An evaluation of Talking PenDown*. Unpublished MSc thesis, University of Southampton.

Keeling, R. and Whiteman, S. (1990) *Simply Spreadsheets*. Sutton Coldfield: KW Publications.

Keeling, R. and Whiteman, S. (1993) *Maths through Databases*. Sutton Coldfield: KW Publications.

Kerslake, D. (1977) *The Concept of Graphs in Secondary School Pupils aged 12-14 years*. Unpublished MPhil thesis, Chelsea College, University of London.

Laurillard, D. (1995) 'Multimedia and the changing experience of the learner'. *British Journal of Educational Technology*, 26(3), 179-189.

Lewis, M. and Wray, D. (1995) *Developing Children's Non-fiction Writing*. Leamington Spa: Scholastic.

Light, P. and Blaye, A. (1990) 'Computer-based learning: the social dimensions' in Foot, H.C., Morgan., M.J. and Shute, R.H. (Eds.) *Children Helping Children*. Chichester: John Wiley.

Longworth, N. (1981) 'We're moving into the information society: what shall we teach the children?' *Computer Education*, June 1981, 17-19.

Lunzer, E. and Gardner, K. (1979) *The Effective Use of Reading*. Oxford: Heinemann.

McCraw, P.A. and Meyer, J.E. (1995) 'Technology and young children: what teachers need to know' in Willis, D.A., Robin, B. and Willis, J. (Eds.) *Proceedings of SITE95*: sixth annual conference of the Society for Information Technology and Teacher Education. San Antonio, Texas, March 1995.

McFarlane, A. (1997) 'Developing graphing skills) in McFarlane, A. (Ed.) *Information Technology and Authentic Learning*. London: Routledge.

Mawdsley, E., Morgan, M., Richmond, L. and Trainor, R. (Eds.) (1990) *Historians, Computers and Data: Applications in Research and Teaching*. Manchester University Press.

Means, B., Blando, J., Olson, K., Middleton, T., Morocco, C., Remz, A. and Zorfass, J. (1993) *Using Technology to Support Education Reform*. US Government Office of Research and Office of Educational Research and Improvement.

Medwell, J. (1996) 'Talking books and reading'. *Reading*, April 1996, 41-46.

Meek, M. (1991) *On Being Literate*. London: The Bodley Head.

Mercer, N. (1993) 'Computer-based activities in classroom contexts' in Scrimshaw, P. (Ed.) Language, Classrooms and Computers. London: Routledge.

Mercer, N. (1994) 'The quality of talk in children's joint activity at the computer'. *Journal of Computer Assisted Learning*, 10(1), 24-32.

Minns, H. (1991) 'Mrs Mopple's Washing Line: Using Touch Explorer Plus in the nursery' in *Primary Language: Enriching the Curriculum with Computers*. Coventry: National Council for Educaitonal Technology.

Murray, D. and Collison, J. (1995) 'Student IT capability within as school-based primary ITT course'. *Journal of Computer Assisted Learning*, 11(3), 170-181

NAACE (National Association for Advisers in Computer Education) (1997) *Implementing IT*. Coventry: BECTa.

Nanlohy, P. (1995) *Computer based texts*. Paper presented at the World Conference Computers in Education, Birmingham, July 1995.

NCET (1996a) *Developing local support arrangements for the effective use of IT*. Coventry: National Council for Educational Technology.

NCET (1996b) *Managing IT in Primary Schools: a planning tool for senior managers*. Coventry: National Council for Educational Technology.

NCET (1996c) *Finding Out! Using Reference Materials on CD-ROM*. Coventry: National Council for Educational Technology.

Neate, B. (1992) *Finding out about finding out: a practical guide to children's information books*. London: Hodder and Stoughton.

Noss, R. (1986) 'Constructing a conceptual framework for elementary algebra through Logo programming'. *Educational Studies in Mathematics*, 17, 335-337.

Oliver, R. and Perzylo, L. (1994) 'Children's information skills: making effective use of multimedia sources'. *Education and Training Technology International*, 31(3), 219-230.

Oxfordshire County Council (1996) *Progression in Information Technology/Information Technology Opportunities Across the Curriculum.* Wheatley: Oxfordshire Computer Education Unit.

Papert, S. (1980) *Mindstorms: Children, Computers and Powerful Ideas.* Brighton: Harvester Press.

Perera, K. (1986) 'Some linguistic difficulties in school textbooks' in Gillham, B. (Ed.) *The Language of School Subjects.* London: Heinemann.

Powell, P. (1990) 'Information processing in Primary History topic work'. *Teaching History*, July 1990, 11-14.

Pratt, D. (1995) 'Young children's active and passive graphing'. *Journal of Computer Assisted Learning*, 11(3), 157-169.

Preece, J. (1983) 'Graphs are not straightforward' in *Psychology of Computer Use*, 40-56. London: Academic Press.

QCA (1998) *Information Technology: A Scheme of Work for Key Stages 1 and 2.* London: QCA.

Quee, J. (1991) 'Park Mead County Middle School database project', *Group Work with Computers* unpublished project report. Brighton: University of Sussex.

Riel, M. (1989), 'The impact of computers in classrooms'. *Journal of Research on Computing in Education,* 22(2), 180-189.

Riel, M. (1990) 'Co-operative learning across classrooms in electronic learning circles'. *Instructional Science*, 19, 445-466.

Riel, M. (1992) *AT&T Learning Circle.* Symposium presentation at the International Conference, Technology and Media Division of the Council for Exceptional Children, Albuquerque.

Robinson, M. (1994) 'Using Email and the Internet in science teaching'. *Journal of Information Technology for Teacher Education*, 3(2), 229-238.

Robson, S. (1987) 'No one can see the awful mistakes you've made: word processing with six and seven year olds'. *Primary Teaching Studies* 2(1).

Rogers, L. (1994) 'Data Logging' in Underwood, J. (Ed.) *Computer Based Learning: Potential into Practice.* London: David Fulton.

Ross, A. (1984) *Making Connections.* London: Council for Educational Technology.

Ross, A. (1989) 'Fossils, Conkers and Parachutes: Children's Data from Science Experiments', *Primary Teaching Studies* 4(2).

SCAA (1995) *Information Technology: the New Requirements.* London: SCAA.

SCAA (1996a) *Monitoring the School Curriculum: Reporting to Schools (1995/6).* London: SCAA.

SCAA (1996b) *Information Technology and the use of language.* London: SCAA.

SCAA (1997) *Expectations in IT at Key Stages 1 and 2.* London: QCA Publications.

Sharp, P. (1995) *Computer assisted learning to develop literacy skills: a manual for learning support assistants.* Hampshire County Council: Hampshire Educational Psychology Service.

Smith, H.M. (1997) 'Do electronic databases enable children to engage in information processing?' in Somekh, B. and Davis, N. (Eds.) *Using Information Technology Effec-*

tively in Teaching and Learning: Studies in Pre-Service and In-Service Teacher Education. London: Routledge.

Somekh, B. (1997) 'Classroom investigations: exploring and evaluating how IT can support learning' in Somekh, B. and Davis, N. (Eds.) *Using Information Technology Effectively in Teaching and Learning: Studies in Pre-Service and In-Service Teacher Education.* London: Routledge.

Somekh, B. and Davies, R. (1991) 'Towards a pedagogy for information technology'. *The Curriculum Journal,* 2(2), 153-167.

Spavold, J. (1989) 'Children and databases: an analysis of data entry and query formulation'. *Journal of Computer Assisted Learning,* 5, 145-160.

Steadman, S., Nash, C. and Eraut, M. (1992) *CD-ROM in Schools Scheme: Evaluation Report.* Coventry: National Council for Educational Technology.

Stephenson, P. (1997) 'Using control information technology' in McFarlane, A. (Ed.) *Information Technology and Authentic Learning.* London: Routledge.

Stevenson, D. (1998) 'Progress against the Stevenson Report', address given at the NAACE Annual Conference. *NAACE Journal,* Spring 1998.

Stradling, B., Sims, D. and Jamison, J. (1994) *Portable Computers Pilot Evaluation Summary.* Coventry: National Council for Educational Technology.

Tabberer, R. (1987) *Study and Information Skills in Schools.* Windsor: NFER-Nelson.

TTA (Teacher Training Agency) (1998) *Initial teacher training National Curriculum for the use of Information and Communications Technology in subject teaching.* London: Department for Education and Employment

Underwood, G. and Underwood, J. (1996) *Gender Differences in Children's Learning from Interactive Books,* proceedings of SITE96, seventh annual conference of the Society for Information Technology and Teacher Education.

Underwood, J. and Underwood, G. (1990) *Computers and Learning.* Oxford: Blackwell.

Underwood, J. (ed.) (1994) *Computer Based Learning: Potential into Practice.* London: David Fulton.

Underwood, J. and Brown, J. (Eds.) *Integrated Learning Systems: Potential into Practice.* Oxford: Heinemann.

Vaughan, G. (1997) 'Number education for very young children ' in Somekh, B. and Davis, N. (Eds.) *Using Information Technology Effectively in Teaching and Learning: Studies in Pre-Service and In-Service Teacher Education.* London: Routledge.

Walkerdine, V. (1982) 'From context to text: a psychosemiotic approach to abstract thought' in Beveridge, M. (Ed.) *Children Thinking Through Language.* London: Edward Arnold.

Watson, D.M. (1993) *The Impact Report.* London: Department for Education/King's College London, Centre for Educational Studies.

Wegerif, R., Collins, J. and Scrimshaw, P. (1996) *CD-ROMs in primary schools: evaluation summary.* Coventry, National Council for Educational Technology.

White, S.H. (1995) 'Pre-service teachers develop multimedia social studies presentations for elementary grades' in Willis, D.A., Robin, B. and Willis, J. (Eds.) *Proceedings of SITE95:* sixth annual conference of the Society for Information Technology and Teacher Education. San Antonio, Texas, March 1995.

Whitebread, D. (1997) 'Developing children's problem solving: the educational uses of adventure games' in McFarlane, A. (Ed.) *Information Technology and Authentic Learning*. London: Routledge.

Wray, D. (1995) *Teaching Information Skills Through Project Work*. London: Athenaeum.

Index

V

W